# THE

# SOCIOLOGY

# OF

# CITIES

# THE
# SOCIOLOGY
# OF
# CITIES

---

## *JOHN SIRJAMAKI*

STATE UNIVERSITY OF NEW YORK AT BUFFALO

## RANDOM HOUSE
### NEW YORK

TO VERNE AND ERIC

# PREFACE

The United States is one of the most highly urbanized countries in the world today. Three of every four Americans live in cities, and they continue to increase proportionately. They live more and more in great cities or their suburbs which constitute vast regional groups of cities or metropolitan areas. Over 60 percent of Americans now live in 212 metropolitan areas. In some heavily populated sections of the United States, these metropolitan areas run into each other, creating supermetropolitan areas, attaining a magnitude of urban settlement never before realized in human history. The American population also continues to expand. It is now approaching 200 million inhabitants and soon will exceed that. This huge population fills the cities, spilling into their suburbs and regions, and makes metropolitan areas the predominant form of urbanization today.

While this relentless growth of cities persists, the importance of cities in American society has diminished steadily. The United States has matured as a nation-state and is no longer a state of cities and commonwealths. This means that the American people compose a nation with a common civilization, language, institutions, and traditions, and that, furthermore, they have their social life and order in the national and not in urban communities. Americans are active in the national community through the federal system of government, the national economy, national religious bodies, public and private schools and universities, modern media of communication, and large-scale organizations. So culturally homogeneous has American society become that people move freely about in the United States, living comfortably wherever they settle and in whatever activities they engage. With the ascendance of the national community, they dwell in cities but have loose ties and often small affection for them and expend only a part of their lives and endeavors in them.

In these developments lies the urban paradox of our times: the people flock to cities, and cities swell into metropolitan and megalopolitan areas; but the national community provides the social organization of their lives and activities and in some respects makes urban communities obsolescent. As cities become engulfed in sprawling masses of urbanized populations, they lose their character as independent, free-standing cities, and exist in a complex metropolitan symbiosis with each other. They keep their separate municipal governments, but their utility as urban communities is impaired. As metropolitan areas they constitute metropolitan economies and nascent metropolitan communities, but lack metropolitan governments, and the cities are largely incapable of cooperating to perform their public services. For these reasons, they are assailed by urban and metropolitan problems which they cannot resolve, and turn increasingly to the state and especially the federal government for assistance. The latter, too, maintains a welfare state which succors the people in all their distresses, not only those which originate in cities.

Still, cities are not going to disappear. In fact, they continue to grow and prosper. Human beings need fixed places of abode and permanent groups for their existence and work, and cities are these local places and groups in modern society. The people live in cities to enjoy a civilized existence, and to attain the standards of living which American society makes available to them. In the stores, workshops, and offices of cities they earn their livelihood;

they establish homes and found families in them; their children attend schools in them; they pursue social and cultural activities there and live out their lives. If cities are no longer the centers of cultural creativity—and they are not—at least the people find cultural opportunities and aspire to the higher reaches of American civilization in them.

I have written this sociology of cities from the perspective of the national community, and the social and cultural changes which it has wrought in urban communities. For the most part, I have concentrated on American cities, and tried to analyze the developments which have occurred in them. But to understand them, it is necessary to know something about the cities of the past. Otherwise the significance of present events is hard to ascertain.

When cities first appeared in the ancient world, they made possible, through an urban organization of human society, the rise of great civilizations. The urban community was indispensable then for human progress; now it has limitations which make it archaic to some degree. To comprehend this sequence of events, and to determine the roles of cities in societies today and tomorrow, it is necessary to compare cities through time and across cultures. In this book I have compared cities at several periods in history, and used American cities as examples of modern types of cities. I have not written a history of cities, but I have used historical evidence to evaluate cities and to analyze the social organizations to which they gave rise. Therefore I have tried to be both scientist and humanist in appraising them.

As a sociologist, I have wanted to help to restore urban sociology to a large conception of cities and to a large construction of the urban and national communities. Conversely, I have resisted the reduction of urban sociology to urban ecology, which deals with the physical organization of cities, or to urban demography, which concerns the vital statistics of their populations. Ecology and demography are estimable sociological disciplines, but neither one encompasses cities adequately nor should they be made to. Each discipline contributes to an understanding of cities, but when they are made central in urban sociology, they diminish it as a science or occupy it with studies of secondary importance.

I have dealt with cities as urban communities, analyzing their social organization and the institutions upon which this rests. As much as I could, I have tried to be continuously sociological in point of view and to address myself to readers, both students and colleagues, who are sociologists. But I hope that other scholars of cities, whatever their interests are, will read this book to reacquaint themselves with urban sociology.

JOHN SIRJAMAKI

*Buffalo, New York*

# ACKNOWLEDGMENTS

The scholarly enterprise is a cooperative one, and while its seminal ideas begin with individuals, they are embellished by many others and finally come to rest in the public domain. My knowledge of cities comes from the many scholars who have studied them and published their findings in books, monographs, and journals over the course of time. My indebtedness to other urban sociologists is obviously great. I have acknowledged my dependence on some of them in the notes, but many others whose names do not appear are important also. I owe a special gratitude to the historians of cities, whose data I have used so much in this book. I hope they will feel my use of their ideas acceptable, if not always competent.

From Maurice R. Davie, now living in retirement in New Hampshire and removed from cities, I received my first scholarly introduction to the study of cities and a training in urban ecology. I continue to follow his ecological analysis of cities, which I believe, with him, provides a useful basis for an institutional analysis of cities.

To my friend and former colleague at the University of Minnesota, Professor Don Martindale, I owe many ideas, some of which I have acknowledged in the notes and others which, inadvertently, I have not. Through our many discussions and from his own writings I obtained an improved theoretical understanding of cities. His own contributions to urban sociology are considerable, not only through his translation of Max Weber's *The City*, but through his analyses of communities, social and cultural change, and sociological theory.

The faults and shortcomings which remain in this book are my own.

J.S.

# CONTENTS

CHAPTER XII     *The Government of Cities*

CHAPTER XIII     *Cities Today and Tomorrow*

# T A B L E S

# F I G U R E S

# THE
# SOCIOLOGY
# OF
# CITIES

# · I ·

# *The Sociology of Cities*

## What Is a City?

Cities share the life and civilization of their societies so completely that they have a variable countenance for those who live in or study them. They are, first of all, large aggregations of people settled densely in limited areas of land and, as such, are different from villages, hamlets, and other places of habitation. They are both human agglomerations and the masses of buildings which contain them. In another sense, cities are an advanced form of human association which enables heterogeneous people to live and work together and to achieve some sense of community.

Cities are also centers of commerce and industry. Their workshops and factories produce a wide range of economic goods and services and employ urban dwellers in a variety of non-agricultural occupations. Cities are populations with some degree of self-rule, which they exercise through municipal governments. They are also centers of learning and cultural progress; historically, cities bred the civilizations of the world, and today they are still locales for the higher forms of civilization. Etymologically the word "civilization" is derived from *civitas*, the Latin word for city, and it meant originally the cultivated life of city people, in contrast to the rude life of peasants. Finally, a city has a name, an identity, and a personality and almost seems a living being to its inhabitants.

These different aspects of cities suggest the traits which distinguish them from other agglomerations. Clearly cities "are" people, and the agglomeration of people in them is one feature of cities. Urban dwellers live in masses of population rather than in scattered groups of families, as rural peoples do. They range in numbers from thousands to millions. A demographic definition of cities, which also emphasizes their ecological traits, is commonly used by sociologists: A city is a relatively large, dense, and permanent settlement of socially heterogeneous individuals.[1]

People must reach a certain level of economic and social organization before they can settle in agglomerations. They need adequate means of subsistence, political leadership, suitable living arrangements, a high degree of cooperation in performing the tasks of life, and a common system of values. Moreover, to remain settled in cities they must achieve and maintain a standard of living higher than they can elsewhere. In short, people require urban order, culture, and institutions to support their agglomeration in cities, and to realize a coveted way of life therein.

As their second characteristic, cities are populations which subsist by exchanging manufactured goods and specialized services for food, raw materials, and other commodities. They carry on commerce and develop industries to produce these goods and services, which employ their population in a great number and variety of tasks and occupations. With wealth earned from economic pursuits, they buy the necessities of life, including the agricultural surplus produced by rural populations as well as the articles of their own manufacture. Thus cities are places of business and manufacturing, which exist through a division and specialization of economic activities with other urban and rural populations, and involve a high degree of cooperation and mutual interdependence.

Urban populations regulate these many activities extensively to assure their stability and prosperity. Therefore, cities have an economic organization which determines their economic enterprises and institutions. This organization comprises commercial, industrial, financial, and other firms which carry on business; markets, labor force, means of transportation, and systems of communication; and the business practices by which they transact the production, distribution, and exchange of economic goods and services. City dwellers earn their own living within this economic organization.

As their third characteristic, cities have a political organization which enables their inhabitants to act collectively in their civil life with legal authority and in perpetuity. They have municipal governments, elected and appointed officials, legislative councils, courts, and other public agencies. Through them city dwellers secure leadership, administer political offices, keep law and order, provide municipal services, and meet other political needs.

In modern countries, cities are reduced to jurisdiction over their own inhabitants and lands and they are restricted even in this. They have governments and powers stipulated in municipal charters granted by higher governments, or specified by administrative acts of these governments. Thus, they differ from the cities of antiquity, which were city-states governing not only their own urban dwellers but other urban and rural populations residing in their territories as well. These ancient cities were fortresses with armies and militias, and their inhabitants were capable of waging war. Now national governments exercise this kind of sovereignty, limiting the cities' right of self-rule.

Urban dwellers also have to organize their social and cultural activities to meet common needs of existence, and the multiplicity of associations which results from this is a fourth feature of cities. Thus they organize religion, education, the family, welfare activities, medical care, and entertainment. Specifically, urbanites establish churches, schools, welfare agencies, hospitals, and a host of other associations, through which they secure specialized services for themselves and add to the culture of their cities. And whenever new problems arise, still more associations are created to deal with them.

With economic, political, and cultural organizations to maintain their existence, urban populations also need a social organization—a fifth characteristic of cities. Social organization holds the urban agglomeration together and enables city dwellers, despite their numbers, density, and heterogeneity, to cooperate in their common activities, and create an urban civilization. While the specialization of persons and tasks in an intricate division of urban labor results in interdependence among city dwellers, the social order also permits them to segregate into social and cultural groups, and to stratify into classes, within which they pursue family and social activities. The social order rests on the economic, political, and other institutions common to cities, and on an integration and grouping among these institutions. It may take different forms in different cities but it functions in all of them.

Two views of cities emerge from this discussion: one which considers them from the point of view of agglomerations, the other from the point of view of organization. Both are essential. All countries define cities as agglomerations having some legally specified minimal population, usually from 2,000 to 5,000 inhabitants. Iceland's low is 300, and India, the Netherlands, and Japan have a high of 10,000, 20,000, and 30,000 inhabitants, respectively; the United States specifies a minimum of 2,500 inhabitants. But some nations merely define cities as agglomerations which have an urban form of government or perform administrative functions of local government.[2] From the point of view of organization, cities are aggregations which have an economic, political, and social organization, pursue urban lives and activities, and support a complete culture. This defines them as urban communities and not merely as urban agglomerations, and puts them into a sociological perspective. This is the concept of cities followed in this book.[3]

## The City as a Community

The term "community" denotes territorial aggregations of population, but the kinds and territories of such aggregations differ widely in the world. They may be bands, tribes, villages, cities, or nations; [4] metropolitan areas are communities; modern countries, which are nation-states, are national communities; today we even speak of a world community. These diverse communities inhabit their lands differently, and make different use of land in their social life and order. Bands, tribes, and villages, which derive their subsistence from the land, make territory a basis of their communities; but cities and nation-states, with higher cultures, never do so or at least not to the same extent.

For these reasons, the meaning of communities as territorial aggregations is confused. To make sense of the term, however, the number of communities may be reduced to two, villages and cities, and contrasted in their social organization and culture. If villages among primitive peoples are considered first, the anthropologists' definition of community, which applies to definite territorial groupings and is unambiguous, may be introduced and compared with the sociologists' use of the term in their studies of cities. In addition, a comparison between village and urban communities will serve both to put them into historical perspective and to make explicit the reasons why the village community tends to give way to the urban in every country in the world.

Anthropologists use "community" to designate the aggregations of families which inhabit a territory and which have formed into social groups because of their common residence, occupations, culture, and descent.[5] These are local groups, one step removed from family and kinship groups, and they occur in all societies because human beings must cooperate in order to survive. In such groups they benefit from larger numbers, division and specialization of labor, improved food getting, mutual aid and sharing, stable family existence, social life and companionship, and protection. Neighboring families who live on the same land and have similar occupations are likely to form such groups; to the already existing and more or less natural ties of residence and propinquity are added social and cultural bonds as well.

Communities thus come to possess three principle features of identity which amplify our earlier definition. First, they are territorial groupings of people who reside in the same area and associate in groups determined by their life and work. Second, they are groups who support a common culture and pursue the round of daily and seasonal activities together. Third, communities have a social life; their members are identified with them, develop loyalties to them, and have primary relations in them. While some communities are homogeneous, others are not, and their members are differentiated into subgroups or stratified into classes.

Among primitive peoples, the band and village are the usual local communities. Tribes that subsist by collecting, hunting, and fishing, and must migrate from one source of food supply to another in their territories, commonly live in bands of related families, with an average of fewer than fifty members. But tribes that subsist by agriculture and require fixed settlements live in villages. These villages consist of groups of families, surrounded by their farm lands and other territories which they divide into fields for cultivation and other use. Their populations traditionally have ranged from 250 to 1,000 or 1,250 persons, with a mean of 300 to 400 persons; but today they are as large as 5,000 or even 10,000 persons in some countries of Asia and Africa.

Generically these are communal villages, stemming in the western world from the Neolithic villages which sprang up in the grassy uplands of the Near East approximately 8,000 years ago. Their inhabitants live by farming and herding, sometimes also by fishing or hunting, and are largely self-subsistent. These communities are relatively self-contained, with stable cultural and religious practices, and ordinarily they have a sufficient natural increase to perpetuate themselves through generations of time. Accordingly, communal villages have been the most perdurable form of settlement ever to exist among human beings. The bulk of the world's population has always lived in such villages and does so today.

Despite their wide distribution, historically and geographically, communal villages are similar in their social organization and cultural life. Their inhabitants follow much the same cycle of agricultural activities through the days and seasons: they plow the land, plant and harvest crops, care for farm animals, make tools and articles by hand, maintain their families and homes, contend with the weather, and commune with nature. They govern their lives and these activities through family and kinship groups which differ in various societies, taking the form of nuclear or extended families, large households, sibs, clans, moieties, or phratries. Some villages, for example, comprise a single clan, and are ruled by its chiefs or heads. Families and kin groups, not their individual members, own or have rights to the land and cultivate it. They also perform basic social roles in procreating, rearing, socializing, employing, educating, punishing, and protecting their members, and in fixing their status and activities in the villages. Their dominance is reinforced by other cultural practices: marriage customs, rules of residence after marriage, and kinship obligations, as well as by land tenure, inheritance, and authority systems.

But these villages differ in various societies and in various periods of history. Some villages have been autonomous, but most of them have existed as communities in larger societies, and have been subject to other governments or to the control of other peoples. Thus village populations have been, at one time or another, free peasants who owned and cultivated their own lands, but they have also been tenant farmers, serfs, and slaves. Moreover, some have had a bare subsistence economy, while others have been integrated in the national economy of their societies, growing cash crops, raising farm animals, using farm machinery, paying taxes, and following other dictates or innovations originating outside their villages. They have also differed in their local government, having much or little of it according to whether their societies have been tribes, city-states, or nation-states. Finally, their communities have been stratified variously into clans, classes, castes, or other strata.*

In contrast to communal villages, cities rest on economic bases of commerce and industry, not of agriculture, and are never self-subsistent. Their inhabitants engage in economic pursuits not only for subsistence but for profit: the business of cities is business. Furthermore, their economic activities are specialized, involve urban populations in an intricate division of labor, and create interdependence among cities. Urban dwellers work as individuals and not as families: they use their earnings to subsist; their work is their employment or career, which they follow through their lifetimes. Because their employments are varied and involve

---

* A second type of village, called a trade village, is the kind which exists in the United States. These villages are inhabited by individuals and families engaged in commerce and service industries which provide for the economic wants of farm families residing in their hinterlands. A small proportion of farm families also live in them. Most farm families, however, exist on farmsteads distributed over the United States, and belong to various rural communities.

different skills, experience, education, and ways of life, city dwellers, individually and as groups, are socially and culturally heterogeneous, providing cities with a population base which is far different from that of villages. Their political base exists in local municipal governments whose powers and activities are in turn restricted by state and federal governments. Unlike the ancient city-states, modern cities are not autonomous.

With these modes of existence, cities clearly are not villages grown large or excessive; they are territorial aggregations of another kind, with a different organization of human life and enterprise. Cities are made up of diverse populations who cooperate extensively in a network of activities and who are mutually interdependent for the necessities of life but who exist in separate social and cultural groups. They represent the fortuitous association of dissimilar persons and groups who, through their collective enterprise, provide the goods and services on which they subsist in cities.

The characteristics of urban communities accordingly differ from those of village communities. First, they have a social organization which rests on diverse associations and institutions deriving from an economic division of labor and from specialized social and cultural activities. This organization enables urban dwellers to build urban cultures and to cooperate in their tasks of life, and makes their permanent settlement possible in cities. Moreover, it permits them to found still other associations or to institutionalize new practices to solve fresh problems of existence as they arise, and therefore to adapt to changing conditions of life. For these reasons, they live rich, variegated lives in cities, and also extend their urban organizations and institutions throughout their societies.

Second, urban communities possess, and indeed require, socially heterogeneous populations to carry on highly diversified social and cultural activities in cities. Such variety among urban dwellers assures variety also in their subcultures, and provides persons and groups with manifold talents and experiences necessary to specialized enterprises. Fresh migrants, moreover, drawn to cities by diverse specialized opportunities in them, perpetuate heterogeneity in urban populations, and add to subcultures in cities. Over the course of time, migrants assimilate to cities, but they are nevertheless hindered in this by competition and conflict among urban populations as they struggle for wealth, status, and power which are never distributed equitably among them. For these reasons, urban populations may approach but never reach more than a relative homogeneity among themselves.

But the social order of cities serves to hold these miscellaneous populations in their unity and diversity. Urban populations exist variously in subcommunities, which are social and cultural groups held together by distinctive sets of institutions, providing members with subcultures as well as individual and group identification. But populations are also divided into socio-economic strata, which may be economic classes, status classes, castes, orders, or estates, according to the system of stratification which exists. Urban dwellers, moreover, belong to organized groups variously associated with economic, family, and other organizations, and form into groups based on ties of family or neighborhood. Finally, urban dwellers also change their subcommunities or classes through improvements in their fortunes; social mobility is institutionalized in cities.

Third, the social order of urban communities no longer is based on family and kin groups, but rather on many organizations and institutions among which the family of course is included. These organizations carry on their separate activities at levels of competence beyond the capacities of families to perform. The family relinquishes to or shares with them its economic, educational, religious, and other activities, while retaining its own specialized activities of procreation and socialization. But the state assumes control over families in matters of marriage ceremony, inheritance of property, rights of spouses and children, and divorce. The church, too, regulates families in some respects. Thus family organization changes in cities: nuclear families displace extended families, although lineages and kindred are retained, and kinship obligations of mutual aid attenuate although they never vanish entirely.

Finally, the role of territory in characterizing urban communities lessens in importance, although it never disappears completely. Urban dwellers value their ties of habitation and propinquity less as they become increasingly involved in organized social and cultural activities and as they take advantage of modern travel and communications facilities to increase their participation in the national community. Even when they want to maintain local ties, they are sometimes discouraged from doing so by the size, density, and heterogeneity of cities.

In order to understand modern cities, it is helpful to formulate a definition of communities in which territory is not a central concept. Such a definition regards communities as human aggregations which have a social order, culture, and institutions, and constitute complete systems of human interaction. These communities inhabit certain lands, but make secondary use of them in creating their social and cultural life. We follow this definition of communities in this book.[6]

## The Social Organization of Communities

In the last hundred years, confronted with the rapid urbanization and industrialization of their countries and the consequent weakening of village and rural life, European sociologists have tried to explain the cultural distinctions between cities and villages. To these sociologists, such developments signified the passage of their countries from one type of social order to another, or, in terms of this discussion, from village to urban communities, with such changes in social life and cultural activities as have been remarked upon. They gave various names to these two kinds of social order, of which *Gemeinschaft* and *Gesellschaft,* that is, communal and associational societies, are the better known, and most sociologists continue to use these typological concepts today.[7]

A *Gemeinschaft* social order is found in village communities. Family and kin groups, which are the principal organizers of social and cultural activities, are the paramount social entities in such communities. They follow custom and tradition, using magic and religion to control their members. They designate their members' status and do not tolerate individualism. In cities, where a *Gesellschaft* social order exists, specialized organizations rather than family groups carry on, through a division of labor, activities which maintain and create an interdependence among the populace. Political and economic organizations especially rise to prominence in urban communities: the state, government, courts, and law establish a political order; business organizations, using markets, money, commercial law, and other economic practices, produce and exchange goods and services. The family and kin group is only one among many groups that carry on specialized activities. Not family controls, but public controls, enforced through legislation and public opinion, keep order in cities. Persons win status through their roles in organizations, thus by their own achievement rather than by family ascription.

Sociologists have found this typology of societies, conceived in ideal-typical terms, useful for a number of reasons. Its generalizations have been at least approximately valid. Moreover, it makes possible analysis of societies both as wholes and in parts. Finally, it facilitates cross-cultural comparisons, analyzing social organization throughout history and serving to explain certain kinds of social change.

But this dichotomy of types oversimplifies the social order of societies, and needs further elaboration. Not all societies fall readily into one social order or another; nor are those in the same order identical in social organization. While cities, metropolitan areas, and nation-states have a *Gesellschaft* social order, they differ in the sets and hierarchies of institutions paramount in their social organization. Similarly, a world community, as it comes into being, develops a social organization based on still another alignment of institutions. Although modern societies are highly urbanized, villages still persist in them, some with a *Gemeinschaft*, others with a *Gesellschaft* order. In the latter case, the way of life in rural communities changes as agriculture becomes commercialized.

To understand the social orders of societies properly, some expansion of the typology through construction of other categories is desirable. Instead of doing this directly, one method which accomplishes the same purpose is to identify the major types of communities which occur in societies, and to analyze the social organization of these communities. For this reason, indeed, the wider definition of communities was advanced: communities are organized groups which support a complete culture and provide their members with a total human experience through the days and seasons of each year and over the normal course of their lives. Defined in this way, communities represent the significant groupings and hence the fundamental organization of human life and activities in societies. By comparing them, the distinctive organization of each community can be established and its place in history determined as well.

To have total cultures, communities must solve the universal problems of human existence and aggregation: economic subsistence, socialization of the human personality, and social and political control of individual and group behavior. At the various levels of civilization, communities possess cultures which meet these necessities in different ways and with different degrees of competence. Not only do they organize their social and cultural activities in diverse ways, but they also institutionalize their activities variously: that is, they invest them with different meanings and with different moral standards. Institutions may be formally defined as the system of norms which order and stabilize human behavior in established patterns of activity. In this discussion they are the standardized solutions to the problems of collective life in communities.[8] The social organization of various communities thus rests on different sets of institutions.

But communities also differ in how they institutionalize new behavior and in how the institutions in their social order cohere. Among primitive peoples, since family and kin groups, and to a greater extent tribes, institutionalize new activities, a high degree of coordination ordinarily occurs among new and existing institutions. In modern societies, many autonomous organizations which carry on specialized activities may create new institutions. For example, to solve novel problems they devise cultural solutions which, if accepted by their society, become institutions. However, since organizations tend to create new institutions only in their specialized areas, new institutions may conflict with existing ones. Any of these—family, economic, political, religious, and military institutions, for example—may conflict with each other. An autonomy of organizations and differentiation of institutions characterize a *Gesellschaft* social order, causing both a separation of activities and compartmentalization of status and roles within it.

However, if communities are to persist as organized groups, they must overcome divisiveness in their institutions. They do this by two general means. One is a functional integration of their social and cultural activities which unifies their communities: this forces a pattern over all their enterprises. The other means is a normative integration of their communities, which is similarly dictated by a human strain for consistency in the mores. This means that communities can develop a social order which rests on some number, grouping, and ranking of institutions in which the more important ones, or those which they think deal with the more significant activities of human existence, are transcendent over the others, making their norms and values standard for individuals and for their communities. Thus communities achieve an accommodation among their institutions.

In such communities, however, the accommodation seldom occurs without struggle. The paramount institutions are those which provide the major access to wealth, prestige, and social power, and their rulers are those who control the organizations related to these means. This generally permits the rulers to enrich and elevate themselves.

Through self-interest, they are driven to defend these institutions and to reduce other groups to inferiority in their communities. They do not always succeed, however. Other groups sometimes conquer them, causing other institutions or some new grouping of institutions to prevail, and thereby initiating social and cultural change. By imposing on the community a social organization that restrains conflict among competing interests,[9] the conquering social groups can maintain a temporary balance.

This discussion of communities has perhaps suggested how they may be utilized for the analysis of the social order of societies. The types of communities which societies have depend on the civilizations, modes of settlement, economic development, governments, and time and place of these societies in history. As societies advance culturally and economically, they adopt new types of communities, and therefore acquire other forms of social organization and different institutions. Thus societies experience social and cultural changes through a succession of types of communities and through mixtures of communities which persist in them.

In world societies, to name the types of community, village and tribal communities occur among primitive peoples; band communities occur in some of them also. Urban communities, based on city-states, were dominant in the societies of antiquity; in them rural peoples existed in villages and tribal communities. Most modern countries are nation-states, and national communities are dominant; however, urban and metropolitan communities, village or rural communities, and various subcommunities also persist. Some Asiatic and African countries, undergoing rapid economic development and political centralization, have both national and village communities, with urban communities also present.

## The Sociological Study of Cities

Sociologists study cities by two methods of analysis, one general and abstract, the other particular and concrete. With the first method sociologists consider cities as urban communities and analyze their social organization and cultures. With the second method sociologists investigate the cities of particular countries at separate periods of time. The first method studies cities historically and cross-culturally; the second studies cities *qua* cities from diverse points of view and in varying empirical detail.

While both methods are necessary and supplement each other, the first is particularly valuable for the sociological study of cities. This is because cities are never identical urban communities in all times and places, and they perform different cultural roles in their societies. Therefore the variable relationships of cities and societies need careful explication in order to place analysis of them into proper perspective. Cities differ because they exist in societies whose social and political organization variously rests on tribes, villages, city-states, and nation-states, and they have accordingly an urban organization based on different sets and hierarchies of institutions. Moreover, they have different cultural importance in societies whose dominant communities are variously village, urban, or national communities. In the national communities of western countries, the significance of cities as urban communities is greatly reduced, and as social groups they are weakened and even becoming obsolete. But in these same countries in the medieval period, cities comprised urban communities which exercised a major part in the social and cultural events of that time. To analyze cities in diverse societies past and present, the comparative method, using historical and cultural data, is indispensable.

Because cities are both alike and unlike, some classification of them into categories is necessary in an analysis. A comparative study of cities requires that they actually be comparable with each other, that is, that they be compared within the same class of cities or, when the occasion arises, with different classes of cities. In this book, therefore, they are divided into four ideal [10] types of cities based on the paramount institutions in their social organization.

These ideal types of cities are as follows: religious-political cities, political-commercial cities, commercial cities, and commercial-industrial cities. Used as examples of these ideal types in this book are, respectively, Sumerian cities (3000–2400 B.C.) and Mesopotamian cities (1790–1595 B.C.), Roman cities (A.D. second century), medieval European cities (A.D. 1250–1300), and modern American cities. In the chapters which follow, each type of city is discussed both at the historic summit of its development and in terms of the particular people who brought it to fruition. Thus, the ancient Sumerians founded religious-political cities and the Mesopotamians later made them general throughout the ancient Orient; the Romans of the Early Empire made their cities into political and commercial centers of the then-known world; medieval Europeans established commercial cities and brought urban civilization back to western Europe; and the present cities of the United States are prime examples of commercial-industrial cities. The discussion of these peoples and their cities makes possible the use of historical evidence in dealing with them, and preparing the way for a sociological analysis of their social life and order.

**N O T E S**

1. Louis Wirth, "Urbanism as a Way of Life," *American Journal of Sociology*, 44 (July, 1938), pp. 1–24.

2. United Nations, *Demographic Yearbook*, 1952, pp. 162–186.

3. Max Weber, *The City*. Translated and edited by Don Martindale and Gertrud Neuwirth (New York: The Free Press of Glencoe, 1958), pp. 80–81. See Martindale's prefatory remarks also, pp. 50–56.

4. R. M. MacIver, *Society* (New York: Farrar & Rinehart, 1937), p. 144.

5. George Peter Murdock, *Social Structure* (New York: Macmillan, 1949), pp. 79–90.

6. Max Weber, *The City*, pp. 80–81; R. M. MacIver, *Community* (London: Macmillan, 1920), p. 23; and Don Martindale, *American Social Structure* (New York: Appleton-Century Crofts, 1960), pp. 131–133, 305–308, 483–505.

7. Ferdinand Tonnies, *Gemeinschaft and Gesellschaft*. Translated by Charles P. Loomis and published as *Fundamental Concepts of Sociology* (New York: American Book Company, 1940); Henry Sumner Maine, *Ancient Law* (London: 1861); and Émile Durkheim, *The Division of Labor in Society*. Translated by George Simpson (New York: The Free Press of Glencoe, 1947).

8. Don Martindale, *Social Life and Cultural Change* (Princeton, N. J.: Van Nostrand, 1962), pp. 39–40.

9. George Vold, *Theoretical Criminology* (New York: Oxford Press, 1958), pp. 204–205.

10. The term "ideal types of cities" means constructed classes of cities determined by their crucial characteristics which are hypothetically conceived but nevertheless are objectively possible in reality and are causally relevant to cities and to urban organization. Max Weber: *The Methodology of the Social Sciences*, translated by Edward Shils and Henry A. Finch (New York: Free Press of Glencoe; 1949), pp. 89 *ff*.

# · II ·

# *Cities of*
# *the Ancient World*

## The Rise of Ancient Cities

Cities first appeared in three places of the world, apparently independently of each other: in southwestern Asia, about 3500 B.C.; in northern China, about 2000 B.C.; and in Central America, about 600 A.D. The first cities in Asia were in Mesopotamia (now southern Iraq) and in Egypt. By 3000 B.C. they had spread eastward to the Indus River Valley, the area which is now West Pakistan, and westward to Crete. By 2000 B.C. they were widespread throughout the Near East. The first Chinese cities emerged in the Hwang Ho River Valley, spreading to other river and coastal areas of China. The first American cities were in Mexico and Peru and were flourishing when Spanish explorers discovered them in the sixteenth century.

Of these the Mesopotamian cities are the best known, owing to archeological excavations and scholars' reconstruction of the life of their inhabitants. These people were literate, and left written records which greatly elaborate the mute testimony offered by the ruins of their cities.

Historically they appear to have created the first civilization to exist on earth.

This remarkable emergence of cities in Asia, after men
had lived in small bands for a half million years and had
scarcely developed Paleolithic cultures, is a complex matter
and cannot be fully explained at this time.[1] But scholars
at least agree that the appearance of cities depended, in
part, on the prior attainment by certain tribes of Neolithic
culture, which provided the economic and population bases
for their later urbanization. The earliest of these tribes were
peoples who lived in the grassy uplands of the Near East.
About 6000 B.C. they apparently learned to domesticate
plants and animals and became food producers rather than
food gatherers. Some of them, possibly because of over-
population, left these hills about 4400 B.C., occupying and
extending their agriculture to the fertile plains below.
About 4000 B.C., certain other tribes settled in the swamps
at the head of the Persian Gulf, where they learned to live
on the banks of the Tigris and Euphrates Rivers.

The gradual development of farming over these millennia
provided these ancient peoples not only with subsistence,
but with an agricultural surplus that made their further
progress toward a Neolithic culture possible. Because they
had to live near their fields and herds, they came to settle
in villages and to cultivate a community life. (See Chapter
One for a discussion of these Neolithic villages and their
later wide distribution.) To carry on agriculture, they invented or improved stone tools, including axes, hoes, sickles,
and blades. (The word "Neolithic," meaning "new stone,"
indicates their advanced stone technology.) They also invented pottery for the cooking and storing of foods, and later,
weaving.

The Sumerians actually founded the first cities. A people
of unknown origin, according to their own legends they
lived previously in mountainous country, possibly in Iran,
and migrated to southern Mesopotamia where they probably

overcame a native population. They established their cities on the plains of the lower Tigris and Euphrates rivers, on delta land recovered from the Persian Gulf by the silting action of the rivers. At times the land must have seemed an enemy to the Sumerians, for they were alternately threatened by floods which swept away their dwellings and by droughts which forced them to irrigate their fields. Nevertheless, they persevered and built their cities, making their lands highly fertile by watering them. They succeeded also in developing a distinctive urban life and order, which reached its height in the Mesopotamian civilization when their cities were united with those of Akkad to form Mesopotamia.

## The City-State: Urban Social Organization

Although these Mesopotamian cities arose from a Neolithic culture base, at their height they were not just larger Neolithic villages with a more elaborate culture. These settlements were different from villages, and their form of social organization was entirely novel in human experience. These first cities organized human beings in a modern way, making it possible for people to live together on a scale and density unknown before that time. Not only did they constitute a new kind of human community, but they also changed the men who lived in them.

In the first place, their inhabitants were citizens who owed their primary loyalties to the cities, not to their clans or tribes. As citizens, they enjoyed the right to live in the cities, to pursue urban trades, to take part in urban activities, and to be protected by the cities. But as citizens they also had duties: to obey the laws, to bear arms when needed, to pay taxes, to work on public projects, and to worship the cities' gods.

In the second place, these cities were politically organized to exercise the powers of a state. A state institutionalizes and makes lawful its own use of force to rule its people and to execute other public actions and policies. Thus these cities were city-states, that is, cities which held the powers of a state over their own inhabitants, as well as over other peoples living in cities and villages in the territories surrounding their walls. They were governed by priest-kings (aided by religious and secular nobilities) who ruled by decree, made public laws, appointed judges, levied taxes, commanded armies, waged wars, and protected the welfare of cities.

Third, institutions other than family and kinship groups formed the basis of the social order in these cities. These included political institutions that were important because their rulers, the political elite, exercised the powers of state. The religious institutions, which were really the source of all economic and political power, were even more important. Urban religion was a conglomeration of various tribal religions which the priests had fused together, adding other institutions of their own creation, such as the pantheons of both city and cosmic gods, rituals of public worship, and theologies. Since religion was the dominant force in men's lives in early antiquity—no other had such awesome, supernatural sanctions—the priests themselves became a rich and powerful class, and the cities were in fact theocratic societies and centers of cult worship, presided over by priests.

Finally, the culture of these cities spread, forming the basis for a more sophisticated civilization far removed from its Neolithic origins. The inhabitants of these city-states demonstrated a cultural inventiveness which produced some remarkable accomplishments. In addition to creating cities and developing productive agriculture, they were able to transport things in bulk by utilizing the wheel, oxcart, and sail, thereby making commerce possible. They understood the metallurgies of copper and bronze and used these metals to manufacture various artifacts as well as war weapons. They dug large-scale irrigation canals, built

temples, and fortified their cities; their buildings were
monumental in size. Moreover, they invented writing, composed a literature, knew arithmetic and algebra as well as
astronomy, and created a representational art.

To sum up, these cities were complete urban communities, with religious and political institutions dominating
their social order. They are sometimes referred to as temple
cities and historically the Sumerian cities are their prototype. For the most part only those people active in religion
or government lived in them: priest-king and secular nobility, the priestly class, government officials, soldiers and
some merchants. There were, of course, free workers and
slaves, who performed the menial tasks of life. But most of
the population of the Mesopotamian city-states was formed
by the peasants who lived in Neolithic villages distributed
over the lands belonging to the cities. The peasants rarely,
if ever, visited the cities or had anything to do with them.

## The Cities of Sumer

Upon settling in cities, the Sumerians entered a formative
or protoliterate period of development from 3500 to 3000
B.C., reaching a cultural maturity in their classical or Early
Dynastic Period, from 3000 to 2400 B.C. There were a
dozen or more autonomous Sumerian cities, each with
about 100 square miles of territory, located near each other
in the Tigris-Euphrates plain of southern Mesopotamia.
This proximity brought their populations into frequent conflict over land and water rights, often provoked by the shift-
ing course of the rivers which affected the irrigation and
therefore the fertility of their fields. After 3000 B.C., they
fought almost constantly with each other and with maraud-
ing tribes who coveted their wealth. Their cities were destroyed and rebuilt many times during these wars and
various dynasties were created, but they were all short-
lived. This succession of urban empires along with the in-

ability of the Sumerians to unite in a stable urban society characterized the Early Dynastic Period.

These city-states were comprised of populations assembled around temples and shrines of tribal deities and organized by priests into religious subcommunities. Their priest-kings maintained an autocratic control over them. They had rigidly planned economies and were nearly self-subsistent from the cultivation of surrounding farm lands and from some trade and production. In modern terms their social order approximated a theocratic socialism.

The rationale for the existence of these cities and their domination by priests lay in Sumerian theology, which asserted that each city belonged to a tutelary god for whom the inhabitants had been created and that the god wished the citizens to work hard and run the city's affairs efficiently. The priest-king, or *ensi,* was this god's representative on earth and steward of his lands and properties. He discovered the god's wishes through divination and presages and put these commands into effect. In this way the priest-king kept the god in good humor, persuading him to continue to protect his people. The people, in turn, honored the god by building a temple for his earthly abode and gratified him by making the city prosperous. This necessitated that the people obey their priests, acquire the discipline of work, and cultivate loyalty to the group.[2]

## The Temples as Social Organizers

There were usually several temples in each city, and they were the basis of its social organization. The main god possessed the most important temple, but other gods, often his relatives and perhaps his associates, had temples too. In Sumerian theology, each temple was accounted the private estate of the god who inhabited it; he owned the temple, its buildings, lands, property, and its people were his slaves. The temples also functioned in a number of other ways to produce a common life and culture in the cities.

As residences of the gods, the temples were, first of all,

the cities' centers of religious activities and, as we have
noted, the priests presided over these activities. Second,
the temples were economic organizations, controlling the
city's industries. By virtue of the god's ownership, the
temples owned most of the land outside the cities as well as
farm animals, tools, seed grain, pastures, wood lots, and
vineyards. They also supervised fishing. Inside the cities
the temples kept granaries and warehouses in which food
commodities and raw materials were stored. They also
maintained workshops of various kinds.

When the growing season arrived, the entire populace,
whether priests, craftsmen, or slaves, worked in the fields.
Each temple allotted its members a private parcel of land,
rations of seed, and the use of implements and draft animals to raise crops for their dependents. The temple members paid a rent for these allotments in produce and money.
Members also worked on communal lands held by the temple which were used to support its personnel and to maintain its buildings. The productivity of their agriculture,
aided by two growing seasons, was large, diversified, and
abundant. The Sumerians raised barley as their principal
grain as well as emmer wheat and spelt. They had herds
of goats, cows, pigs, and sheep, which they used for milk
and meat. Fish, however, was their main source of protein.
They planted beans, peas, onions, and radishes, and they
had dates, pomegranates, figs, and other fruits. All these
foods were stored in temple warehouses and granaries in
the cities, to be eaten throughout the year.

During the other seasons, the populace pursued other
economic activities, both in the temples and in the cities.
Many of them toiled in the temple workshops; these included potteries, kitchens, breweries and textile and handicraft industries, in which they produced tools, weapons,
jewelry, statuary, and other manufactured goods. They
worked as cadres to repair drainage and irrigation canals
and on other public projects, both for their temples and for
the cities. Since the Sumerians lacked timber, building

stones, and metals, their merchants, working through the temples, traded for these commodities with other cities and some foreign countries. Some priests, known as scribes, kept school in the temples. When floods, wars, or other crises arose, the priests, scribes, and general population left these occupations to serve as citizens and soldiers, returning to their work when it was safe to do so.

The third way in which the temples produced a common life and culture was by holding their members together as subcommunities. Each person belonged to one of the temples; the members of each temple were known collectively as the people of the god who owned it.[3] As this god's slaves, they lived and worked together, sharing the same social and cultural existence. Inevitably, they formed into subcommunities based on the temples and their associations in them, developing sentiments of individual and social identity. Thus the temples, not the family and kinship groups whom the temples embraced, served to produce social order in the cities.

Finally, while the temples were not political associations, their head-priests served as political leaders in the cities. The *ensi* of the main temple, whose deity was the principal god of the city, was the city's priest-king. As this god's surrogate on earth, the *ensi* had a reflected divinity of his own. He commonly appointed members of his own family as the *ensis* of the other temples, and thus coordinated the activities of the several temples within the city. His leadership consisted of administering temple activities [4] and ruling the city. He was king, commander of the army, and chief judicial authority; he governed by decree, appointed judges to enforce his laws, commanded professional soldiers, and engaged in wars. (In the protoliterate period, a popular assembly of elders who ruled the cities had appointed one of their members as a *lugal*, or temporary chief, to lead them in wars and other crises, but priest-kings eventually displaced these leaders.)

The temples dominated the cities physically as well as economically and socially. Each walled temple area comprised several buildings grouped together and bounded by walls. Within the enclosure stood the temple, usually in the form of a *ziggurat* or tower, shrines, the high priest's residence, courts, workshops, administrative offices, schools, granaries, stables, and sheds.

With this social organization of their cities and their high degree of inventiveness, the Sumerians created the first civilization. As a means of keeping accurate records of the temples' commercial transactions, they invented writing, first using word pictures, then word symbols. But they soon used it for other purposes. They created a literature which included mythology and poetry, kept official records which reveal something of their history, and codified their laws into the first legal system in the world. The Sumerians also devised a system of numerical notation which stimulated their invention of mathematics, notably arithmetic and algebra; mathematics encouraged their efforts in astronomy. Sumerian craftsmen, working with copper and bronze, and at times with gold and silver, produced graceful and delicate art objects as well as various tools and utensils. As the *ziggurats* testify, the Sumerians knew how to build arches and vaults and how to build on a grand scale. They founded schools and created a class of literate priests who made all these achievements possible. As a postscript, we should add that their civilization, too, was plagued by war, slavery, and prostitution.

## The Cities of Mesopotamia

Sargon I, Semitic king of Agade, conquered the Sumerian cities about 2500 B.C., uniting them with the cities of Akkad in his state of Mesopotamia. Thus he was the first to combine Sumerians and Semites in a single society and to begin the fusing of their cultures. But when Sargon's dynasty ended about 2400 B.C., Sumerians and Semites renewed their enmities. About 1790 B.C., another Semitic king, Hammurabi, again conquered the Sumerians, and united them in his kingdom of Babylon; this is known as the First Dynasty of Babylon. Under Hammurabi and his successors, the two cultures merged harmoniously, once more enjoying peace and prosperity. The Mesopotamian civilization they composed reached its apex of development. Fortunately, these kings left numerous records of their reigns, among them the Hammurabi code which was a compendium of detailed public laws of the Sumerian and Semitic cities. The code reveals a great deal about the social, cultural, and political life of the time.

As rulers of an urban empire, the Hammurabi kings possessed much greater powers than did the priest-kings of the Sumerian cities. Moreover, they augmented their powers by weakening those of the priestly strata, and reducing the participation of priests in government. In addition to being an absolute monarch, Hammurabi claimed divinity (although not godhead) in his own right and not merely as a surrogate of a city god. This claim allowed him to make succession to his office hereditary. His actual powers rested largely on his control of the state and its armies. He created a secular class of military nobles to support him and to oppose and weaken the influence of the priestly class.

Hammurabi located his government in a palace. With its complex of buildings and rooms, its court of nobles and attendants as well as the soldiers, priests, scribes, civil officials, and harem who occupied them, the palace was the most important edifice in Babylon. Hammurabi's regime was a prototype of the despotic oriental monarchy that later prevailed throughout the Near East and in northern Africa.

## Religion

Despite the power of the king, Mesopotamian cities were still religious cities, and the priests, although weakened, remained potent and were far more numerous than ever before. Under their influence, the people remained faithful to the gods; indeed, their habit of infusing religious precepts into everything they did blurred the distinctions between the sacred and secular aspects of life.[5] However, religion had a different role in the social order of these Babylonian cities than in the cities of Sumer.

One important difference was the multiplication of gods and religions in Babylonia which breached and changed the unanimity of religious life that had existed in Sumer and Akkad. The Sumerian and Semitic gods were assimilated into a Babylonian religion to which Hammurabi added a new pantheon of national gods. For instance, under Hammurabi, Marduk, who had been the city-god of the city of Babylon, became the chief god of the new cosmic religion of the Babylonian dynasty and was made the creator of the universe. He was thus elevated to the top of the new national pantheon of gods. At the same time, the various urban populations continued to revere their traditional city-gods and to observe their ritual worship. They also worshiped family and tribal deities in a domestic religion in which the father served as the priest of his family. In addition, the Babylonians, like the Sumerians, believed in a host of demons or spirits, attributing good and ill fortune in human affairs to them and perpetuating practices of magic and divination as means of coping with them.

The polytheism of the Babylonians, with its various levels of religious worship, hierarchy of gods, and elaboration of religious beliefs and practices, indicates both complexity and contradiction in the Mesopotamian cities that did not exist in Sumer. This religious diversity, along with the number and heterogeneity of the Mesopotamian priests, led to the priests' further stratification. The priests of the temples, especially those who served important gods, constituted a priestly upper class. These head-priests and their families also belonged to the aristocratic class of the cities and

intermarried with royal and noble families. The priests who
were scribes were part of the intelligentsia but of lesser
prominence than the head-priests. A second stratum of
priests was magicians and a third was soothsayers or di-
viners. These latter priests served both public and private
clients who wanted supernatural guidance in handling
their civil or private affairs.

Another difference in the religious life of the two civilizations was the diminished role of the temples in the social
order of Mesopotamian cities. In the Babylonian empire,
the temples could no longer maintain a unity of state, society, and religion nor contain the people in subcommunities. Therefore they were detached from the state—with
Hammurabi's assent—and became independent organizations. To win their loyalty to his regime, Hammurabi gave
them various special privileges. Thereafter, the temples
took on new activities, notably commercial services. They
served as banks, made and registered business contracts,
loaned money with or without interest, and repurchased
Babylonian war prisoners from slave merchants. They also
increased the scale of their economic enterprises, added
facilities for artists, and provided recreation and diversion
for the people. These temples were houses of worship,
places of business, banking, amusement, and centers of
economic production with large numbers of priests, scribes,
artisans, soldiers, merchants, musicians, slaves, and prosti-
tutes living or working in them. In some ways the temples
resembled modern corporations. The high priests were like
a board of directors, managing their numerous activities to
win wealth, power, and prestige.

The temples continued to dominate commerce and agriculture, but, owing to their changed circumstances, they no
longer monopolized these areas of enterprise. In agriculture, the king himself was a formidable competitor. Representing the state, he amassed large estates, cultivating
them with the use of tenant farmers, serfs, or slaves.

Other royal families, military leaders whom the king re-
warded with grants of land and elevated to the nobility,
and wealthy merchants also acquired estates. Free peasants living in Neolithic villages owned lands, too. Their
numbers increased as tribes dwelling in the empire were
converted into sedentary farmers. Having to compete with
the temples, the palace, and the rich city families for land
and markets, the peasants had a hard struggle to exist.
Often in periods of economic distress or civil strife, they
lost their holdings and were reduced to tenantry or serfdom
on the large estates.

The king was also active in trade and production, usually
in the administration of state enterprises but sometimes for
his private gain. This explains why his palace resembled
the temples; it too had attached to it workshops and other
buildings where artisans labored. Free merchants, established in their own businesses, engaged in both foreign
and domestic trade; they had become highly important in
commerce. A few of them participated in the manufacture
of some of the goods they handled, usually by helping to
finance a shop or household to produce them. Through the
efforts of the merchants, but more largely as a product of
temple and palace workshops, free workers—most of them
skilled artisans—also existed. As wage-earners they constituted an urban labor force, differing from the slave
laborers who toiled in temple, palace, handicraft, domestic,
and rural enterprises.

*Social Life*

Hammurabi's code not only signified the reign of law in
Mesopotamia, but was an intimate mingling of religious and
civil law as well. In these cities, omitting religious rites
was comparable to committing theft or murder.[6] Nevertheless, Hammurabi appointed magistrates and judges from
the military class—not ecclesiastics—to enforce the provisions of the code; priests continued to administer oaths to

litigants and witnesses who appeared before them in the courts.[7]

Hammurabi's code recognized the existence of social classes in the cities and treated them unequally before the law in their rights and duties, as well as in the nature and severity of their punishments. The code throughout favored the aristocracy which consisted of royal, military, and priestly families united by intermarriage, wealth, and style of life. A second class, comprising merchants, shopkeepers, artisans, free workers, and peasants, were commoners who had a legal status inferior to that of the aristocrats. Slaves constituted a third and servile class; unless one parent was a free person, they were legally little more than chattels, whether captured in war, purchased, or born in their masters' houses.

In those sections dealing with economic activities, the code recognized and protected land as private property, differentiating between land given by the king for military service, which was inalienable, and other land whose owner had rights of sale, lease, mortgage, and bequest of it. The code also supported other property rights in provisions which dealt with the sale and purchase of goods, leases, partnerships, and interest on loans. Furthermore, it designated the duties of tenants, workers, and professions, setting the scale of their rentals, wages, and fees.

The code's regulations of marriage and family were similarly numerous. It affirmed the husband and father as the head of his family, although women otherwise enjoyed an unusual independence. It recognized monogamy as the usual form of marriage, but allowed polygamy under some circumstances. It sanctioned arranged marriages, dowries, concubinage, and divorce, and the punishment of adultery with death. The code did not mention clans or tribes to which the people might be attached.

Today the code is best known for its criminal laws which emphasized retaliation, at least insofar as the aristocratic class was concerned. Its *lex talionis* specified: "If a man destroy the eye of another man they shall destroy his eye; if a man knock out the tooth of another man of his own rank, they shall knock out his tooth." The code recognized many kinds of crime and sanctioned death by drowning or by impaling for many of them: rape, kidnapping, incest, robbery, cowardice in battle, brigandage, even watering beer. Cases of witchcraft or false accusation warranted trial by ordeal—for example, accused persons were thrown into the river to swim or sink and were adjudged innocent if they swam to shore. Both the number of crimes and the severity of their punishment, especially the crimes committed by slaves, suggest that the cities found it hard to assimilate large numbers of culturally diverse peoples and so dealt harshly with their felonies.

## Size and Appearance

Most Mesopotamian cities were relatively small in size, having from 5,000 to 25,000 inhabitants—40,000 at the most; rural populations of similar or smaller numbers lived in their territories. One estimate for the third millennium gives Ur a population of 24,000 inhabitants; Lagash, 19,000; Umma, 16,000; and Khafaje, 12,000.[8] Another estimate for Ur for the second millennium is 34,000 inhabitants, with perhaps a larger number living outside it.[9] The urban dwellers for the most part were persons of privilege and wealth, belonging to royal, military, priestly, governmental, and merchant families; suburban inhabitants, in contrast, were inferior and servile populations who were more often engaged in rural industries.

The cities were protected by walls pierced by gates and were heavily fortified. Temple precincts and the king's palace with their clusters of buildings were the most prominent structures; the *ziggurat* of the main temple was the highest edifice. The people's homes were crowded in irregular masses in the available space within the cities' walls. Wealthier families lived in one-, two-, and three-storied houses of brick and stone. These homes, with their rooms built around an interior court, had thick walls and flat roofs waterproofed with pitch. The homes of the poor were of much meaner quality, usually hovels made of mud and reeds, located near or outside the city walls. Bazaars with stores and workshops were located near the gates, where they were accessible to merchants, peasants, and strangers. Other shops were scattered among the homes of residents. Only one street was planned. Extending from the main gate to the main temple, it was used for religious processionals and for military purposes. It also served the people as a promenade on which to stroll, enjoy music, dance, gossip, or otherwise divert themselves.[10] For their daily movements the inhabitants used narrow, twisting paths between buildings which had been trod over the ages. They were provided with water brought by aqueducts and tunnels. Garbage was dumped into the streets.

## Other Cities of Early Antiquity

As other cities of antiquity arose in different parts of the world, they resembled Mesopotamia's in having a social organization based mainly on religious and political institutions. In some cases, this was due to the influence of Mesopotamian urban culture diffused through trade, war, etc. But other cities far removed from Mesopotamia apparently followed a similar course of cultural development, creating comparable urban communities of their own. The latter cities nevertheless differed in important respects, which suggests that they might be classified as sub-types of religious-political cities. However, since most of these cities have not been excavated at present, enough is not yet known about them to make a detailed classification.

In Egypt, where cities appeared in the Nile River Valley about 3000 B.C., nearly the same time as those of Sumer,

a comparable growth of urban communities and civilizations did not take place. Instead semi-divine pharaohs who
acquired monarchical powers of state ruled a largely rural
society by means of administrative districts, or nomes, and
delegated authority to local officials. Each pharaoh resided
near the place where, during his lifetime, he constructed
his pyramid and tomb, and he located his government in a
nearby city. At his death priests maintained his cult in a
temple at the pyramid. The next pharaoh moved his residence to his own pyramid and his government to a city
near it. No permanent capital existed in Egypt until the
middle of the second millennium B.C., when Thebes became its first stable urban community.[11]

Cities also appeared in a third river valley, the Indus
Valley in West Pakistan, producing the Indus civilization
which flourished from 2500 to 1500 B.C. Intensive excavations of several Indus cities reveal that they were walled
and dominated by huge fortresses. Large palaces and temples, and great tanks apparently used for ceremonial bath-
ing, were located on the tops of the fortresses. Presumably
these cities were theocracies, ruled by priest-kings and
priests. They were, like the cities of Mesopotamia, centers of
an extensive agriculture. Excavations have revealed granaries for food storage and mills to manufacture flour. Special
quarters in the mills for workmen suggest that there were
slaves.[12]

The cities of ancient China were also religious-political
cities, not unlike those of Mesopotamia. Semi-divine rulers,
priests, warriors, and merchants lived in them, organizing
the rural populations of their hinterlands in agriculture.[13]

The Mayans in Central America had ceremonial cities
filled with temples and other religious buildings, and inhabited by ruling and priestly strata; they had no other
population. By means of city-states, semi-divine kings assisted by priests and warriors ruled the Mayans, who lived
in villages scattered in their territories.[14] Only two cities in

the New World were cities in a modern sense and both of them still existed when the Spanish explorers appeared: Tenochtitlan, the great city of Mexico, and Cuzco, the Inca capital in Peru.

NOTES

1. For some tentative explanations see Tom B. Jones, *Ancient Civilization* (Chicago: Rand McNally, 1960), pp. 18–20.

2. Sabatino Moscati, *The Face of the Ancient Orient* (Chicago: Quadrangle Books, 1960), p. 21.

3. Henri Frankfort, *The Birth of Civilization in the Near East* (London: Williams & Norgate, 1951), p. 60.

4. Thorkild Jacobsen, *The Intellectual Adventure of Ancient Man*, H. and H. A. Frankfort *et al.*, eds. (Chicago: University of Chicago Press, 1946), pp. 188–189.

5. Moscati, *The Face of the Ancient Orient*, pp. 298–299.

6. Moscati, *The Face of the Ancient Orient*, p. 86.

7. Ralph Turner, *The Great Cultural Traditions* (New York: McGraw-Hill, 1941), I, p. 141.

8. Henri Frankfort, "Town Planning in Ancient Mesopotamia," *Town Planning Review*, 21 (July 1950), p. 104.

9. Cf. Leonard Woolley, *Excavations at Ur* (London: Benn, 1954), p. 193.

10. Lewis Mumford, *The City in History* (New York: Harcourt, Brace, 1961), p. 74.

11. Henri Frankfort, *The Birth of Civilization in the Near East*, p. 83.

12. Tom B. Jones, *Ancient Civilization*, pp. 78–80.

13. Ralph Turner, *The Great Cultural Traditions*, I, pp. 407–438.

14. Sylvanus Griswold Morley, *The Ancient Maya* (Stanford: Stanford University Press, 1946); and Paul Rivet, *Maya Cities* (New York: Putnam, 1960).

# · III ·

# *Cities of*
# *the Classical World*

## The Rise of Political-Commercial Cities

From Mesopotamia and Egypt, which were the great centers of culture in the ancient Orient, cities spread through that arc of fertile land stretching between them called the Fertile Crescent. In this part of Asia Minor, cities were numerous and widespread by 1595 B.C. when the Hammurabi dynasty fell. The people who inhabited these cities—in what is now Syria—developed agriculture and urban trade and enjoyed a civilized life comparable to that of the city dwellers of Mesopotamia. But as they prospered, they attracted the attention of other peoples who coveted their wealth, mountain peoples to their north and desert peoples to their south. These were nomadic tribes of hunters and horsemen who attacked the cities periodically. Usually the urban dwellers repelled them. If not, their cities were pillaged or razed. Some conquerors settled in the cities, founding dynasties built on the indigenous civilizations. Later on, they, too, were assaulted and sometimes defeated by still other urban dwellers and nomadic tribes.

This cycle of war on cities and between cities, succession

of urban empires, and diffusion of urban cultures persisted in Asia Minor until 500 B.C. During its course various
peoples—Kassites, Hittites, Hurrians, Hyksos, Egyptians,
Assyrians, Minoans—rose to prominence for limited periods. Each of them retained certain aspects of the Mesopotamian-Egyptian civilization, but embellished it with additions of their own. They enriched it further when, after
1500 B.C., they began to borrow cultural traits from peoples living near their territories who had different traditions from their own, notably the Jews of Palestine and the
Persians of Iran. They also borrowed from more distant
peoples in India, China, Greece, and the western Mediterranean lands with whom they came into contact through
trade.

About 500 B.C., the Persians conquered the peoples of
Asia Minor, uniting them in a vast empire which stretched
from Libya to India. But shortly thereafter their thrust
westward to the Mediterranean Sea was repelled by the
Greeks, who had by then strong cities of their own. The
Greek victory foretold a geographic shift of the great world
civilizations from the river valleys of the Near East to the
shores of the Mediterranean. Alexander the Great assured
this shift when, with his Macedonian armies, he overthrew
the Persian empire in 330 B.C., thereby ending the ancient
hegemony of the Orient.

## The Cities of Asia Minor

During this period the cities of Asia Minor remained city-
states, with each retaining considerable autonomy even
when it belonged to an urban empire. The upper classes,
made up of royal, noble, priestly, and military families,
continued to predominate in the cities, but large numbers
of merchants, free workers, and slaves also lived in them.
Moreover, the city dwellers remained nearly economically
self-subsistent, raising their food supply on lands near the
cities, insuring an agricultural surplus by cultivating new

land, forcing rural populations to farm these lands, and improving the methods of tillage.

The city-dwellers subsisted on local agriculture because they lacked suitable means of transportation to haul food commodities over long distances, and did not improve transportation facilities much during the entire period of antiquity. This lack of transport also caused them to depend on local artisans in each city for manufactured goods and services, thus hindering the development of domestic trade. However, they did have to carry on a foreign commerce with other cities and countries to get metals, stone, wood, and other raw materials, which they needed to build their cities and to supply their industries when these commodities were scarce or unavailable locally.

The rise of absolute monarchs and the growth of urban empires corresponded with significant changes in the cities themselves. Since wars determined the fate of empires and the character of the empires depended on the cities they arose from, the expansion of military institutions in the cities was inevitable. The growth of professional armies was accompanied by the rise of a new military class. At the same time, technological refinements demanded by war, such as the development of bronze and iron weapons and the use of chariots, required the cities to be veritable fortresses.

As the institutions of war and the political institutions related to them grew, so did the kings' power. We have already seen that, except for the Egyptian pharaohs, kings were regarded not as gods but as demigods. Their power rested on both religious and civil foundations. They had complete control over the military, and the growth of the military vastly augmented the kings' strength. The kings expanded their powers still more through their control of courts, taxation, police powers, and the other institutions of government. Their regimes represented the oriental monarchy at its height.

As the kings became stronger, they reduced the political powers of the priestly strata by removing them from the civil administration of government, developing in their stead patrimonial staffs of public and bureaucratic officials. At the same time, the kings sought to control the priests, and to use them to buttress their regimes. Therefore the kings supported the religion and the priesthood, both vastly important in the cities. The urban communities continued to be theological societies; their sacred institutions were wedded to the secular. The temples also remained places of worship and of business, but they no longer maintained the people in subcommunities.

## The New Merchant Class

Since urban empires consumed great quantities of food, manufactured goods, and raw materials, urban dwellers necessarily had to expand their economic activities over the centuries. After the manner of the people of Mesopotamia, they were able to increase the agricultural surplus of the land and to enlarge the output of economic goods and services by handicraft industries. With somewhat more difficulty, they were also able to expand their foreign trade with other cities and with areas of natural resources. In Mesopotamia the state and temples had carried on this commerce, with free merchants assisting them, usually under their supervision. But these merchants came gradually to control foreign trade in the later empires, and to conduct it with economic gain and the acquisition of riches and power as their principal concern. In the process they emerged as a distinct, powerful class.

Several things explain this emergence of a merchant class and appearance of a profit motivation. First, they represented a necessary specialization of labor in this period. Many of them were literate, highly skilled, and experienced in trade, and they did their work much better than either state or temple officials had. Second, the

wealthy royal, noble, military, and priestly families, invest-
ing their fortunes in land and slaves, became a *rentier*
class which disdained commerce as a source of livelihood.
In the third place, merchants, once they became wealthy,
bought or exacted special privileges of trade from kings,
who valued their economic services even when they de-
spised them as persons and as a class. Also, the kings kept
public peace and order throughout the empires, which
enabled merchants to carry on trade with greater safety
and security. And finally, merchants extended the range
and speed of their commercial operations by making the
improvements in sailing vessels and chariots which the
smelting of iron and other technological advances had
made possible after 1200 B.C.

There were other developments which benefited merchants, and nourished mercantile sentiments in them. As
Hammurabi's code discloses, private ownership in land and
property already existed in the cities of Mesopotamia,
providing a means for the acquisition of wealth and the
pursuit of economic self-interest. We have already seen
that the temples, too, developed such business practices
and legal institutions necessary to commerce as the use of
contracts, commercial law, interest on loans, loans secured
by mortgages, accumulation of capital for investment, and
still others. Later on, the Babylonians continued to elaborate these institutions and to diffuse them among the
peoples with whom they traded. After 1200 B.C., the
coinage of money greatly facilitated business transactions
and the accumulation of wealth. (Throughout antiquity,
prices of economic goods and services were set by law or
custom, as Hammurabi's code shows, and never by the
competition of buyers and sellers in the market place.)

As foreign commerce expanded, other urban dwellers
also undertook business ventures for the sake of profits.
The first urban peoples to commit themselves aggressively
to business, however, were the Phoenicians. After 1000

B.C., they sent their ships to all the shores of the Mediterranean Sea in pursuit of trade. The Babylonians did not lag far behind. After 600 B.C., they rebuilt Babylon with great splendor as the capital of the neo-Chaldean empire of south Mesopotamia, making it the greatest commercial city of the world at that time. Significantly, its rulers were an oligarchy of rich merchants. By 500 B.C., Athens and other Greek cities were bustling commercial centers whose inhabitants were devoted to business. The Hellenistic cities of the fourth, third, and second centuries B.C. and the Roman cities of the early empire were even greater commercial centers. So was Carthage, which was ruled by mercantile oligarchies for many centuries until the Romans destroyed it.

The rise of an essentially commercial capitalism in the cities affected them in many ways. For one thing it made them busy centers of trade and production, linked to each other by international commerce and united by their business cultures and ethos. Consequently their inhabitants, whatever their nationalities, came to think of themselves as urban peoples whose natural habitat was the city, who could live comfortably in each other's cities, and who were more like each other than they were like the rural peoples of their own societies. Another effect was that urban dwellers intensified their striving for wealth, power, and prestige, becoming increasingly differentiated in their possessions and occupations, styles of life, and privileges. They were stratified into rigid classes based on their social and cultural distinctions, which were recognized and enforced by law. In general, the classes of nobility monopolized the wealth and led lives of luxury, while the lower classes earned a meager subsistence and often barely survived.

A third effect of this commercial capitalism was to fill the cities with a heterogeneous population. Many people came to the cities through commerce, others as migrants seeking fortunes, still others as war captives or slaves. As the mixtures of urban inhabitants increased, their loyalty and identity with their cities decreased so that they sometimes clashed in civil war when their sufferings became too hard to bear.

Finally, the growth of the merchant class led to a great increase in the number, size, and distribution of cities. They were the social, political, and cultural centers of empire and affluence.

## Roman Cities

The urbanization of the ancient world reached its apogee with these cities. They were, in ideal type, political-commercial cities whose political, economic and family institutions were paramount in their social order and whose religious institutions were only secondary. The cities of the Roman Empire in the second century A.D. were mature, prosperous cities of this type and are treated as examples of it in this section.

The Roman Empire under the Principate * in the second century was a great state, ruling over 50 to 60 million people, with some three and one-half million square miles of territory, an area so vast that it was virtually coextensive with the civilized world of the time. Politically the Empire was a confederation of city-states, held together by the civil administration and military forces of the central government at Rome. The city-states were largely self-governing in most of their urban affairs. Their foreign and military policies, however, were determined by Rome, and they provided political bases for imperial taxation, jurisdiction, and military conscription. This was in keeping with the Roman policy to govern all peoples and territories by

* From 27 B.C. to 285 A.D., the Roman emperors were called *princeps*, or limited, not absolute, monarchs. Therefore historians designate this period as the period of the Principate or Early Empire.

means of cities and a municipal administration of their affairs. Therefore, the Romans retained or expanded the conquered city-states which they added to the empire, and founded new cities in territories where they did not exist previously, as in Europe, where they attached rural lands to them. There were only a few provinces which had no cities, and these were mainly in imperial domain lands.

In the second century, the Roman Empire was politically stable, and its diverse Italian, Hellenic, and provincial peoples—at least the urban upper classes among them— were sufficiently Romanized to feel part of the empire. By then, too, the emperors were conducting their office and duties with a concern for the entire empire and had reduced some of Rome's former gross exploitation of the provinces for the sole benefit of Italians. Throughout the provinces, they reformed the collection of taxes, used trained bureaucratic personnel in imperial offices, conferred Roman citizenship on provincial people, recruited the Roman armies, and elevated some provincial ruling families into the equestrian order. In Roman courts the emperors dispensed the same justice to Italians and provincials alike. Rome's development of civil, criminal, and public law was complete by then, and the civil law, based on legal principles and judicial precedents, was its single greatest achievement. While Rome was the capital of the Empire, constitutionally it differed very little from cities of the province.

Two types of cities, distinguished by their forms of municipal government, existed in the Empire: Hellenic cities in the east and Italian cities in the west. Hellenic cities were the former Hellenistic city-states and other cities founded by the Greeks in the east and modeled after the Greek municipalities. Italian cities were the Roman cities of Italy and other cities founded by the Romans in Europe and Africa.

On conquering the Hellenic cities, the Romans interfered

relatively little in their internal affairs in the beginning, permitting the inhabitants to continue with their social and cultural activities and to speak the Greek language. Under the Principate, however, the Romans reversed this policy, restricting the popular government and urban democracy to which the Greeks were accustomed. The Romans transferred from popular assemblies to councils the power to initiate legislation and to elect magistrates, and they made the councils into permanent bodies of ex-magistrates holding their seats for life. In Italian cities, which had assemblies, councils, and magistrates copied after the Roman government, they similarly weakened the assemblies, strengthened the councils, and limited the selection of magistrates to rich men. In effect, they gave control of the cities to wealthy, upper-class families, reducing, if not eliminating, the political activities of ordinary citizens in their own governmental affairs.

The cities were city-states; councils and magistrates governed both urban dwellers and the rural populations residing on the lands which belonged to the cities. Among the important duties of the city governments were the construction of public buildings, roads, bridges, aqueducts to bring in fresh water, and sewage disposal tunnels. They kept a close watch over the business and industries of their cities, supervising prices, weights and measures, and the quality of coins in the markets. They also provided fire and police protection. In addition, they staged many public games and festivals, supported the gods of the city and the local priesthoods, contributed to the support of teachers of grammar and rhetoric and sometimes of athletics. Finally, they collected taxes levied by the Roman state on the people.

To defray the expenses of cities, the magistrates were expected to donate large sums of their own money; they were never paid for their services while in office. When the empire entered into economic depression in the third century, magistrates were often unwilling or unable to make these financial contributions and sought to avoid office. The emperors thereupon made the magistracies both compulsory and hereditary. The cities, however, derived some revenues from indirect taxes, profits from monopolies, and land rents. But inadequate municipal finances was always a serious problem in the Roman cities.

## Economic Organization

The municipal functions of Roman cities suggests, perhaps, how the empire and its cities were organized economically. The Roman economy, in modern terms, approximated a mixed state-private commercial capitalism, with the state active in public works and in certain industries involving large funds or labor forces, while individuals and families engaged in trade, production, and agriculture. Most cities were still largely self-subsistent. Their food and raw materials were supplied locally. They depended on local artisans working in households or shops for manufactured goods and specialized services.

Most urban populations could not trade food products and manufactured goods because transportation, whether by land or sea, was still too costly, hazardous, and slow. Rome and several other large seaport cities were exceptions, however. Lacking an adequate agriculture in their areas, these cities had to import huge quantities of food and commodities to support their citizens. In addition, Rome, the capital of the empire, consumed great quantities of goods and needed an array of services, which it had the military power and tax resources to command from all parts of its vast empire.

In general, the state was responsible for the construction and maintenance of roads, aqueducts, canals, palaces and other public buildings, and fortifications and city walls. Sometimes it entered into the production of the materials used in these projects, such as bricks, tiles, cement, and lead pipes, which it manufactured in competition with private business firms. More important, it held monopolies in mining, metal working, sometimes in textiles, and it owned fleets of ships and maintained wharves and warehouses. The state pursued a policy of economic imperialism by using its powers to promote the welfare and prosperity of empire and people; it fortified trading posts, founded colonies, destroyed hostile tribes, suppressed piracy, built military highways, and established a single currency throughout the empire. Its unremitting surveillance of private enterprise was intended to ensure the economic stability of the empire.

Commerce and agriculture flourished in the private sector of the Roman economy but manufacturing did not. There were three types of commerce: a retail trade in the cities, a regional trade among the cities and provinces, and a foreign trade with other countries. Local retail trade, carried on by a few large merchants, many small shopkeepers, and peddlers, involved the sale of commodities and services produced on nearby farms or in households and shops in the cities. For the most part, only large seaport cities took part in regional trade, with Rome the focus of a network of trade routes which bound them together. These cities, for example, Lyon and Massilia in Gaul, Damascus and Palmyra in Syria, and Thessalonica in Macedonia, assembled foodstuffs, raw materials, and some manufactured products from their regions, and shipped them on to Rome and other large cities. As inventories of the warehouses of Rome attest, the total quantity and variety of these goods were enormous. Foreign trade with the countries of Asia, India, even China, consisted of luxury goods, jewelry, wines, perfumes, and spices, and was carried on by foreign merchants and freedmen.

Roman agriculture flourished under the Principate. With the pressure of growing cities and the inordinate demands of the state and the military, the Romans were forced to

organize agriculture efficiently, extend it to all provinces of
the empire (to Europe, in particular), and to increase its
total productivity. The large Roman farms or estates,
known as *latifundia*, were the dominant form of landhold-
ing, and practiced diversified farming and cattle raising.
These *latifundia* were operated with slaves and tenant
farmers, although farmers were preferable because, by the
second century, the supply of slaves had diminished with
the cessation of foreign wars.

To native methods of farming, the Romans added
practices which they had borrowed from Greece, Carthage,
Gaul, and elsewhere, and developed a prosperous agriculture. They managed their vineyards scientifically, planted
many fruits, vegetables, and grasses for fodder, and attempted to breed better livestock. In addition, they improved cultivation by manuring fields, by ploughing in
fodder crops after grazing, and by leaving fields fallow.
But because they made few advances in the technological
improvement of farm tools and machinery, they did not
fundamentally change the character of agriculture in the
ancient world.[1]

In striking contrast to their agricultural practices, the
Romans showed far less initiative and enterprise in urban
industry. They did not advance, for the most part, beyond
a household and shop organization of production and the
handicraft methods of manufacture. In some industries,
however, such as in the manufacture of articles from
bronze and silver, pottery, glass making, and textiles, they
sometimes founded factories which utilized a division and
specialization of labor, employing as many as two hundred
persons in some workshops, but they always used manual,
never mechanical, power in these operations. Such factories existed mostly in Hellenic cities, where the state,
temples, or wealthy merchants owned them, and they used
both free and slave laborers. They did not mass produce
manufactured goods or make important technological advances in manufacturing.

A number of reasons which explain why the Romans lagged in developing industries illuminate further the character of their economy. In the first place, they did not mass produce manufactured goods because they lacked a mass market for the sale of such products. Neither rural nor tribal populations, which comprised 90 percent or more of the total population of the empire, had wealth, opportunity, or incentives to buy manufactured goods; the state, the military, the temples, and the rich families could get them in sufficient quantities from local artisans or through export trade.

In the second place, wealthy urban families invested their capital preferably in land, sometimes in mortgages or loans, occasionally in trading ventures, but almost never in industry. They were a *rentier* class that lived on incomes derived from the land, but did not reinvest their capital in industrial enterprises which would have created new wealth because these were risky and speculative. Not only was land the safest and most lucrative investment, but ownership of *latifundia* conferred prestige.

Third, wealthy families were disinterested in making technological advances or introducing labor-saving devices in industry, because slaves were a plentiful and cheap labor force. Slaves did much of the work of the Roman economy; not only did they labor in the mines, shipyards, textile shops, and other industries, but they were doctors and schoolmasters, shopkeepers and clerks, actors, gladiators, even architects.[2] Nor did Roman law protect patent rights in inventions which would have encouraged the utilization of inventions in industries. Moreover, most Romans were apathetic toward science and the application of scientific discoveries to their industries. A fourth reason for Rome's industrial lag was that under Roman law the corporation as a form of organization was permitted in public but not in private enterprise; since businessmen could utilize only individual ownerships or partnerships, they were, in effect, restricted to small-scale enterprises.[3]

In the second century, freedmen and their descendants, Greeks, Syrians, and other provincial peoples, dominated commerce and manufactures in the Roman cities. They operated businesses of every kind, were manufacturers, filled the trades and professions, entered the civil service at its lower ranks, and managed *latifundia* and farms. Successful business men among them used their wealth to buy high offices in government, others bought land and slaves, still others were elevated to the equestrian order. They cultivated the commercial virtues, making the aggressive pursuit of wealth an end in itself. In the process, as they imparted their parvenu qualities to other urban dwellers, they made the ethos of capitalism paramount in the cities.

## Social and Cultural Life in the Cities

### The Size of the Cities

No more than 10 percent of the empire population—or about five million persons—lived in cities, and, in the second century, approximately one million of them lived in Rome. Since Rome was the political, military, and cultural center of the Empire, important, successful Romans had to live there, and people from all parts of the world traveled there for the same reason. Large populations also lived in the older Hellenistic cities—Alexandria, Corinth, Pergamum, Ephesus, Thessalonica, Athens, and others; one or two had nearly 500,000 inhabitants and several had more than 100,000. But most cities were much smaller than this, especially in the west, as evidenced by the large number of cities in relation to the total urban population. The Romans apparently intended that the new cities which they built in Spain, France, and England should not exceed 50,000 inhabitants, and probably they did not.[4]

With cities spread from Iraq to England, the urban populations of the empire were diverse both ethnically and culturally. In Rome and in the eastern cities, Hellenized Greeks and Romans were the predominant population, with many other groups, free and unfree, scattered among them. The ethnic mixture was greater in Rome and in seaport cities accessible to merchants, sailors, peasants, and others. The cities of Europe were populated by Romans, Hellenized Gauls, and native groups.

The Romans emphasized cultural rather than ethnic distinctions among their populations, accepting as Romans any peoples or races who were urbanized and acculturated to Roman life. War, commerce, and slavery abetted the mixing of peoples among them, and their amalgamation through intermarriage was always considerable. The basic stock of the Romans changed at least three times through these intermixtures over the course of time.[5] Roman civilization was based on Graeco-Roman culture, but this was a culture of cities and urban dwellers. The rural peoples retained their own traditional ways of life, and most of them were scarcely touched by Roman culture. Within the empire, there were actually three different areas with distinct cultures: the Hellenized East, which was the empire's creative center despite Rome's political supremacy; the Latin West—Italy, Africa, and Spain; and the Gallic West—France and Britain.[6]

*Social Stratification*

Not all urban dwellers had equal access to the cultural life of their particular cities. They were stratified into social orders which were nearly hereditary, which afforded different paths to wealth, power, and prestige, and which forced different styles of life on them.

There were three social orders: senatorial, equestrian, and plebian. The first two comprised the hereditary and secular nobility, who were essentially a single class of

aristocrats living in the city of Rome; the third was the
class of free workers found in all cities. In the provincial
cities, the rich, ruling families, whose members sat on the
councils and were magistrates, composed a curial class of
aristocrats; they were nearly at the level of the equestrian
order of knights, and could be elevated to it by the
emperor. A large number of poor citizens, almost 300,000
in 200 A.D., existed as a de-classed group in Rome. They
lived on subsidies provided by the state and by wealthy
families, and refused to work at all. They were a proletariat
of consumers, not producers.[7] The rural populations—
peasants, tenant farmers, and slaves—were not included
in the urban orders, and some were hardly accounted
civilized.

There was very little mobility between orders. Emperors
appointed new members to the upper orders, not to
liberalize them, but to replenish their ranks or to reward
their friends. Some wealthy persons succeeded in climbing
to a higher order, and the emancipation of slaves elevated
the status of vast numbers of persons who could, thereafter,
advance within the lower order. As democracy grew weaker
under the Principate, the orders became, if anything, more
rigid.

The Roman senators and their families who constituted
the hereditary senatorial order were a powerful aristocratic
class that monopolized the prerogatives of the empire. In
addition to sitting in the Senate, they alone were eligible to
the highest political offices and to military commands and
were greatly deferred to by the inferior social orders. They
possessed enormous wealth, which was, indeed, a qualifica-
tion for the Senate. These were the people who ordinarily
invested their capital in lands and slaves.

The knights, a secular nobility, occupied the next highest
civil and military posts in the empire, such as personal
offices under the emperors, provincial administrative posts,
municipal offices, and army commands. They engaged in

trade and production more frequently than senators, owned land and slaves, served as bankers, and were, indeed, the successful businessmen of the empire. Although they needed smaller incomes to hold their rank, some knights were much wealthier than senators as a result of their economic activities. The emperors appointed new members to this equestrian order from eligible wealthy Italian and provincial families, and, from the knights, new members of the senatorial order. While preserving social distinctions between them, under the Principate, senators and knights often acted together in self-interest to maintain their class privileges and to retain their closeness to the emperors.

After the aristocrats came the plebian order, which comprised a wide assortment of urban dwellers: whites, Negroes, and Orientals; citizens and non-citizens; freeborn, freedmen, and slaves. The upper stratum among them, the *honestiores*, included persons who had annual incomes of 5,000 sesterces or more: merchants, manufacturers, shopkeepers, some artisans, lesser army officers, civil servants, and others. Their lower stratum, the *humiliores*, consisted of persons with little or no capital: most artisans; some tradesmen; workers in such industries as cloth making, metal working, and brewing; sailors; dock workers; and mule drivers employed in transportation. Not much is known about the plebs of the cities other than that the *humiliores*, at least, made a precarious living and that most of them were abjectly poor. Their poverty was due to the inadequate employment in urban industries, and the constant competition of slaves in nearly all places of work. For the *humiliores* the amenities of cities scarcely existed.

The plebian order, however, improved its economic circumstances through an increase in the number and size of handicraft industries and through their own greater control of these industries as free workers, which the empire's prosperity promoted. At this time the emperors also encouraged tradesmen and workers in these crafts to organize into guilds, which became the principal associations of the working class and their main social outlets. These guilds were variously trade, professional, religious, and funerary associations, enrolling alike employers, employees, free citizens, freedmen, and slaves. They were modeled on municipal governments, with patrons, president, other officers, and a treasury maintained by dues, fines, legacies, and other contributions.

In addition to helping members during periods of hardship and giving them burial after death, the guild's functions were social in nature: they provided their members with fellowship under public and religious auspices. In no way did they correspond to modern trade unions; they did not bargain collectively about wages, hours, or conditions of work, although some associations tried to advance the economic interests of their members. Nor did the guilds undertake political activity. This was discouraged under the Principate. In the third century, however, when the empire was afflicted with troubles and facing decline, emperors made the guilds into semi-public bodies and charged them with the performance of public duties.

## Religion

Religion was an important element in Roman cities under the Principate, even though it no longer exerted a major role in the urban social order. Religions abounded in the cities—above all, in Rome—and people were either active in one or another of them or sought the help of the gods in their activities. Emperor and state controlled religion, using it to support the government and to unify the people.

The official religion prescribed the worship of a pantheon of Greek and Roman gods. Colleges of priests conducted its rituals and processions from imposing temples in the cities. It embraced the worship of auxiliary deities, too, such as the gods of Fortune, Chance, and Peace, as well as the Roman Empire itself in the cult of Roma and Augustus. Urban dwellers also worshiped their city gods, sometimes their tribal gods, too, some of whom were elevated to the status of state gods.

A great number of Oriental religions, partly Hellenized by contact with Greek civilization, existed in Rome and the other cities, brought there by merchants, soldiers, sailors, and slaves. Mithraism was the most widespread of these eastern religions, while gnosticism, a blend of religious, astrological, and philosophical ideas, existed in Rome in at least thirty forms. Primitive Christianity was one of these Oriental cults until it became the state religion of the late Roman Empire in the fifth century. Astrology and magic also had their followers, and, whatever religion they espoused, most people resorted to them periodically.

As in the other cities of antiquity, domestic religions also persisted; the Romans venerated clan and tribal gods, their *lares* and *penates,* and observed rituals of worship addressed to them in their homes. The emperors tolerated these domestic religions so long as their adherents publicly acclaimed the state gods as well and did not threaten the stability of the state or provoke resistance to Roman rule in the provinces. But they persecuted the early Christians and Jews who refused to comply with the first injunction, and suppressed the Druidism of the Celts of Gaul and Britain for violating the second.[8]

By the second century, however, despite the support and subsidies of the emperors, the state religion had fallen into decadence. Many Romans, deprived of political activity under the Principate, lost their enthusiasm for the state religion, and tired of the rites. They either neglected to attend services or attended from expediency and scoffed at the gods. Instead they went to the chapels of the Oriental religions, attracted to their elaborate ceremonies of worship, their amelioristic theologies, and their evangelism. These cults gave some Romans both a sense of faith and a discipline of behavior intended to make possible a life beyond the grave. Others turned to astrology or magic, read the Greek philosophers, made a religion of business, or lost their faith entirely.

## Physical Plan

Roman cities did not conform to any single city plan. Many older Greek and Hellenistic cities were largely un-planned, with the exception of their fortifications, civic centers, and water supply. Some of these cities resembled overgrown villages with their huddle of buildings, narrow winding streets or alleys, and crowded neighborhoods. Rome itself was much like these older cities, even though the Romans, who were good engineers with a large con-struction industry, used Greek concepts of city planning and rebuilt many of the city's older sections. Rome, of course, had a huge population with which to contend, and though its walls were extended several times, they severely constricted the inner space of the city. The resulting density led to overcrowding and an indiscriminate mixture of public structures, temples, and residences, although there was greater uniformity in buildings in the forum and the market place.

Because they were so important, the forum and market place were located near the intersection of the two principal streets, which were straight and bisected the city. But most other streets were short, discontinuous, narrow, curving, and generally unplanned. They contributed to the jumble of buildings and to the confusion of Roman neighborhoods.

Wealthy Romans lived in single-family houses built around an interior court, with running water, sewage disposal drains, and other conveniences. But the plebian population inhabited tenement buildings six and seven stories high which often were flimsily built. These buildings lacked running water except on the ground floor and had no sewage disposal facilities at all. Inserted among the tenements were a colosseum, amphitheater, public baths, and other edifices in which the emperors provided the people with circuses and public spectacles. Rome got its fresh water by means of great aqueducts which carried it from long distances away, its sewage emptied into the Tiber River.

The Romans might have wished to live in cities they built in the provinces, which copied the newer Hellenistic cities and followed Greek ideas of city planning.[9] These cities were intended for 50,000 inhabitants at most. The planners grouped public buildings in areas based on function, topography, convenience, and tradition, and related them to the gridiron system of streets. Among these buildings, which reveal the social and cultural activities of the people, were a city hall, a theater, gymnasia, a library, a stadium, and public baths. However, the planners paid relatively little attention to private houses, which made up neighborhoods in the areas not used for public purposes. These Hellenistic cities were celebrated in the classical world for their beauty, comfort, and public hygiene. Even by modern standards, they were very livable, having glamor, color, and an individuality of their own.

## Evaluation of the Roman Cities

Through these cities, which served as urban and regional governments, the Romans ruled a world empire and brought Graeco-Roman civilization to maturity. The cities were centers of thriving business and production; they provided a social and cultural life for their inhabitants; they were always civilized places in which to live. Through them, the Romans maintained a Roman peace throughout their territories, organized and extended agriculture to new peoples and countries, brought millions of acres under cultivation, introduced cities and civilization to a Europe whose people heretofore had lived in tribes, and left a

legacy of Roman law and political administration. Perhaps
the cities themselves, with their order and sophistication,
were the greatest legacy.

Yet the Roman cities and their empire were built at the
cost of incessant wars of great destruction, and the flagrant
exploitation of the conquered peoples. The weakness of
their bases eventually destroyed the prosperity of their
cities and brought them to ruin.

One serious weakness was a Roman city's inevitable
parasitism on the rural populations and territories where
it was located. As we have noted, no more than 5 to 10
percent of the people of a province lived in the cities, yet
this small minority systematically extracted an agricultural
surplus and other wealth from a great rural majority by
such means as enforced labor, enslavement, taxes, tithes,
and military conscription. Moreover, the city made little,
if any, economic or cultural return. The rural populations
lived in agricultural villages, continued illiterate, and were
too removed and too poor to afford urban goods and
services. Even urban trade was mostly one-way, involving
the transportation of agricultural commodities and raw
materials from the provinces and foreign countries to the
cities; its main beneficiaries were the state, the armies,
and the rich families. Thus, throughout the empire wealth
moved from the country to the cities, and seldom the
other way.

This pattern of exploitation existed within the cities as
well. A relatively small number of rich city families lived
comfortably, but at the cost of political disfranchisement
and economic insecurity for the plebian population, which
was often not far from destitution and whose subsistence
was always precarious. The Romans did not establish industries which might have employed rural populations displaced from agriculture. Instead, they used the land for
their own enrichment. Many *latifundia* owners were
absentee landlords in Rome or some other city, where they

were mainly concerned with living well.[10] From an economic point of view, the cities were overpopulated in
terms of available employment; urban commerce was never
extensive enough to employ more than a small number of
the city dwellers. The cities also lacked sufficient industries to employ more than another small percentage of
their inhabitants. There was only the manufacturing, in
households and shops, of goods that were not exported.
The plebians, who were free citizens, survived by the
forced labor of numerous, relatively cheap slaves who were
employed in every kind of economic activity. These slaves,
who performed much of the cities' work, were a constant
economic threat to the free workers whose conditions of
existence they depressed. The magistrates sought to rec-
oncile the lower social orders to their mean lot by doles
of bread and by public spectacles, but these were never an
adequate substitute for jobs. And in periods of depression,
the upper orders increased their exploitation of the inferior
orders, which sometimes provoked the latter into rebellion
and fierce combat, with much brutality on both sides, and
many casualties. These practices bred a cruelty and
violence beneath the civilized veneer of the urban popu-
laces.

Finally, the persistence of cities as city-states was another weakness. The cities did not have good municipal
governments, nor did they govern their rural populations
and territories well. Oligarchies of rich families ruled them
to perpetuate their own advantages and to advance the
interests of the state. They eliminated the participation of
citizens in government and largely destroyed the democracy
which previously the cities had enjoyed. The lack of
adequate public finances was the particular bane of cities,
but magistrates did not seek to strengthen urban fiscal
policies or to improve municipal administration by con-
sultation with other city or empire officials. In their
activities as heads of city-states, they tended toward

particularism and localism, which prevented such co-operation. For this same reason, they seldom developed a high sense of responsibility for their rural populations— except, of course, to keep them hard-working and submissive. Despite their legal and administrative abilities, the Romans could not organize their cities successfully, nor enable them to withstand the eventual dissolution of the empire.

**NOTES**

1. W. F. Heitland, "Agriculture," in *The Legacy of Rome*, ed. Cyril Bailey (Oxford: Clarendon Press, 1923), p. 512.
2. Herbert Heaton, *Economic History of Europe* (New York: Harpers, 1948), rev. ed., p. 52.
3. Arthur E. R. Boak, *A History of Rome to 565 A.D.* (New York: Macmillan, 1955), 4th ed., pp. 377–378.
4. Lewis Mumford, *The City in History*, p. 209.
5. Ralph Turner, *The Great Cultural Traditions*, II, p. 1332.
6. Ralph Turner, *The Great Cultural Traditions*, II, p. 949.
7. W. W. Tarn and G. T. Griffith, *Hellenistic Civilization* (London: Arnold, 1952), 3rd ed., p. 119.
8. Arthur E. R. Boak, *A History of Rome to 565 A.D.*, p. 389.
9. R. E. Wycherley, *How the Greeks Built Cities* (New York: Macmillan, 1949).
10. A. H. M. Jones, *The Greek City from Alexander to Justinian* (Oxford: Clarendon Press, 1940), p. 268.

# · IV ·

# *Cities of Medieval Europe*

### Urban Renaissance

After the fall of Rome, the Eastern Roman empire survived as the Byzantine empire for another thousand years, retaining its Hellenism. Constantinople, its capital, became one of the great cities of the world, while other cities also flourished in its territories and throughout the Near East.

But the Western Roman empire fell apart and, with it, the Roman cities in Italy which were disorganized politically; these declined economically and lost most of their inhabitants. Some survived as small cities and villages during the next centuries, a few rising again to eminence in the tenth century and thereafter with the revival of trade.

In Europe, as the native populations resumed control of their lands, they were unable to maintain the previously existing Roman cities and institutions. Instead, they entered into a prolonged period of cultural decline and political decentralization, now known as their Dark Ages, during which they separated into numerous kingdoms and lesser principalities and lapsed into feudalism. They were also converted to Christianity. The Catholic Church became not only a powerful international state among them, but the principal architect of the medieval synthesis of their societies.

The few European cities which did remain were greatly reduced in size. Often they comprised mere clusters of dwellings, grouped about a monastery, palace, or castle, and were ruled by a bishop, king, or feudal lord. These cities served mainly as administrative centers for religious and political jurisdictions. Some were episcopal cities, from which bishops governed their dioceses, and which might be laid out along the boundaries of the former Roman municipalities. Others were political cities, serving as capitals of kingdoms, counties, or of other civil divisions. There were also hamlets, or burgs, in which soldiers were garrisoned to protect nearby rural populations.

With the revival of trade in the eleventh century, European cities began to recover from their near eclipse.[1] This revival was due in large part to population increases in areas which had to import food because of famines— which were frequent at the time—or low agricultural productivity. Those cities whose agriculture could not feed an expanding population became centers of commerce: Venice first, followed by Genoa, Pisa, Amalfi, Gaeta, and other Italian cities, as well as many in southern France. Later cities appeared in northern Europe, Flanders, the Rhineland, northern France, the British Isles, and at North and Baltic Sea harbors. Later, the Crusades provided a further stimulus, from the eleventh century through the thirteenth, to the renewal of trade between Europe and the Orient.

This growth in trade increased the total wealth of Europe, stimulating a demand for greater production and exchange of commodities and for luxury goods from the Near East. The Italian cities dominated a revival of Mediterranean commerce with the Orient, but north

Europeans carried on some trade with the Near Eastern cities via the rivers of Russia.

The merchants who conducted this trade—many of them Jews and Syrians from the eastern Mediterranean, who dealt in silks, furs, spices, and other luxuries—established warehouses and other facilities in cities located on their travel routes where they had access to local markets and where local rulers protected them. They settled, however, not inside the cities but immediately outside their walls, in places subsequently known as suburbs, which were also enclosed by walls during the eleventh and twelfth centuries. Other people whose livelihood depended on large-scale trade, such as shopkeepers, artisans, and laborers, also settled in the suburbs. The suburbs eventually outgrew the original urban centers and developed into medieval cities. Some long dormant Roman cities such as London, Paris, and Cologne revived under the impetus of trade; new cities were founded, and some grew out of burgs; but other Roman cities and many burgs not favorably located for trade failed to grow.

## A Degree of Freedom

Nevertheless, neither cities nor commerce fitted conveniently into medieval society, and urban dwellers came into conflict with the king or lord who governed them, and to whom the land they lived on often belonged. His sovereignty over them was autocratic. He ruled them as a part of his larger rural domains, but extracted from them special urban rents, tolls, and taxes. They wanted freedom from feudal and seignioral restraints in order to carry on trade and production; they wished to keep for themselves as much of their profits and property as they could. In self-interest they also sought both a measure of control over the laws governing their enterprises and ways to resist the lord's levies.

Led by the more intrepid and experienced merchants,

urban dwellers organized into communes—to which they bound themselves by oath—in order to act together in their dealings with feudal lords and outsiders. Through the communes they established governments to hold property in common, manage their affairs, build defenses, and enforce law and order among themselves. Thereafter, by negotiation, purchase, coercion, and military force, they won from their rulers certain rights of trade and manufacture, along with a number of civil liberties which made them relatively autonomous. Communes thus served a revolutionary function in enabling city dwellers to exist outside the feudal social order in European countries.

To protect their trade and to wrest further social and economic privileges from sovereigns and feudal lords, urban dwellers formed merchants' guilds of both merchants and artisans, also often oath-bound. The guilds were corporations which carried on commerce and production in the cities and sought to ensure the prosperity and welfare of their inhabitants. Often commune leaders were also the large merchants in the guilds, and the communes and guilds were closely associated in controlling the cities. For these reasons, guild regulations had the status of quasi-public laws binding on the urban dwellers whether members of the guild or not.

Not all feudal lords opposed the growth of cities and the subsequent expansion of trade and markets within their jurisdictions. On the contrary, many welcomed the increased revenues they got from the cities through taxes, rents, and imposts on growing urban businesses. When short of money, they were often willing—or were forced by communes—to sell added economic privileges for cash. Some rulers founded new cities on their lands in anticipation of income from them, and, in order to attract migrants, granted civil liberties similar to those enjoyed by older communes elsewhere.

In the twelfth century many kings and lords of England and France actively encouraged the rise of cities. In Germany, the greater lords rather than the kings founded many new cities, drawing settlers to them by granting municipal charters copied from Freiburg's or Magdeburg's. Sometimes, seeking allies in their conflicts with nobles, the kings would strengthen communes by granting them new economic and political rights to win them to their side.

Unlike secular lords, church prelates seldom either encouraged the growth of cities or willingly surrendered their control of ecclesiastical cities and their special privileges. The Church was the greatest owner of property in Europe, with vested interests in feudalism, and it welcomed no threat to its economic dominance. Its monasteries and cloisters, with their work forces of clerical and lay brothers, were great economic organizations, often competitive with urban communes and guilds. Moreover, the Church hampered the commerce of cities by its sanctions against usury and other business practices. Also, bishops and abbots were not so hard pressed for money as lords—or, at least, they were less willing to sell social or economic privileges for cash. As a result, the communes in Italy and especially in Germany engaged in long, bitter strife with ecclesiastical rulers, removing them by force of arms from the civil administration of their cities.

Through accumulated social and economic rights that were written into municipal charters to protect them from revocation or erosion, urban inhabitants gradually won freedom from feudal restraints and acquired the civil liberties necessary to their urban existence. Their major achievement was to win status as urban citizens of cities; they did not need to remain serfs or villeins. Thus they won the rights of person and movement which derive from citizenship. Usually the charters stipulated that any serf who took refuge in a city and lived there a year and a day without being recovered by his master was thereafter a citizen. "City air makes a man free," as a German proverb expressed it. Such freedom attracted new settlers from the land to the cities.

Urban dwellers secured other rights. They could acquire and dispose of land, buy, sell, and bequeath property, and could hold a perpetual market; that is, they could engage in trade at any time and according to their own rules. Moreover, they had a special body of commercial law, known as the law merchant, enforced in their own courts to regulate business practices necessary to their economic activities. Urban citizens were thus a third estate, less powerful than the two estates of the nobility and clergy, but free, privileged peoples nevertheless, who lived amid a vast, unfree population tied by serfdom to the soil.

Not all urban populations were equally successful in winning emancipation or in getting strong city charters. Most cities, in fact, never won more than the minimal civil rights to govern themselves and to carry on trade. The majority of European cities, especially in France, southern Italy, England, Spain, and Germany, accepted the sovereignty of kings and states and a limited autonomy under their charters. Even such great cities as Paris, London, Palermo, Rouen, and Bordeaux had such restricted powers, and two sets of officials, their own and the king's, who commonly administered their affairs. Exceptions were the North Italian cities; these developed into city-states, resembling the Roman municipalities in their governments, state enterprise, military power, commercial capitalism, and political particularism. Some German cities in the Rhine and Danube river valleys were virtually free cities and some communes in southern France and in the Low Countries held considerable power, partly because they controlled their own militia. But most medieval cities, with their limited rights of self-rule, were kindred to them only in their commercial activities.

### Economic and Political Organization

With the main exception of the Italian city-states, the medieval cities of Europe in the period from 1250–1300 were, in ideal type, commercial cities. After 1300 and especially after 1400 the cities changed in character considerably, but in the late thirteenth century most were small trade centers and market places for their residents and the rural populations dwelling in their areas. Their economies were also partly agricultural. Inhabitants grew some of their food and grazed livestock in fields outside the cities, although they bought most of their foodstuffs from nearby feudal estates and from other local sources. For non-local commodities and for luxury goods—when they could afford them—they depended on the appearance of foreign merchants at fairs held once or twice a year. Urban dwellers earned their livelihood in trade and in household industries providing manufactured articles and services. Many kinds of artisans—bakers, butchers, blacksmiths, potters, and others—worked in their homes and shops. They made their articles on order, not in anticipation of demand. Because of the high cost and inconvenience of transportation, cities seldom entered these goods in foreign trade. They depended instead on their own local artisans. To a great extent, medieval cities and their surrounding areas were relatively self-subsistent. One result was the individuality which accompanied their relative isolation.

The larger cities advanced beyond this local self-sufficiency. They were variously active in foreign commerce, manufacturing, finance, or in all three. The northern Italian city dwellers, for example, carried on an active overseas commerce with the Near East and the Orient and an overland commerce with other European cities. Over the Mediterranean they transported fabrics, weapons, metals, timber, and sometimes slaves to the Near East, returning with spices, wines, silks, wools, dyestuffs, medications, and jewelry. Urban populations in northern Europe were similarly engaged in trading raw materials and foodstuffs (metals, timber, hides, fish, grains, salt, and wool) with other European cities and with the Near East, although they did not entirely neglect such luxury goods as wines, furs, and jewelry.

Some large merchants, especially in Italian and Flemish cities, manufactured some of the goods they traded, textiles in particular. They produced these goods by a "putting-out" system of manufacturing: they supplied artisans with wool or other materials to convert into finished goods in their own homes or workshops. The merchants later sold these goods in markets or fairs. They did not often hire the workers and assemble them to work under supervision in shops. When they did, however, as sometimes they did in Flemish textiles, these merchants became industrialists and the workers became wage-earners of a modern kind.

As urban dwellers developed foreign trade and industries, they also established banks, credit agencies, and other commercial services to facilitate their operations. The Italian cities, in particular, specialized in financial activities. To hold or attract more business, the cities also provided other facilities such as markets, ports, highways, and canals.

## Regulating Business

The pursuit of commerce was the city dweller's reason for being, whatever the size of the city. All urban peoples wanted to expand their economic activities in order to strengthen their place in feudal European society and to ensure their own welfare and prosperity. Therefore, they used whatever economic, political, and military powers were available to protect their businesses and tended to let considerations of economic self-interest determine their urban policies and actions. They believed that urban governments properly should support the economic enterprises of all inhabitants, not merely those of a few wealthy persons among them.

Urban governments had two methods of accomplishing their purposes: to create monopolies to prevent the spread of trade and industries to villages or other rural places, and to regulate them in complete detail so as to favor their own inhabitants against foreign merchants and feudal lords and protect them against their own excessive competition or cupidity. The degree to which cities succeeded in maintaining monopolies and in enforcing their regulations differed. Italian city-states and, to some extent, cities with strong communes could succeed at it—often, indeed, pursuing policies of economic imperialism. But most cities were more restrained in these matters.

Urban dwellers had several ways of implementing their economic policies. They tried to limit buying and selling in city markets to themselves, in order to restrict the competition of foreign merchants in retail trade and to subject feudal estates and peasants to their rules. Whenever possible, they protected the persons, goods, and interests of their citizens in and out of the cities. Upon merchants and artisans they conferred the privilege of organizing guilds and carrying on trades in the cities. They also tried to attract entrepreneurs and artisans to their cities while preserving their own trade secrets with utmost care. In addition, they fixed wages, prices, and standards of manufacture, and regulated markets to prevent monopolies, speculation, fraud, or other abuses. Finally, they protected the consumer from the dishonest practices and avarice of sellers and tried to ensure him of ample food supplies at fair prices.

Mayors and magistrates of cities controlled the guilds and administered these regulations in order to promote stability and prosperity of business and to protect customers. But they entrusted to the guilds the responsibility for enforcing

the regulations in their own trades or occupations and for
safeguarding the welfare of their members. As we have already noted, this made the guilds quasi-public associations.
On some occasions, when their own interests were benefited, church and feudal lords enforced some of the business regulations of cities.

By the late thirteenth century, the many merchants' and
artisans' guilds which existed in the cities indicated an increasing specialization of labor. Some guilds were founded
by tradesmen or artisans who broke away from the earlier
merchants' guild when wealthy merchants began to dominate it. These guilds were also initially oath-bound organizations. Other guilds were formed when sufficient numbers
of artisans were employed in new or expanding trades and
were motivated by self-interest to establish separate associations of their own. In the thirteenth century they were
mainly economic organizations concerned with protecting
their members within the guild itself and in their contacts
with other guilds and with the cities. They provided a common social life for members, but not traditional services of
mutual aid.

In a spirit of thoroughgoing protectionism, the guilds
tried to establish monopolies in their respective trades. This
meant that, when successful, they determined the quantity
and quality of goods and services, fixed prices and wages,
established conditions of work, and controlled the admit-
tance into guilds and the training of apprentices. They inflicted severe penalties against members or outsiders who
violated their rules or threatened their power. Through
their regulations they sought to provide equal economic opportunity for members and to prevent any one of them
from gaining an unfair competitive advantage over the
other members. In the small markets which then existed,
a member could often improve his business rapidly only by
taking away business from other members. For this reason,
the guilds steadfastly opposed free enterprise in the cities.[2]

## The Emergence of Capitalism

The guilds succeeded, in general, in imposing their monopolies and regulations in retail trade and in craft industries which supplied only local markets, but they could not control the foreign merchants who carried on an international or inter-regional commerce. Urban dwellers valued their commodities and services too highly to alienate them by excessive restrictions on their activities. Besides, such merchants, having business organizations, specialized personnel, economic capital, often political connections, and considerable experience in dealing with cities and urban monopolies, could resist the encumbrances which city officials and feudal lords attempted to impose on their commerce. If not, their own cities protected them, or they banded together in merchants' organizations or they combined into leagues of cities—such as the Lombard and Hanseatic leagues—to protect themselves and their enterprises.

These foreign merchants, the capitalists of their time, laid the foundations for capitalism in medieval Europe. Since they engaged in commerce and manufacturing for profit, they sought to multiply their gains by increasing production through new or better sources of raw materials, expanded markets, improved technologies, and sound financing. In addition, they began to separate business management from the ownership of capital and from the employment of labor. Unlike the guilds, they encouraged economic competition. In later centuries, these capitalists helped to destroy the monopolies of cities and, indeed, the entire feudal order of Europe.

## Municipal Government

By the thirteenth century, many cities possessed charters which were the basis for their governments and which assured them certain political liberties. In general, their governments were vested in municipal corporations whose members were elected, although only a small number of inhabitants had the rights of suffrage. These officials were, under various names, mayor, magistrates, aldermen, and judges. The corporation passed ordinances, enforced statutes, kept the peace, constructed public works, levied and collected taxes on real estate and duties on imports, and performed much the same functions as city officials do today.[3] A few families ordinarily controlled the corporations in most cities in this period. They were often the rich merchants who, through their leadership and wealth, had evolved into a class of aristocrats. These merchants assumed the important political posts or appointed members of their families to them. As they were in their own businesses, they were highly capable in public office and developed municipal administration into an efficient, skillful vocation. The Italian cities which were often embroiled in bitter urban politics imported persons from other cities to manage them. These *podestas* were prototypes of modern city managers.[4]

This domination of cities by large merchants inevitably provoked the hostility of small traders, artisans, and workers. Their artisans' guilds were one means of resisting it (see above). When, later on, these guilds limited their membership and discriminated against apprentices, journeymen attempted to form their own separate guilds. Eventually the lower classes organized themselves into associations to protest and often rebelled openly against the patricians.[5] (These associations were known as *popolo* in Italy and by other names elsewhere.)

The resulting class wars which such organizations precipitated occurred mostly in the fourteenth and fifteenth centuries and were reminiscent of similar urban struggles in the Roman and Greek times. However, the *popolo* could not dislodge the patrician families from their political control of the cities for very long and their protest movements ended unsuccessfully.

## Religious and Social Life

Urban dwellers had close, important, but ambivalent ties with the Catholic Church to which they all belonged. They had more trouble with prelates of the Church than with secular lords in getting charters of civil liberties and in forcing a separation of state and church in city government. Sometimes they even directly opposed the prelates' ecclesiastical powers. This opposition developed later into strong anticlerical movements against the Church when it resisted social and economic changes the people wanted. Furthermore, an estate of urban citizens could not readily absorb into the cities the clergy who belonged to another and superior estate claiming their main loyalties.[6]

In addition, the Church was highly critical of the commercial activities of urban dwellers and attempted to impose its own economic policies on them. The doctrines which the Church had developed to regulate feudal agriculture tended to rationalize the general insufficiency of goods. They asserted that economic activities should be carried on to provide the needs of subsistence—not to make money—and should be judged by ethical—not profit—standards enforced through the Church's own canon law and courts. Thus, it maintained that a "just price" should be charged for goods and services; it should cover the costs of raw materials, expenses of manufacture, wages, and profit, and should not exceed the individual's ability to pay at his social level.

According to the Church, charging excessive prices in order to increase profits was avarice, which it condemned as a cardinal sin. In its policies, the Church was concerned to keep the relations of buyer and seller and lender and borrower on a humane, non-commercial basis. Therefore it condemned usury as a heinous practice, although it later exempted certain business loans from this interdiction.

The Church played an important role in the cities' life. Its cathedrals and churches were prominent. Urban dwellers were devout Catholics in a century when a believer was obsessively concerned with salvation. They attended services, accepted the canons of the Church, joined orders and fraternities connected with the Church as lay members, and participated in the religious pageants and parades, which were always colorful events in the medieval cities. In their guilds, as in their other secular organizations, they observed religious rituals. They venerated certain saints of the Church as the religious guardians of their cities, much as urban dwellers of antiquity worshiped their gods.

The Church maintained its jurisdiction over educational, welfare, and family institutions. It provided a variety of services which showed its awareness of the cities' heterogeneous, even cosmopolitan, inhabitants and their needs. Through cathedral schools and universities, it made higher education possible for sons of wealthy merchant families. The universities were ordinarily organized as corporations of their faculties, with only priests eligible to teach a curriculum strongly theological in content and tone.

Religious orders cared for the cities' distressed populations—the sick, the poor, widows, orphans, lepers, travelers, and wayfarers—whose numbers multiplied. They maintained orphanages, hospitals, and almshouses and made alms-giving and care of the indigent a religious duty incumbent on all. In its ecclesiastical courts the Church enforced its control over marriage and the family. It supported the small patriarchal Christian family by denying divorce and remarriage, instituting the religious officiation of marriages, and substituting marriages based on self-choice of spouses for marriages arranged by parents. So complete was its jurisdiction over family institutions that the late thirteenth century has been called "a golden age of canon rule."

Most city dwellers were a mercantile and artisan population, whose numbers and varieties multiplied as division of labor increased. As the church urbanized, it too added its own diverse personnel to the cities. Other people sought the cities to escape serfdom, to avoid punishment for crimes, to seek educational opportunities, to enjoy urban liberties, and to live a civilized life. A variety of inhabitants thus daily commingled, especially in the large cities—monks, shopkeepers, students, soldiers, a legion of craftsmen, goldsmiths, brewers, glassmakers, dyers, weavers, merchants, knights, and clergy, and many others. However, merchants were the persons who most typified the medieval cities.

There were two social classes existing in medieval cities: an upper class of merchants, manufacturers, public officials, and lesser nobility; and a lower class of artisans, shopkeepers, and workers. Nonetheless, as urban citizens and as free people in feudal Europe, the two classes existed in a condition of relative equality. They were united by a belief in the dignity of labor and respect for their crafts and workmanship. They were neither capitalists nor proletarians in the modern sense, but rather an urban community, all of whom were proud to work for their living.

Their social life acquired an urban character as they multiplied and prospered. The city enlivened it with intellectual excitement, aesthetic sensibility, often gaiety and color. The people spent most of their social life in the guilds, enjoying the company of fellow artisans and holding banquets, shows, masquerades, and processions which were both private and public spectacles. They joined in similar entertainment when city officials, church organizations, or other guilds held them, and they attended jousts and tourneys staged by knights. On their numerous feast days and holidays, citizens gorged themselves on food and wine, caroused in taverns, gambled, or played sports. They saw mys-

tery plays and comedies and listened to street-singers de-
claiming epics and romantic tales or singing ballads.

There was also a sinister, often violent, side to urban
life—frequent fights, robberies, and murders. The people
showed a brutality and callousness of feeling toward human
suffering which, however, characterized all medieval society, not just the cities.

Urban dwellers were devoted to their own city and
fiercely partisan about its civic virtues. Because they could
appreciate their privileges, they took their status and responsibilities as citizens seriously. They worked at their
jobs, supported their families, paid taxes, obeyed the myr-
iad rules and regulations, served in the urban militia, and
joined the watch and ward and the fire brigades. Moreover,
they zealously took part in political life, especially in the
cities of north Italy.

## The Physical City

The physical plan of the medieval city reinforced the de-
votion of its inhabitants and also gave each one a certain
individuality. Each city was a fortress. It was surrounded
by walls, surmounted by towers, pierced by gates, and further encircled by a deep moat, which might be kept either
wet or dry. At night with the gates locked and the draw-
bridges over the moat lifted, the inhabitants, safely enclosed within the walls, could sleep without fear of attack.
Within the city, streets wide enough for the passage of carts
ran between the gates. Another street encircled the city inside the wall, permitting quick access to any part of it. The
other streets, however, developed without plan and were
crooked, narrow alleys, ten feet wide or less, appearing even
narrower because the upper stories of buildings projected
over them, sometimes nearly touching each other.

The center of each city was a public square or market
place, facing the principal church, the town hall, the guild
hall, and some shops. The houses, which had pointed gables

and slate-covered fronts, were built of wood or clay. Their ground floors were used as workshops and their upper floors as residences.

Except for patricians' homes, houses were simply constructed, with furniture and appliances of primitive simplicity. Yards and gardens in the rear relieved the austerity. Families seldom enjoyed much privacy or showed much interest in these homes. Often the houses of artisans of the same trade stood together on the narrow alleys, segregated into neighborhoods. Sometimes, also, enclaves of the population who were subject to feudal or ecclesiastic jurisdiction and not to that of the city government resided in the cities.

Only a few streets were paved with cobblestones and there were no sidewalks. Into these streets inhabitants threw their garbage and other wastes, to be consumed by hogs and other animals which ran free. Drinking water was drawn from rivers, if cities were located on them, or from springs and wells, which were often contaminated. So nearly non-existent was their public sanitation and so little attention did they pay to personal hygiene that medieval urban dwellers suffered recurrent decimating plagues and epidemics. Their knowledge of medicine was, of course, deficient. To some extent, however, the smallness of the cities and especially the proximity of the countryside served to restrict the spread of diseases.

In the absence of reliable census data, only estimates of the size of medieval cities are available. Thirteenth-century Florence, Venice, and Milan had about 100,000 inhabitants; and Asti, 60,000 to 80,000 inhabitants. At the end of the thirteenth century, Paris had 240,000 inhabitants; Douai, Lille, Ypres, Ghent, and Bruges, about 80,000; and London, 40,000 to 45,000. Only a few cities had populations of 50,000 to 100,000; a city of 20,000 was considered a large one; and most cities fluctuated in size from 5,000 to 10,000 inhabitants.[7] Of western Europe's population of 60,000,000 persons in the second quarter of the fourteenth century, about 10 percent lived in cities, the majority in cities with 6,000 inhabitants or less.[8]

## The Importance of Medieval Cities

Medieval cities resembled the Roman municipalities from which they arose in having mercantile populations devoted to trade and production and in developing urban civilizations stemming from the Graeco-Roman culture. Excepting some Italian cities, they did not, like the Roman cities, become city-states. As self-governing cities, they restored many urban political institutions to Europe, but they used these institutions mainly in the service of their commerce. Hence, in ideal type, they were commercial, not political-commercial cities, and had a form of urban community which differed from that of the Roman cities.

In part, this difference was due to the fact that the inhabitants of medieval cities accepted the rule of royal, feudal, or ecclesiastical lords from whom they received liberties and rights of self-rule as stipulated in their municipal charters. In a historical perspective, medieval cities laid the foundations for the development of the nation-state, which appeared in Europe after 1500. Secondly, medieval peoples, unlike the Romans, did not control the church and politicize it to serve their own self-interest. The Catholic Church was itself a powerful state as well as an international church, and, while it gave up civil administration of cities, it surrendered little else to them.

Political sovereigns and the Church seldom exercised unchecked restraint on the cities. Instead, urban dwellers influenced both of them in their separate activities, deriving some of their own political uniqueness in doing so. Kings used cities as military allies in their struggles with lords, recruiting administrative staffs, soliciting members of Parliament, relying on them for armies and tax revenues, encouraging urban traders and manufacturers to promote the general prosperity, and making urban business practices the basis of their national economic policies. Kings depended on urban populations extensively because they were far superior to feudal lords in administering the affairs of state. Urban dwellers were accustomed to politics, trained in municipal government, and experienced in business. Some were better educated than the clergy, and, above all, they were zealous to protect and increase their civil liberties. Conversely, urban populations used kings to prevail over lords, to protect and expand their municipal charters of rights, and to employ military and political force to defend their commerce and supplies from attack. Thus, they hastened the rise of monarchical states in Europe, later enlarging their own participation in the administration of them.

Urban populations also helped to weaken the political power of the Church, not only through their struggles with prelates for control of cities, but also by weakening the Church's economic strength through their part in destroying feudalism and transforming the character of medieval agriculture. In developing their trade and production, they provided consumers and markets for the purchase of farm commodities and raw materials. Feudal lords and peasants, able to sell their produce in cities, were motivated to increase their profits by improving their methods of land cultivation and animal breeding. Thus began a commercialization of agriculture, eventually ending the self-subsistent manorial farming of medieval times. Village populations, emulating urban dwellers in wanting freedom from serfdom, agitated against their manorial and seignioral restraints and succeeded in getting some political rights for themselves. Eventually, millions of men and women were able to flee the villages for cities, where they became emancipated citizens and played their part in the great European social and cultural movements of early modern times.

Medieval cities also differed from Roman cities in that

medieval commercial and artisan classes were dominant and had an importance and respect which similar Roman classes never had. Merchants and workers took their place beside the nobility and clergy of medieval society, competing with them for wealth, prestige, and power. So great an impetus did they give to economic productivity that they made labor honorable. Furthermore, they took pride in maintaining standards of discipline and honesty of workmanship. Under their own leaders, and following their own rules and regulations, they organized and protected their separate crafts, associated in them as equals, and there developed sentiments of community. Through their guilds, furthermore, they got training in managing their own affairs, and in the experience of citizenship which prepared them to advance urban political democracy.

As a result, all urban dwellers shared in the prosperity of cities and the benefits of urban civilization—although never equally. They worked in new or expanded occupations which permitted them to earn their livelihood in labor which they liked. Over the course of time, they improved their standards of living—rising to higher levels of consumption, building larger houses, wearing better clothes, pursuing personal pleasures, and acquiring a sense of personal hygiene. They cultivated the arts, encouraged learning and literature, supported schools and universities, patronized shows and pageants, and in other ways fostered the social and intellectual life of cities. Eventually their larger fortunes enabled the richer families to pursue the good life as an end in itself, causing a thoroughgoing secularization of life which was at variance with the theological bases of medieval society.

The flaw of these cities, like that of Roman cities, was the political particularism of their populations. Each city was, in a sense, a small state in itself. Its inhabitants enjoyed the rights of citizens, but denied these rights to other populations residing elsewhere. They struggled to establish trade monopolies and to control economic enterprises for their own exclusive benefit. Not only did the inhabitants of different cities exploit peasants and other peoples living in their regions, but they were competitive and hostile to each other, engaging in wars between cities or forming military alliances among cities to wage wars. Thus, the democracy which they practiced in the cities was limited largely to themselves.

For these reasons, the cities could not provide adequate political and economic bases for the European nations which appeared in modern times. Nor could they prevail against the great states which then emerged, whose monarchs and parliaments limited the cities' rights of self-government and reduced them to municipalities. When this happened, and their freedom of action as autonomous cities and city-states was ended, the age of great cities was over.

**N O T E S**

1. Cf. Robert S. Hoyt, *Europe in the Middle Ages* (New York: Harcourt, Brace, 1957), pp. 247–252.

2. Robert S. Hoyt, *Europe in the Middle Ages*, pp. 431–432.

3. Paul Farmer, *The European World* (New York: Knopf, 1951), p. 266.

4. Max Weber, *The City*, pp. 130–131.

5. Max Weber, *The City*, pp. 157–164.

6. Max Weber, *The City*, pp. 192–194.

7. Henri Pirenne, *Economic and Social History of Medieval Europe* (New York: Harcourt, Brace, 1936), p. 173.

8. J. W. Thompson, *Economic and Social History of Europe in the Later Middle Ages* (New York: Century, 1931), p. 603.

# · V ·

# *Cities of the Western World*

## The Early Modern Period in Europe

The growth of cities and the expansion of trade and industry which had taken place in Europe in the thirteenth century decreased in the next two centuries. Urban populations encountered economic and political troubles during these centuries which undermined the prosperity of their cities. Europe experienced a gradually contracting economy, a slow decline in total population, severe rivalry among cities or leagues of cities, state action in increasing taxes while repudiating debts and debasing currencies, wars and the rising cost of fortifications and armaments, and class struggle in cities. These events also affected feudal lords and rural populations, who suffered, in addition, from agricultural disturbances which reduced prices for commodities but increased costs for land and labor. Although not uniformly in all countries, and with different rates of recovery, European cities were economically stagnant by 1500, at the end of the Middle Ages.

But certain social and political movements, some already

underway in the late Middle Ages, others making an appearance now, led to the growth of nation-states in Europe, and ushered in its early modern period. Among these movements was the rise of monarchs who gained control over their people and lands, notably in France and England, Spain and Portugal, the Scandinavian countries, the Holy Roman Empire, Italy, Germany, and the Low Countries. By commanding armies, possessing national treasuries, and using bureaucratic officials to administer the affairs of governments, these monarchs reduced lords and cities to their rule. With this centralization of power, feudalism became extinct in western Europe. During this time, too, the Catholic Church was wracked by the movements of Reformation and Counter-Reformation which produced a century of religious wars after 1560. In the fourteenth century in Italy—and later in other European cities—there was a cultural renaissance, initially in the arts and humanities and later in science and other branches of learning. Finally, late in the fifteenth century, the Europeans discovered the American continents, established trade routes, and founded colonies there. Subsequently, Asia and Africa were also opened to European trade and colonization.

In this early modern period, monarchs strove to unify their nations politically and to make them economically strong and prosperous. They devoted much of their efforts to a struggle for empire and wealth by colonizing and exploiting the New World. As a result, economic activities in Europe well into the eighteenth century centered about getting, transporting, and distributing goods the world over. As Europeans developed this international commerce, they created a commercial revolution that transformed their economies and eliminated from them the last vestiges of feudalism. At the same time they realigned themselves politically and economically. The countries bordering on the Atlantic and favorably located for world trade—which, for the first time, included Portugal and Spain—rose to dominance. Those in the interior of Europe lagged behind in economic development, while Italian cities, well located for Mediterranean but not for Atlantic trade, lost their superiority when their commerce declined.

Although not all European nations underwent the commercial revolution equally or at the same time, they all were affected by certain aspects of it. One of these was the organization of their economies by means of mercantilist institutions. ("Mercantilist" refers to the governments' actions and policies in modern national states in promoting and regulating commerce, industries, agriculture, and shipping for the purpose of increasing their countries' economic resources, ensuring their general prosperity, and strengthening them in their economic competition and political rivalry with other countries.) In essence, monarchs adopted the practices of medieval cities by establishing a political control of economic activities in order to advance the general welfare of their people, and made these into national policy. A mercantilist economic system lasted in European countries until the nineteenth century, when it was displaced by a free enterprise capitalism which supported doctrines of laissez faire.

In order to aid commerce, stimulate manufacturing, and revive agriculture, monarchs employed various political and economic policies. They adopted uniform weights and measures, introduced single currencies, removed the internal restraints on trade and manufacturing levied by lords and cities, imposed uniform regulations on trade and industries, and improved internal systems of transportation, including roads, rivers, and canals. In addition, they endeavored to make their nations economically self-sufficient by practices which reduced their dependence on other countries for economic goods and services. Thus, they encouraged the growth of diversified industries, hoarded gold and silver as national wealth, sought to maintain a favorable balance in foreign trade, built merchant marines, and maintained armies with modern armaments.

Still another aspect of this commercial revolution was the gradual triumph of capitalism and the emergence of merchants and bankers as the principal figures in it. In the Middle Ages, only the merchants who engaged in foreign trade could be termed capitalists because only they conducted their business on principles of free enterprise, economic competition, and production for profit. Now all merchants became capitalists, and adopted these same institutions of capitalism in their economic activities to the extent that the mercantilist policies of their countries permitted them.

Some merchants acquired such large fortunes that they began to lend money to monarchs, lords, and other businessmen, and developed into bankers. Such bankers were prominent in the Italian cities, which became the financial centers of Europe; later Antwerp usurped this function, and, still later, Amsterdam. In the northern European countries, the new Protestant churches extolled the economic activities of businessmen as secular vocations or callings through which they served God, praising their modes of life and motivations as well. This "Protestant ethic," as Weber called the religious sanction of business enterprise, was, in essence, a redefinition of the Christian morality of medieval times by the rising commercial classes to adapt it to the changed circumstances of their city life.

Merchant capitalists were responsible for a third development of the commercial revolution, an increase in household manufacturing by means of an expanded "putting-out" system of production which subsequently promoted the growth of other industries. In the Middle Ages, some merchants participated in the manufacture of textiles and other economic goods which they carried in trade. Now in the early modern period, merchants made this practice general by taking control of the industries which produced the goods they sold, and in which household production was practicable. They "put-out" the manufacture of commodities into the homes of workers and then collected the finished articles which they sold in markets. At the least, under this system they supplied raw materials to workers who provided their own tools and labor; at the most, the merchants owned the materials and tools, hired workers at wages, and managed the complete manufacturing process. Entire families, including women and children, worked in this household industry. A few efforts by merchants at this time to assemble workers in workshops and to supervise their labor were unprofitable to them and unsatisfactory to laborers.

Using their accumulated capital and new business techniques, these merchant-entrepreneurs promoted new industries and, when profitable, invigorated old ones. Mining, one of these revived industries, was expanded because of advances in technology, the demand of the new nation-states for armaments, and the increased demand of industry for metals. Another renewed industry was shipbuilding, which was encouraged both by countries that wanted to build their own merchant fleets and by the need for ships to carry on world trade. Other industries, such as printing and publishing, expanded to meet the increased demands of literate populations for books and periodicals.

Gradual improvements in agriculture were a fourth development in the commercial revolution. The breakup of feudalism was accompanied by the increasing commercialization of farming which led to such improvements as growing cash crops, putting more land under cultivation, unifying individual field strips into larger farms, and treating soil to increase its fertility. The growing of crops for sale also wrought important changes in the ownership of land. With the waning of feudalism, landlords changed the traditional obligation of serfs into money rents whose amount they fixed according to custom or feudal rule, and which they made unchangeable to protect, as they thought, their own future income and interests.

After 1450, however, European prices inflated for more than a century. The peasants benefited from higher prices for farm produce while their rents remained the same; but landlords suffered from rising prices for the goods they bought with their relatively fixed incomes. They were often forced to sell or lease their lands to peasants, who eventually evolved into a class of free farmers in western Europe.

In Eastern Europe the feudal lords and landlords benefited from rising prices and an increased demand for their grain and forest products. As their wealth and power grew, they forced the peasants even more deeply into bondage, keeping them serfs well into the eighteenth and nineteenth centuries.

These events were accompanied in Europe by a rise in the total population which began to expand slowly after 1450, then more rapidly after 1600. The estimate for 1650 is 100 millions. Thereafter it increased at accelerating rates, to 140 millions in 1750, 187 millions in 1800, 401 millions in 1900.[1] In 1950 it was 541 millions.[2]

The individual European countries did not increase in population at similar rates or in the same periods of time, but eventually all of them shared in the conditions of cultural progress which made their population growth possible. A decrease in death rates while birth rates remained high permitted a rapid natural increase in population. Medical advances, such as the professionalization of doctors, discoveries in pathology and the growth of hospitals; social advances, illustrated by improved diets, higher standards of living, and greater economic security; along with the increasing interest in public sanitation and personal hygiene —all these developments contributed to the growth in population. After 1810, birth rates in England and later in some other European countries began to fall for the first

time, but the large decrease in the birth rate occurred in
the present century.

## The Uneven Growth of Cities

As the nation-states became dominant in Europe, cities,
slowly abandoning their medieval practices, took on a modern guise. But relatively few of them, mostly the political
cities, benefited from the developments of the commercial
revolution in the early modern period and grew in importance and size. Most other cities were at first adversely
affected by the changes. Many declined in population.
These were reduced, for the most part, to trade centers and
places of local production for their rural environs, serving
as marketplaces for a predominantly agricultural Europe.
There are a number of reasons for the uneven growth in
European cities at this time.

Under the mercantilist system, monarchs and parliaments established political control over their national economies and thus became important factors in the distribution
of wealth, power, and prestige, Moreover, they, and mercantilist policies in general, became subject to manipulation
by individuals or groups who sought to use the powers of
state or the national wealth to advance their own economic
interests. Thus, merchants, manufacturers and land owners appealed to monarchs and parliaments to adopt public
policies in the name of mercantilism when they really
wanted to profit privately by such measures. Even monarchs rationalized their dynastic ambitions by mercantilist
arguments when they imposed taxes to pay the costs of
government or to defray the costs of war, or when they took
advantage of their powers to accumulate great private fortunes.

As a result, capital cities, or cities where powerful rulers
resided, grew in this period; but provincial cities serving
only trade functions remained small or declined in popula-

tion. Into the political cities flocked those who wanted to live near the seat of government or who were employed in the political, military, or economic affairs of state. Paris, for example, had 180,000 inhabitants in 1594. In 1600 London had 250,000 inhabitants; Naples had 240,000; Milan, over 200,000; Palermo, Rome, Lisbon, Seville, Antwerp, and Amsterdam, about 100,000.

Another factor in the provincial city's decline in these centuries was the loss of some of its industries. Thus it could not support large or growing populations. Merchant entrepreneurs, in organizing their "putting-out" system, located their manufacturing, when feasible, in villages or in farm homes to avoid the restrictions which cities imposed on them. In the villages merchants hired peasants full- or part-time who were glad to supplement their income with cottage work in which all members of their families could participate. Moreover, the lack of guilds in the villages made costs there less than in cities. Some villages were even located on rivers where water power was available. This dispersion of industries outside cities was safe now because monarchs maintained peace and order throughout their countries.

Some industries, notably textiles, but also the manufacture of metal wares, leather work, and others, were suitable to household production, and they were distributed widely throughout many rural areas. How considerable this rural industry became is indicated by an estimate made in 1739 that some 4,250,000 men, women, and children in England were "engaged in manufactures"[3]; they constituted nearly a half of the English population at that time.

Thus urbanization and industrialization, now regarded as invariable partners, were dissociated from each other; growing industries were dispersed instead throughout societies. While national manufacturing thereafter increased in size and output, cities were affected mainly by such added trade as these industrial advances provided. Thus

England had fewer large cities then than did Italy or Spain but was more industrialized than either of them. Indeed, in the early modern period, India and China had more large cities than Europe. Even American cities compared favorably with European cities. At least the Spanish conquistadors marveled to find such cities as Tenochtitlan and Cuzco, which were quite as large and imposing as their own.

The intrusion of industry had a twofold effect on the villages involved. On the one hand, these villages, in acquiring industries, widened their economic base and ceased being solely agricultural. Instead, village dwellers became industrial workers, earned larger incomes, improved their standards of living, took on urban ways of life, and became socially and intellectually oriented toward their larger society. At least some villages developed into miniature cities, as it were, attaining relatively urban prosperity and sophistication. In many of them industrialization thus worked a social revolution.[4]

But the "putting-out" system of manufacturing also had an adverse effect on villagers and on those peasants who took wool or yarn to spin or weave into their homes. This domestic production inevitably led to sweatshop conditions. Family members, often including infant children, worked many hours each day to earn an income which was never enough; their homes, never intended to become places of production, were crowded and cramped; inevitably they suffered from fatigue, disease, inadequate diet, insufficient leisure, and other maladies.[5]

## The Industrial Revolution

With the advent of the Industrial Revolution—that series of technological advances made in the industries of England which transformed their manufacturing methods after 1760—cities took on a new life. The paramount technological advance was the use of the steam engine, perfected in the 1780's, to provide mechanical power to drive machines. Because such engines and machinery were costly, and steam power cannot be conveyed efficiently over distances, they were installed in factories and the factories concentrated in cities. Steam power thus had a centralizing effect; it brought together industries and working population in cities, and led to an accelerated growth of cities thereafter.

The rise of factories made the mass production of goods possible. Factories denote, of course, one or more buildings in which owners, or business firms, have assembled machinery, employ workers under supervision, and use a division and specialization of labor to manufacture standardized parts which are assembled into finished articles. In eighteenth century England, the first factories were buildings located in villages along rivers where merchants gathered frames for spinning and used water power to turn them. They added steam engines, when these became available, to supplement water power with steam power. By 1830 textile factories using only steam power prevailed, and stood in cities and villages wherever their owners desired. Thereafter, factories spread to other industries, by 1850 dominating the manufacture of paper, glass, cloth, pottery, metals, engines, and machinery. The steam engine was adapted to railroads after 1830, to coastal and inland shipping after 1820, and to transoceanic shipping after 1840.

To build and operate factories, large accumulations of capital and new forms of ownership were necessary. In the early decades of the Industrial Revolution, only large merchants, some land owners wishing to exploit the natural resources of their estates, a few bankers, and some manufacturers ventured to construct factories, to gather a labor force and machinery in them, and to develop a mass market for their products. Usually they organized their companies as single or family-owned business firms. They accumu-

lated working capital by using their own funds, borrowing
from relatives, friends, and banks, and reinvesting their
earnings.

After 1850, however, they began to utilize the joint-
stock company, or corporation, as a preferred form of business organization. Through corporations, they could acquire
both larger capitalization and sounder management of
their enterprises. In the first instance, the joint-stock—or
shares of ownership—of corporations were transferable by
sale, giving them legal perpetuity without regard to particular individuals who owned them. Such shares, moreover,
involved only limited liability of ownership for their owners,
which influenced many banks, insurance companies, and
persons to purchase shares with their savings or surplus
funds. This made possible an enormous capital accumulation from the public at large which served to finance the
expansion of manufacturing. In the second instance, corporations made large-scale organization possible with separation of ownership and management, unity of control and
leadership, and bureaucratic administration. Both privately-
and publicly-owned corporations appeared, with the latter
eventually predominating.

These developments provoked still others which wrought
a major transformation in the economic organization of the
European countries in the nineteenth century. One was the
emergence of manufacturers as an economic class and
through them the displacement of mercantile by industrial
capitalism. Another was the abandonment of mercantilism
by Western countries in favor of laissez-faire policies which
espoused minimal public regulation in their national economies. A third was the institution of the free market and its
regulation through the law of supply and demand.[6]

At first these new manufacturers located their factories
in cities not only for reasons of technology, but also because
cities contained an availability of markets, raw materials,
financial agencies, transportation facilities, labor forces,

storage facilities, and residences. Therefore, they chose
cities which possessed, for their purposes, some desirable
combination of these advantages. For the most part, they
selected cities which already had important commercial
activities, were situated on harbors or rivers, and were
served by railroads; but they also installed some plants in
small cities and villages.

In the latter case, they sought to locate their factories
near natural coal and iron deposits, the one needed to
generate steam, the other to provide steel now vital to industry. By doing so, they gave rise to industrial cities and
to industrial regions, which comprised groups of such cities;
both of these new urban phenomena came to exist on a
huge scale. Manufacturers abetted the growth of these
cities, moreover, by new industrial practices. One was the
now familiar system of sub-contracting the production of
standardized parts or supplies, which led to the rise of
many business firms in the same industry. Another was the
appearance of satellite industries which utilized the mechanical power, semi-finished products, industrial supplies,
or services of major industries, or sold goods or services to
them. Both practices led to an aggregation of manufacturing companies in these cities and regions, for example, the
cities of the English Midlands, the Ruhr Valley, and the
northeastern United States.

As industrialization swept England and the Western
countries, their cities were enormously affected by the
acquisition of new industries, and by a growing commerce
stimulated by these industries. They began to grow rapidly,
even chaotically, heralding the modern urbanization of
the world. With a widened economic base and rising
prosperity, the cities attracted rural and village populations. In some cases foreign populations were drawn by
work available in factories or as a result of the growth of
factories. Large cities became larger and nearly all cities
increased in size, some attaining a million inhabitants or

more. London and Paris were the great cities of Europe in the nineteenth century. At the end of the century they— with Moscow, Berlin, St. Petersburg (now Leningrad), and Vienna in Europe; New York, Chicago, and Philadelphia in the United States; and Tokyo and Peiping in the Far East— were the great cities of the world. Table I on page 97 illustrates the rate of growth of the world's largest cities since 1800.

Another effect of industrialization on the cities was a serious deterioration of living conditions, intensified by the rapid increase in population. The industrialists located their factories and railroads to suit their own business needs. They gave little thought to possible deleterious effects of, for example, the smoke and soot that poured unchecked over city neighborhoods and inhabitants. Moreover, industrialists hired unskilled workers for their factories and kept them at work for long hours and little pay. Some preferred to hire women and children rather than men in order to depress wage rates.

Nevertheless, large numbers of migrants—in some cities immigrants, too—flocked to the cities in search of employment. They took whatever work and lodgings they could find, no matter how wretched. Thus cities inherited the social problems that still afflict them: extensive slums, substandard housing, disorganized families, personal and social pathologies, increased crime, and high disease rates. The new industrial cities especially offended in these respects. Yet business classes and government officials who subscribed to the doctrines of laissez faire tolerated and even justified these evils as the unfortunate but inevitable price of economic progress.

To sum up, political, economic, and demographic developments in Europe since 1500 greatly changed their cities. This period witnessed the rise of the nation-states which eliminated the medieval states. National communities thus displaced urban communities as the dominant form of so-

**TABLE I**

Population of the world's largest cities, 1800 to 1950

| | 1950 | 1930 | 1900 | 1850 | 1800 |
|---|---|---|---|---|---|
| New York | 7,891,957 | 6,930,446 | 3,437,202 | 696,115 | 79,216 |
| Tokyo | 4,555,565 | 2,070,000 | 1,819,000 | | |
| Moscow | 4,137,018 | 2,781,000 | 1,174,673 | 332,878 | 188,654 |
| Chicago | 3,620,962 | 3,376,438 | 1,698,575 | 29,963 | |
| Shanghai | 3,489,998 | 3,000,000 | 457,000 | | |
| London | 3,348,000 | 4,396,821 | 4,536,267 | 2,363,341 | 959,310 |
| Berlin | 3,199,938 | 4,227,000 | 2,712,190 | 429,217 | 172,846 |
| Leningrad | 3,191,304 | 2,228,000 | 1,439,613 | 487,300 | 220,200 |
| Paris | 2,853,000 | 2,891,000 | 2,660,559 | 1,053,262 | 547,756 |
| Buenos Aires | 2,660,827 | 2,100,000 | 821,293 | 76,000 | 140,000 |
| Calcutta | 2,108,891 | 1,485,582 | | | |
| Cairo | 2,100,506 | 1,307,422 | 570,000 | | |
| Philadelphia | 2,071,605 | 1,950,961 | 1,293,697 | 121,376 | 41,220 |
| Rio de Janeiro | 2,014,185 | 1,469,000 | 687,699 | 166,419 | 43,376 |
| Los Angeles | 1,970,358 | 1,238,048 | 102,479 | 1,610 | |
| Detroit | 1,849,568 | 1,568,662 | 285,704 | 21,019 | |
| Vienna | 1,798,659 | 1,836,000 | 1,727,073 | 446,415 | 231,949 |
| Sao Paulo | 1,776,000 | 962,295 | 240,000 | | |
| Nanking | 1,755,300 | 633,452 | 270,000 | | |
| Osaka | 1,690,072 | 2,453,000 | 996,000 | | |
| Rome | 1,653,935 | 1,008,000 | 463,000 | 184,000 | 153,000 |
| Peiping | 1,556,364 | 1,297,718 | 1,000,000 | | |
| Bombay | 1,489,883 | 1,161,000 | 776,000 | | |
| Sydney | 1,484,004 | 1,254,000 | 487,932 | 53,924 | 2,537 |
| Mexico City | 1,448,422 | 1,007,672 | 345,000 | | |

SOURCE: Warren S. Thompson, *Population Problems* (New York: McGraw-Hill, 1953), 4th ed., p. 389.

cial and political organization, reducing the cities to municipalities. Cities nonetheless grew enormously with the advent of industry, and the rapid industrialization of their societies was accompanied by an increase in population.

## Modern Commercial-Industrial Cities

In modern cities since the nineteenth century, industries have multiplied their effect by stimulating the growth of commercial enterprises as well as personal, mechanical, and public services. Some part of the wealth which they create is invested in these economic activities, which are necessary in themselves and valuable to industry too. The wages which industries pay workers provide them with incomes to buy food, clothing, housing, and other necessities of life at standards of living which they can afford, or covet. In this way urban populations, possessing purchasing power, constitute vast domestic markets of consumers, which further encourage and support the growth and diversification of urban business. Urban business must handle problems of retailing, communication, transportation, and entertainment, and provide all kinds of professional services. These economic activities, some of which are vast businesses, make the cities into centers of economic consumption as well as of production.

In the language of economists,[7] these consumption-oriented—or service—industries are tertiary industries; the productive—or processing—industries are secondary industries, differentiated from primary, or extractive, industries such as agriculture, lumbering, mining, and fishing. Economists find this typology of industries useful to analyze the economic development of countries. Nations begin to advance economically through the rise of cities and secondary industries, in the manner we have described for modern Europe. In the process, their populations transfer from agriculture to urban industries. Still later, nations reach a further stage of development with the urban growth of tertiary industries. The industries become especially important when manufacturing becomes the chief employer of labor. Thereafter, tertiary industries employ an increasing proportion and eventually the bulk of the labor force. In England, this happened in the 1860's; in the United States, in the 1920's.[8] Tertiary industries provide the specialized goods and services which establish the style and amenities of life in cities; hence their preponderance signifies the presence of an advanced modern economy.

The cities of the West have become, in their ideal type, commercial-industrial cities. With the acquisition of industries, their economic base has widened enormously. They are centers of trade and manufacturing; in them, service, mechanical, and construction industries proliferrate, railroads and airlines are located, and modern communications concentrate; they are filled with stores, offices, factories, and shops; a great number of other social and economic organizations which hire labor exist in them. As a result, their populations are composed of large, highly specialized, diversely employed labor forces which can improve their status in life through economic mobility. One major distinction between ancient and modern cities is the latter's ability to support large populations in relative affluence without the city dwellers exploiting the working classes and the rural populations.

Another distinct difference between modern and ancient cities is the diminished role which non-economic organizations and institutions play in modern urban social life. Politically, modern cities are reduced to local governments, with their legal powers and duties specified in charters issued by state legislatures and variously constrained by both state and national governments. Urban dwellers are citizens of their countries, not their cities, and are politically active in national affairs as well as in municipal activities.

Churches long ago ceased to provide urban populations with a common religious life, or a common set of predominantly religious values. Nor are cities now the sole centers of cultural creativity or the seed-beds of civilization. Cultural innovations may occur anywhere in the society, not just in the cities.

In large perspective, Western countries are now nation-states or national communities with an associational, or *Gesellschaft,* form of social organization. Their form of society is characterized by multiplicity and autonomy of organizations, division and specialization of labor, institutional separateness, and popular adherence to canons of rationality and secularity.

In the cities, economic institutions are paramount in the urban order. Cities of the United States are typical examples of commercial-industrial cities. The chapters which follow explain the salient social and cultural features of such cities and analyze the character of the society in which they exist. To begin this task, a brief historical survey of American cities is desirable.

**NOTES**

1. A. M. Carr-Saunders, *World Population* (Oxford: Clarendon Press, 1936), p. 30.

2. United Nations, *Demographic Yearbook,* 1951, Table 1A, p. 103.

3. R. R. Palmer and Joel Colton, *History of the Modern World* (New York: Knopf, 1956), 2nd ed., p. 226.

4. Lewis Mumford, *The City in History,* pp. 328–329.

5. Paul A. Samuelson, *Economics* (New York: McGraw-Hill, 1951), 2nd ed., p. 66.

6. Karl Polanyi, *The Great Transformation* (New York: Rinehart, 1944).

7. Colin Clark, *The Conditions of Economic Progress* (London: Macmillan, 1951), p. 401.

8. Colin Clark, *The Conditions of Economic Progress,* pp. 403, 407.

# · VI ·

# *The Growth of*
# *American Cities*

## The Economic Growth of Cities

As Americans occupied the continent, they founded many
cities—along the eastern seaboard in colonial times, in the
interior Middle West in the early national life, and finally
in the far western states and territories. Cities fulfilled
three major roles in the growth of the nation. To use the
language of geographers,[1] many cities served, first, as
central urban places which performed comprehensive economic and social services for the surrounding populations.
They made possible the growth of trade and production
locally, and were indispensable to the development of
agriculture. Often they were seats of government, either
local or state. Some had fortresses to protect the inhabitants. In general, the cities were social centers which made
civilized life and urban associations possible and which
extended American culture to the peoples of the frontier.

Second, cities served a transport function. They were
located at points of transshipment of economic goods along
transportation routes and performed essential break-of-bulk

and allied services for urban and regional populations. Third, cities facilitated the economic development of some natural resource. Many were specialized-function cities whose industries were manufacturing, mining, lumbering, fishing, entertainment, and the like.

Cities did not always follow but sometimes preceded the movement and settlement of Americans in the West. In the latter case, they were spearheads of the frontier, securing the lands of the West for the United States and making them safe for future populations.[2] Some cities were gateways through which settlers passed to occupy the rich territories lying beyond them.[3] In short, cities served to organize the settlement of the land and to accelerate the economic development of the United States.

## Typology of Cities

In general, cities that are economic and social centers of their local areas and hinterlands occur widely throughout settled areas. They provide retail and wholesale markets for the assembly and distribution of farm commodities and raw materials, and for the exchange of manufactured goods and personal, mechanical, and professional services. In addition, they have local governments, schools, churches, hospitals, and other organizations which provide social and cultural services to local populations. Once in existence, these cities attract manufacturing or other industries, hence widening their economic base. Consequently, some have grown into large cities in the United States.

Transport cities arise along routes of transportation where some break in transportation occurs: for example, a transfer from water to rail travel necessitating a change in transport facility, at ocean and inland lake harbors and at certain places along rivers. At such places, the processing of the economic goods handled in transportation is economically feasible. This stimulates other businesses involved in packaging, storage, financing, and insuring the goods. Hence these cities abound with commercial enterprises; and, once gaining trade and transportation advantages, they attract industrial activities as well.[4]

Cities appear at places with highly localized natural resources whose utilization gives them a basic industry. Thus manufacturing cities arise in areas having iron and coal deposits, mining cities near ore deposits, resort cities in areas whose climate or geology favors such activities. Manufacturing cities sometimes develop as clusters of such cities because they have major industries which attract satellite industries and services. These, being economically interdependent, encourage the growth of economic regions. This is true even of resort cities.

In the early history of the United States, cities were commercial cities, standing at centrally located places or serving as transportation centers to their hinterlands; none were industrial cities until well into the nineteenth century. Initially they served as trading outposts for European economic expansion to the New World, and then as trade centers for Americans in their settlement of the continent. The cities grew quickly, filling with stores, shops, public buildings, churches, and homes. In addition to trade, urban merchants were also active in other activities, mainly in land sales and speculations and in the construction of canals and railroads. Some also speculated in the founding of new cities on the frontier, anticipating the westward movement of population.[5]

As business centers, the cities were built at places convenient for commerce and transportation, which determined the present geographical network of American cities.[6] The post roads of the colonial period and the turnpikes of the early national period were slow, expensive, and hazardous. Water was the major means of travel and transportation, and American cities in the colonial period were invariably located at ocean harbors and other strategic sites on rivers. After 1807, when Robert Fulton made the steamboat practicable for domestic navigation and Americans could use it for travel or shipping, the cities on waterways became even more important. The dominance of harbor and port cities was further enforced, beginning in 1830, by railroads. Initially, the railroad entrepreneurs conceived of railroads as auxiliary to water transportation and laid railroad tracks from port cities into rural territories and economic areas. Later on, when locomotives proved faster and more efficient carriers than steamships, railroad companies connected cities by projecting their lines across the country, thereby increasing the advantage of location at harbors or on rivers. Thereafter, new cities arose along railroad lines or in areas opened to settlement by the railroads.

Unlike commerce, manufacturing did not thrive in the cities in the early centuries. In the colonial period, the majority of Americans were farmers living in sparsely settled, widely dispersed areas. In 1790, only six cities had 8,000 inhabitants or more and only one had more than 40,000 inhabitants, and their total population was 3.3 percent of that of the United States. Thirteen cities of 8,000 inhabitants or more existed in 1820, and 141 in 1860, and they had respectively less than 5 percent and 16 percent of the nation's population. The rural populations seldom visited cities and, moreover, lacked purchasing power to buy manufactured goods or mechanical services in cities where they were available. Instead, these rural people made many household articles and farm tools, as well as processed food commodities, in their own homes and shops; sometimes farmers sold a small surplus of articles in local markets.[7] Labor and commercial credit were also scarce at this time. The immigrants' preference to settle on the land, which existed in great abundance and was cheap, rather than take employment in urban industries, also served to deter the accumulation of venture capital.[8] Often, businessmen who had funds invested them in commercial enterprises or in land rather than in manufacturing. Finally, the competition with European and especially English industries was severe. Not only were foreign commodities generally superior in quality, but they were available in greater volume and variety than were American-made goods.

Under these conditions, there arose a cottage-and-mill system of manufacturing similar to that which existed in England at this time but more modest in scale. It lasted as a major form of industrial organization well into the nineteenth century. At least three types of enterprise and technology existed as part of the cottage-and-mill system, all employing handicraft production and manual power. A first type consisted of individual craftsmen producing goods and rendering services in homes or shops. In time, their number and variety multiplied. There were carpenters, cobblers, masons, blacksmiths, potters, watchmakers, tailors, and bakers. Some were itinerant workmen.

Mills were a second type of enterprise: grain, lumber and grist mills, tanneries, distilleries, and iron forges. These mills required capitalization in plant and machinery, and employed specialized workers. They were located near sources of water power or raw materials in cities and villages; their products sold locally because high costs of transportation prevented their wider distribution. In seaport cities, whose location made coastal and foreign commerce possible, there was a third type of industrial activity: iron works, ship building, rum manufacturing, meat and food packing, and lumber works. These enterprises exceeded the mills in capital investment and productivity and practiced division of labor, although they still used manual power.

In the early nineteenth century, American enterprisers advanced to factory production of textiles, copying the

English in this respect, and shared in the economic developments which occurred thereafter. What was possibly the first modern factory in America to manufacture cotton cloth was established at Waltham, Massachusetts, in 1814, and the first such factory for woolens, at Lowell, Massachusetts, in 1830. Thereafter, textile factories, using machinery driven initially by water power, then by steam power, were built along the rivers of southern New England, the Hudson and Mohawk Rivers in New York, and the Delaware River in Pennsylvania. Paterson, Fall River, Lowell, and Lawrence emerged as industrial cities at this time, the first of their kind in the United States. After 1840, other industries adopted factories as the necessary technological advances were made in the American economy. Among these were the substitution of coal for charcoal in smelting iron ores, which increased the supply of iron, the Bessemer process of making steel, the use of steel rails by railroads, and engine works. The variety of industries using factories in 1860 is indicated by the leading manufactures of that year, measured by net value of product in each: cotton goods, iron, sawed lumber, boots and shoes, ready-made clothing, flour and meal, steam engine machinery, woolen and worsted goods, and leather.[9]

This spread of factories in American industries caused fewer dislocations in cities and inflicted less hardship on urban dwellers than did the industrial revolution in England at this time. Not only was their adoption relatively slow, but it occurred in various industries at different times and with varying rates of speed, often coexisting with household or mill production. In addition, some industries were either very small or had not previously existed in the United States before the advent of factories. Finally, the scale of manufacturing was insufficient to divert urban dwellers from their main employment in business and personal and mechanical services, and most Americans, of course, still lived on farms.

After the Civil War, and particularly after 1880, the tempo of industrial development and the extension of factories to nearly all industries accelerated in the United States. The next few decades witnessed those great economic events which transformed the Western world (see Chapter V), including the progression of capitalism through successive merchant, industrial, finance, and state phases of development; the rise and fall of laissez-faire ideas of public regulation of the national economy; the utilization of steam, electricity, and fuels as sources of industrial power; the development of the internal combustion engine, the business corporation, scientific business management, and modern forms of transportation and communication.

After 1880, too, mass immigration from Europe swelled to hundreds of thousands annually, exceeding a million persons annually shortly after 1900. Unlike the earlier immigrants who settled on the land, these "new immigrants" settled in cities where they found work in the factories. People who had been mostly peasants and villagers became city dwellers and industrial workers in the United States. With new or expanded industries and populations, cities changed from commercial to commercial-industrial cities. By 1900, too, some cities in the northeastern states had suburbs, and the modern metropolitan age of cities was at hand.

## The History of Urban Government

Americans utilized English municipal institutions in establishing the government of their cities, but, in the process of transferring them to the New World, deleted many remnants of medieval custom. Thereafter, in the course of their national existence, they amended the structure and powers of urban governments in many ways to enable cities to take on new responsibilities which their growth compelled and the political organization of the United States dictated.

In the American federal system of government, cities are municipal corporations controlled by the legislatures of the states in whose jurisdictions they exist. In the colonial period, colonial governors and legislative assemblies controlled cities. At that time, however, the colony, town, and country were more important jurisdictions than cities; in some colonies even village and vestry rivaled cities. Governing bodies accordingly gave cities differing amounts of self-rule.[10] For this reason, cities did not develop a standard form of government or follow uniform municipal policies and practices. Indeed, their diverse circumstances in the New World prevented this. Some, but not all, cities were incorporated as municipalities; some possessed municipal charters but others did not; some were governed by colonial governors, assemblies, or commissioners rather than by their own officials; in some cities the important officials were appointed by the governor or assembly rather than being elected by their inhabitants.

These officials, too, performed diverse municipal duties, some of them political services, others judicial functions now transferred to courts. Only New York City, of the cities with governments based on the medieval English municipal corporation, had a full-fledged representative government by the end of the colonial period in 1775. The New England cities were notable by then for their town-meeting form of government and for having the selectmen serve as town officials in them. Later, New England settlers transplanted this indigenous form of government to some cities, villages, and townships of the Middle West.

Officials in these cities carried on many public activities necessary to sustain the lives and promote the welfare of the people. These included the construction of streets, roads, bridges, and other public projects, regulation of buildings and houses, provision of water and sewage disposal facilities, fire and police protection, and public welfare.[11] In addition, they attempted to regulate the economic life and activities of cities in some detail, as was considered a proper function of government. Thus they followed the protectionist policies of medieval cities in seeking to advance the economic interests of urban dwellers as producers and consumers. To this end, they regulated prices, fixed the quality of goods, set wages, controlled markets, and restricted the right to buy and sell. In some cities, artisans attempted to establish craft guilds and merchants to experiment with the "putting-out" system of household industry, but in neither case with much success. While never able to enforce these regulations completely, especially as the years of the revolution drew on, officials nevertheless pursued their practices of urban mercantilism throughout the colonial period.

These officials were controlled by oligarchies of rich merchants who were anxious to maintain monopolies of trade and production and who dominated the cities not only economically but politically and socially as well. By restricting the right of suffrage largely to themselves and to others whom they trusted, they were able to elect or influence the appointment of magistrates and members of assemblies. Hence they could govern the cities in their own self-interests.

At this time, a "standing order" of classes, resembling the social estates of Europe, existed in cities. These merchants, with some few other families having economic, political, or religious eminence, constituted its upper class and were known as persons of quality. A class of less notable persons and families, known as "the better Sort," was next in status; then followed "the middling Sort," who were shopkeepers and artisans; "the inferior Sort," who were seamen, laborers, apprentices, and freedmen, was the lowest class. While the oligarchies were challenged occasionally by persons of the middle classes, they held on to their powers and prerogatives throughout the colonial period, and, for that matter, well after it too.[12]

After independence, state governments, replacing colonial governors and assemblies, assumed political control over cities in their jurisdictions. State legislatures specifically asserted their power to incorporate cities and to grant municipal charters which established their forms and functions of government. However, the legislatures did not intervene in city administration and the urban upper classes continued, for the most part, to rule them. After 1800, the latter lost much of their political power. At this time, the legislatures began to grant universal suffrage to adult, native-born, white males in their states, thus enfranchising the middle and lower classes, who aligned themselves politically against the upper class. Owing to the steady national economic and political progress of the nation, the old social order collapsed, entirely eliminating the aristocrats from American soil. In the course of re-establishing a new system of classes in nineteenth-century America, the various groups fighting for political control modified their city's government.

Among these modifications, many of which were intended to diffuse political power among various officials and public bodies, were the adoption of bicameral city councils—copied after the two houses of Congress—and weak mayor-council forms of municipal government. While mayors were responsible for enforcing the laws and had the right to veto assembly actions and the limited right to appoint officials to office, their powers of leadership were restricted. Other city officials were elected to office, including some that are commonly appointed today, in order to make them independent of the mayor and to thwart possible coalitions of power among them. Then too, various departments, boards, and collegial bodies, some of them autonomous or nearly so, such as school, library, and park boards, carried on important, often new, services in the cities, services not entrusted to mayors and other officials.[13]

An increase in political factionalism and a deterioration in the quality of urban governments followed these developments. City and state political bosses sometimes won control over local government by organizing the legions of new voters, both native and foreign-born, into blocs of followers. Political parties also entered into the political contests in cities, striving to win offices for their members, and to gain the support of voters in state and national campaigns. Occasionally state legislatures intervened in the administration of cities, sometimes to take over urban functions either neglected or badly performed by city officials and often to restrain the officials of a particular city. City governments had become so debased by the end of the nineteenth century that Bryce declared them "the one conspicuous failure" of American democracy.[14] Andrew D. White was more critical, saying that "with very few exceptions, the city governments of the United States are the worst in Christendom—the most expensive, the most inefficient, and the most corrupt." [15]

There are several reasons for the deterioration of urban governments during the nineteenth century. First, many Americans lost interest in urban government and ceased to participate in municipal politics because elected city governments performed relatively few services which affected them. In this period, elected governments maintained streets and roads, attended to the water supply, provided sewage disposal, and performed similar domestic functions; but independent boards or departments administered other functions: for example, education, the care of the poor, even the police function in some cities.[16] Another reason for political disintegration of urban governments was the corruption of politicians. Moreover, their middle-class background often made them less respectable to Americans used to a ruling aristocracy. Third (a factor stronger toward the end of the nineteenth century),

Americans, believing in the market regulation of business activity, subscribed to laissez-faire ideas of the limited role of government. This did not deter some business men, however, from buying public utility franchises or other special privileges from politicians or city bosses, thus contributing to the dishonesty of urban governments.[17] And finally, Americans organized voluntary associations to carry on social and cultural activities and thus did not need governments to provide services that they could provide for themselves. As early as the 1830's, de Tocqueville observed a public propensity to organize educational, religious, economic, political, and other enterprises and to act collectively through them to meet individual and group goals.

Cities recovered from this political nadir in the twentieth century, and today have relatively efficient and honest governments. Because urban governments direct many important functions, such as education, welfare, health, and transportation, the people will no longer tolerate inept administration or flagrant corruption in officials. Furthermore, today, urban governments, copying state and federal government organization and bureaucratic practices, hire a trained personnel to carry out their activities.

## The American Image of Cities

Americans have had an ambivalent attitude toward cities during much of their history. Since they were predominantly a rural people—the western frontier lasted until around 1890—Americans inevitably nurtured sentiments which extolled the agrarian and deprecated the urban way of life. Thus they venerated agriculture as "the most beneficial and productive object of human industry," to use Jefferson's words, and deplored the commerce of cities and the merchants and laboring classes engaged in it. While not all of them concurred in Jefferson's indictment of the latter—"I consider the class of artificers as the panders of vice and the instruments by which the liberties of the country are generally overturned" [18]—they believed nevertheless that farm and village life was more natural and wholesome than urban existence, and more likely to ensure the nation's prosperity and stability. Indeed, American democracy was, on the whole, bred in rural United States, where doctrines of individualism and liberty took firm hold among the people. Obviously urban dwellers cherished democracy also, but unlike medieval European urban dwellers, whose participation in the social and political movements of their time brought on the modern age in the Western world, urban Americans played no such paramount role in the development of democracy in this country.

Americans found anti-urban attitudes harder to sustain, however, as cities continued to grow, and as their inhabitants obviously lived fuller, more productive, and easier lives than farm populations did. Especially after 1880, increasing numbers of rural youth, weary of their drudgeries and often lonely on the farms, migrated to cities, seeking there the advantages and beguilements they had coveted.[19] European immigrants, mostly peasants, also settled in cities, especially in the large metropolises, making such cities foreign by contrast with the old American rural population. These influxes of migrants and immigrants sometimes stirred hostility in the indigenous urban populations. Some number of migrants, disillusioned with cities, always returned to the land, remembering their urban experiences with rancor. These movements of population intensified the antinomian attitudes of many Americans toward cities; they hated cities because they undermined rural modes of life, but they respected them as necessary to the growth and prosperity of the nation.[20]

These urban-rural antagonisms have abated greatly today, appearing only occasionally in the disguise of economic and political rivalries over the agricultural programs of the federal government, the domination of state legislatures by their rural members, and such public issues as daylight saving time. Only twelve percent of Americans were classified as rural-farm in 1960, and their proportion in the population will dwindle even more in the future. Thus, city-born, city-bred populations, with no experience of rural life except for summer vacations, outdoor sports, and excursions to the countryside, are increasingly numerous. Today agriculture has become more a rural industry, similar to urban industries in many respects, and less a family way of life. The standards of living of urban and rural populations no longer differ appreciably, even if they have not as yet reached equality.

## The Number and Size of Cities

In 1960, 70 percent or 125 million Americans lived in cities. This is the highest urban ratio and largest urban population ever reached in the United States, making America one of the most highly urbanized countries in the world. In addition, of the 30 percent who were rural in residence in 1960, 18 percent were rural non-farm population, meaning that they live in places having up to 2,500 inhabitants, and are more likely to be urban than rural in culture and outlook.

Table II illustrates the percentage of Americans living in urban places for each decennial year since the first national census was taken in 1790. It reveals the steady increase in their urbanization for each decade except 1810–1820, a notable acceleration in their rate of urbanization after 1880, and a preponderant urbanization after 1920.

The designation "current urban definition" of cities for 1950 and 1960 in Table II indicates that the census bureau revised its definition of cities for those years. It calls attention to the bureau's periodic redefinition of terms and alteration of categories to report more accurately the changing conditions of settlement of the American people. In the case of cities, the bureau in 1910 reduced the size

TABLE II

Urban and rural population in the United States, 1790–1960, by percentage of total population

|  | Urban | Non-farm | Rural | Farm |
|---|---|---|---|---|
| 1960 (current urban definition) | 69.9 | | | |
| 1950 (current urban definition) | 64.0 | 20.7 | | 15.3 |
| 1930 | 56.2 | 19.3 | | 22.9 |
| 1940 | 56.5 | 20.5 | | 24.6 |
| 1920 | 51.2 | | 48.8 | |
| 1910 | 45.7 | | 54.3 | |
| 1900 | 39.7 | | 60.3 | |
| 1890 | 35.1 | | 64.9 | |
| 1880 | 28.2 | | 71.8 | |
| 1870 | 25.7 | | 74.3 | |
| 1860 | 19.8 | | 80.2 | |
| 1850 | 15.3 | | 84.7 | |
| 1840 | 10.8 | | 89.2 | |
| 1830 | 8.8 | | 91.2 | |
| 1820 | 7.2 | | 92.8 | |
| 1810 | 7.3 | | 92.7 | |
| 1800 | 6.1 | | 93.9 | |
| 1790 | 5.1 | | 94.9 | |

SOURCE: *Census of Population, 1960, United States Summary, Number of Inhabitants* (Washington: Bureau of the Census, 1961), Table 3, p. 4.

of population necessary for cities from 8,000 to 2,500 inhabitants or more, and, since then, has defined as urban also the thickly settled aggregations residing in suburbs or fringes of large cities. In its present usage, it defines as urban places the cities with 2,500 inhabitants or more; all incorporated and unincorporated agglomerations of 2,500 inhabitants or more; towns, townships, and counties classified as urban; and smaller urban fringe settlements having sufficient density of population measured by either 100 dwelling units or more in closely settled areas or 1,000 inhabitants or more per square mile.

To deal with metropolitan areas, which comprise groups of cities which surround one or more central cities and are functionally interrelated and sometimes physically attached, the census bureau uses two terms—"urbanized areas" and "standard metropolitan statistical areas." Since 1910, when the bureau first took cognizance of such areas by introducing the concept of "metropolitan district," it has redefined its term a number of times. By the term "urbanized area," first used in 1950, it means the metropolitan area considered as a single physical city rather than as many political cities spread contiguously over an area. The bureau hopes its definition will "provide a better separation of urban and rural population in the vicinity of the larger cities" and identify more reliably the actual urban population of the United States. It defined urbanized areas in 1960 as having at least one city of 50,000 inhabitants or more, including the closely settled incorporated places and unincorporated areas surrounding the city which meet criteria of urban classification. Since the suburban areas continue to grow, the boundaries of such regions change from one decennial year to the next. According to this definition, 213 urbanized areas existed in the United States in 1960. (See Figure 1.)

Population data for urban places and urban areas for 1960 are combined in Table III. This table shows that 6,041 urban places exist in the country: 254 central cities, 1,580 suburban cities, and 596 urban places under 2,500 inhabitants inside urbanized areas; and 3,611 cities outside them. About three fourths of the urban population reside in urbanized areas, nearly a half in central cities within them. Of every ten urban dwellers in the United States, five live in the central city and three in the sub-

## TABLE III

Population in groups of urban places in and outside urban areas
classified by size and by percentage of total and urban
population in the United States in 1960

| Type of place and size of area | Number of urban places | Percent of U.S. population | Percent of total urban population |
|---|---|---|---|
| TOTALS | | 69.9 | 100.0 |
| *Within urban areas* | | 53.5 | 76.5 |
| *Central cities,* total | 254 | 32.3 | 46.3 |
| Cities of 1,000,000 or more | 5 | 9.8 | 14.0 |
| Cities of 500,000 to 1,000,000 | 16 | 6.2 | 8.9 |
| Cities of 250,000 to 500,000 | 30 | 6.0 | 8.6 |
| Cities of 100,000 to 250,000 | 66 | 5.5 | 7.9 |
| Cities of 50,000 to 100,000 | 111 | 4.4 | 6.3 |
| Cities under 50,000 | 26 | 0.5 | 0.7 |
| *Urban fringes,* total | | 21.1 | 30.2 |
| Places of 2,500 and more | 1,580 | 15.2 | 21.8 |
| Places of 100,000 and more | 15 | 1.0 | 1.4 |
| Places of 50,000 to 100,000 | 90 | 3.3 | 4.8 |
| Places of 25,000 to 50,000 | 212 | 4.0 | 5.8 |
| Places of 10,000 to 25,000 | 518 | 4.6 | 6.6 |
| Places of 5,000 to 10,000 | 399 | 1.6 | 2.3 |
| Places of 2,500 to 5,000 | 346 | 0.7 | 1.0 |
| Places under 2,500 | 596 | 0.4 | 0.6 |
| *Outside urban areas* | | | |
| Places of 2,500 and more | 3,611 | 16.4 | 23.5 |
| Places of 25,000 and more | 200 | 3.9 | 5.5 |
| Places of 10,000 to 25,000 | 610 | 5.2 | 7.4 |
| Places of 5,000 to 10,000 | 995 | 3.9 | 5.5 |
| Places of 2,500 to 5,000 | 1,806 | 3.5 | 5.1 |
| *Urban areas,* total: 213 areas | | | |
| Areas of 1,000,000 or more | 16 | 28.9 | 54.0 |
| Areas of 500,000 to 1,000,000 | 22 | 8.6 | 16.0 |
| Areas of 250,000 to 500,000 | 30 | 5.9 | 11.1 |
| Areas of 100,000 to 250,000 | 85 | 7.5 | 14.1 |
| Areas under 100,000 | 60 | 2.6 | 4.8 |

SOURCE: *Census of Population, 1960, United States Summary, Number of Inhabitants* (Washington: Bureau of the Census, 1961), Table 5, p. 11.

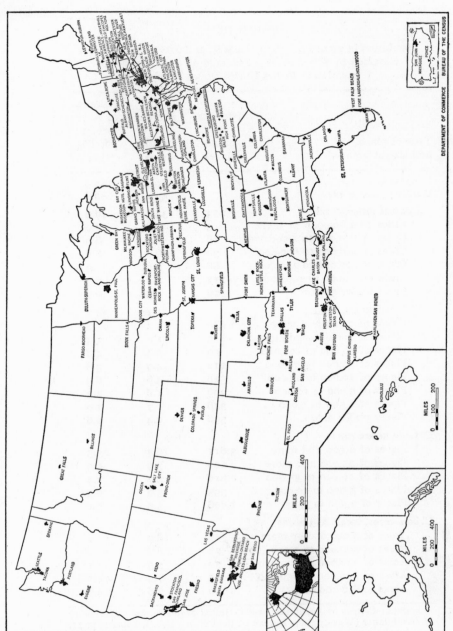

FIGURE 1. Urbanized Areas: 1960

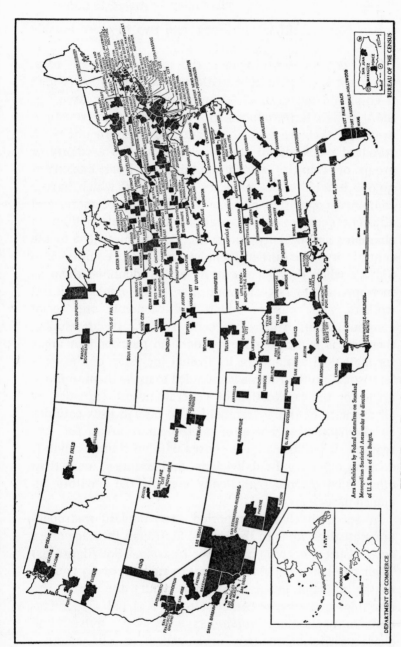

FIGURE 2. Standard Metropolitan Statistical Areas: 1960

urban cities of urbanized areas, and two in cities outside them.

The second term which the census bureau uses, "standard metropolitan statistical area," or SMSA, which it employed in 1960, or "standard metropolitan area," or SMA, which it introduced in 1950, defines metropolitan areas by their central cities and urbanized counties. A standard metropolitan statistical area means a county or group of counties which contains at least one city of 50,000 inhabitants or more, or "twin cities" which have a combined population of 50,000 inhabitants or more, and adjacent counties which are essentially metropolitan in character and socially and economically integrated to the central city. The bureau includes contiguous counties into SMSA's when they meet criteria which identified them as metropolitan places of work, homes of nonagricultural workers, and counties which had economic and social communication with the central city. In developing these areas it provides census data on metropolitan areas for statistical evaluation; its formal inclusion of the term "statistical" in their name is intended to make them uniform areas for the publication of general-purpose statistics by all agencies of the government. The bureau uses counties as the statistical bases of metropolitan areas for two reasons: it publishes more census data on counties than it does on other legal subdivisions; and counties, more than other subdivisions, realistically contain the territory included in such areas.

In 1960, the bureau reported 212 standard metropolitan statistical areas in the United States, an increase of 44 such districts over their number in 1950. (See Figure 2.) Their combined population was 113 million, or 63 percent of the national population. They signify the steady, inexorable amassing of Americans in regional agglomerations of population, which has become the outstanding characteristic of modern urbanization in this country.

Data on the number and rate of growth of metropolitan regions since 1900, when the census bureau first compiled data on them, are provided in Table IV.

As metropolitan areas expand, their populations redistribute themselves, decreasing proportionally in central cities and increasing in suburbs. This means that central cities fill with population, spilling additional populations into the suburban and urban fringe areas. While central cities still hold the larger population, suburban populations are rapidly overtaking them and will exceed them soon. The proportion of urban and suburban populations in metropolitan districts is shown in Table V.

Since 1920, suburban cities have grown more rapidly than central cities in metropolitan areas; from 1900 to 1920, central cities had a greater rate of increase. As suburban cities near central cities are populated, the suburbs farther removed from them attract population and grow at an accelerated rate. These data are shown in Table VI.

These trends in the growth of cities and metropolitan areas had proceeded far enough by 1960 to have several important results, one being the sheer size of metropolitan areas at present. The population of the 24 SMSA's with 1,000,000 inhabitants or more is reported in Table VII.

Another outcome was that many central cities showed a decline in population between 1950 and 1960, suggesting that metropolitan cities in the United States have reached a maximum size. However, some cities in sections of the country which experienced considerable economic development in the last decade continued to grow, notably Los Angeles, Houston, Dallas, New Orleans, and San Diego. The size and rank order of the 25 largest cities in the United States in 1960 and 1950 are given in Table VIII.

A third result was that smaller cities outgrew larger ones in the United States between 1950 and 1960. For cities with 10,000 to 14,999 inhabitants, the increase in popula-

## TABLE IV

Metropolitan districts in the United States, 1900–1960

| | Number of districts | Total population of districts in millions | Percent of U.S. population in districts | Percent of U.S. population increase in districts |
|---|---|---|---|---|
| 1960 | 212† | 113 | | |
| 1950 | 168 | 89 | | |
| 1940 * | 140 | 63 | 47.8 | 53.0 |
| 1930 | 97 | 55 | 44.6 | 70.8 |
| 1920 | 58 | 36 | 34.0 | 55.5 |
| 1910 | 44 | 26 | 28.3 | 41.9 |
| 1900 | 44 | 19 | 25.5 | |

SOURCE: *Census of Population, 1960, United States Summary, Number of Inhabitants* (Washington: Bureau of the Census, 1961), p. 103.

* Warren S. Thompson, *The Growth of Metropolitan Districts in the United States, 1900–1940* (Washington: Government Printing Office, 1947). Figures apply to metropolitan districts as defined by census bureau in these years.

† The Bureau of the Census added four new areas to make a total of 216 SMSA's and revised 57 other areas in 1963. *Current Population Reports*, Series P-23, No. 10, "Standard Metropolitan Statistical Areas in the United States as Defined October 18, 1963." (Washington: Bureau of the Census, 1963.)

## TABLE V

Percent distribution of population in standard metropolitan areas in
the United States, 1900–1960

| | Standard Metropolitan Areas | | | Percent of S.M.A. Population | | |
|---|---|---|---|---|---|---|
| | | | | | In metropolitan ring | |
| Year | Number | Population in millions | Percent of U.S. population | In central city | Urban | Rural |
| 1960 | 212 | 112.8 | 63. | 51.5 | | |
| 1950 * | 162 | 85.6 | 56.8 | 57.7 | 21.2 | 21.1 |
| 1940 | 125 | 67.1 | 51.1 | 61.9 | 20.6 | 17.5 |
| 1930 | 115 | 61.0 | 49.8 | 63.9 | 20.7 | 15.3 |
| 1920 | 94 | 46.1 | 43.7 | 66.2 | 18.3 | 15.5 |
| 1910 | 71 | 34.5 | 37.5 | 66.3 | 17.3 | 16.4 |
| 1900 | 52 | 24.1 | 31.7 | 66.5 | 15.6 | 17.9 |

SOURCE: *Census of Population, 1960, United States Summary, Number of Inhabitants* (Washington: Bureau of the Census, 1961), p. 106.

* Donald J. Bogue, *Population Growth in Standard Metropolitan Areas 1900–1950.* (Washington: Housing and Home Finance Agency, 1953.) Adapted from tables on pages 10, 11, 13, and 28. The number of metropolitan areas do not agree with those given in Table IV because Bogue re-delimited them to conform to the definition of standard metropolitan area used in the 1950 census, and reduced the number of such areas for 1950 because some were reported on town, and not county, bases. Metropolitan rings refer to the suburban and fringe populations contained in the areas.

## TABLE VI

Percent change of population in standard metropolitan areas, by type of place and distance from central city, 1900–1950

| Distance Zone | Standard Metropolitan Areas | | | | | |
|---|---|---|---|---|---|---|
| | 1940–50 | 1930–40 | 1920–30 | 1910–20 | 1900–10 |
| All Area | 19.7 | 8.0 | 24.9 | 24.5 | 29.4 |
| Central cities | 11.8 | 5.1 | 21.4 | 25.9 | 31.5 |
| Satellite areas | 31.6 | 12.6 | 31.0 | 22.2 | 26.0 |
| 0–5 miles | 23.6 | 10.4 | 26.3 | 29.3 | 27.9 |
| 5–10 miles | 36.3 | 15.0 | 41.2 | 23.4 | 29.4 |
| 10–15 miles | 32.2 | 11.6 | 25.4 | 20.3 | 24.9 |
| 15–20 miles | 32.9 | 13.4 | 32.7 | 21.8 | 22.9 |
| 20–25 miles | 30.6 | 13.5 | 34.9 | 20.8 | 24.1 |
| 25–30 miles | 23.2 | 9.6 | 24.2 | 19.0 | 23.7 |
| 30–35 miles | 36.8 | 11.0 | 17.5 | 15.6 | 14.2 |
| 35 miles and over | 27.2 | 9.5 | 18.7 | 9.3 | 25.2 |

SOURCE: Amos H. Hawley, *The Changing Shape of Metropolitan America: Deconcentration since 1920* (New York: The Free Press of Glencoe, 1956), p. 14.

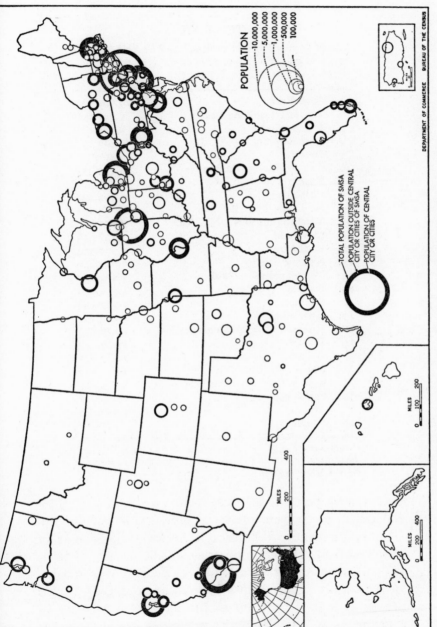

POPULATION

- 10,000,000
- 5,000,000
- 1,000,000
- 500,000
- 100,000

TOTAL POPULATION OF SMSA
POPULATION OUTSIDE CENTRAL
CITY OR CITIES OF SMSA
POPULATION OF CENTRAL
CITY OR CITIES

MILES
0    200    400

MILES
0    100    200

MILES
0    200    400

DEPARTMENT OF COMMERCE    BUREAU OF THE CENSUS

FIGURE 3. Population of Standard Metropolitan Areas: 1960

## TABLE VII

Size of population and rank order of 24 SMSA's with
1,000,000 inhabitants or more in the
United States, 1960

| | | |
|---|---|---|
| 1. | New York | 10,694,633 |
| 2. | Los Angeles–Long Beach | 6,742,696 |
| 3. | Chicago | 6,220,913 |
| 4. | Philadelphia, Pa., N. J. | 4,342,897 |
| 5. | Detroit | 3,762,360 |
| 6. | San Francisco–Oakland | 2,783,359 |
| 7. | Boston | 2,589,301 |
| 8. | Pittsburgh | 2,405,435 |
| 9. | St. Louis, Mo.–Ill. | 2,060,103 |
| 10. | Washington, D. C., Md., Va. | 2,001,897 |
| 11. | Cleveland | 1,796,595 |
| 12. | Baltimore | 1,727,023 |
| 13. | Newark | 1,689,420 |
| 14. | Minneapolis–St. Paul | 1,482,030 |
| 15. | Buffalo | 1,306,957 |
| 16. | Houston | 1,243,158 |
| 17. | Milwaukee | 1,194,290 |
| 18. | Paterson-Clifton-Passaic | 1,186,873 |
| 19. | Seattle | 1,107,213 |
| 20. | Dallas | 1,083,601 |
| 21. | Cincinnati, Ohio–Ky. | 1,071,624 |
| 22. | Kansas City, Mo., Kan. | 1,039,493 |
| 23. | San Diego | 1,033,011 |
| 24. | Atlanta | 1,017,188 |
| 25. | Miami | 935,047 |

SOURCE: *Census of Population, 1960, United States Summary, Number of Inhabitants* (Washington: Bureau of the Census, 1961), p. 117.

tion was 35 percent; for cities with 15,000 to 24,999 inhabitants, 31 percent; but for cities with 100,000 inhabitants or more, 7 percent. However, a large part of the growth in population of cities was because of annexation of surrounding territory. In each geographical division of the country, except the Middle Atlantic and the Pacific states, at least 70 percent of the population increase in cities of 10,000 inhabitants or more was due to extension

## TABLE VIII

Number of inhabitants and rank order of 25 largest cities
in the United States, 1950 and 1960

| | 1960 | | | 1950 | |
|---|---|---|---|---|---|
| 1. | New York | 7,781,984 | 1. | New York | 7,891,957 |
| 2. | Chicago | 3,550,404 | 2. | Chicago | 3,620,962 |
| 3. | Los Angeles | 2,479,075 | 3. | Philadelphia | 2,071,605 |
| 4. | Philadelphia | 2,002,512 | 4. | Los Angeles | 1,970,358 |
| 5. | Detroit | 1,670,144 | 5. | Detroit | 1,849,568 |
| 6. | Baltimore | 939,024 | 6. | Baltimore | 949,708 |
| 7. | Houston | 938,219 | 7. | Cleveland | 914,808 |
| 8. | Cleveland | 876,050 | 8. | St. Louis | 856,796 |
| 9. | Washington | 763,956 | 9. | Washington | 802,178 |
| 10. | St. Louis | 750,026 | 10. | Boston | 801,444 |
| 11. | San Francisco | 742,855 | 11. | San Francisco | 775,357 |
| 12. | Milwaukee | 741,324 | 12. | Pittsburgh | 676,806 |
| 13. | Boston | 697,197 | 13. | Milwaukee | 637,392 |
| 14. | Dallas | 679,684 | 14. | Houston | 596,163 |
| 15. | New Orleans | 627,525 | 15. | Buffalo | 580,132 |
| 16. | Pittsburgh | 604,332 | 16. | New Orleans | 570,445 |
| 17. | San Antonio | 587,718 | 17. | Minneapolis | 521,718 |
| 18. | San Diego | 573,224 | 18. | Cincinnati | 503,998 |
| 19. | Seattle | 557,087 | 19. | Seattle | 467,591 |
| 20. | Buffalo | 532,759 | 20. | Kansas City | 456,622 |
| 21. | Cincinnati | 502,550 | 21. | Newark | 438,776 |
| 22. | Memphis | 497,524 | 22. | Dallas | 434,462 |
| 23. | Denver | 493,887 | 23. | Indianapolis | 427,173 |
| 24. | Atlanta | 487,455 | 24. | Denver | 415,786 |
| 25. | Minneapolis | 482,872 | 25. | San Antonio | 408,442 |

SOURCE: *Census of Population, 1960, United States Summary, Number of Inhabitants* (Washington: Bureau of the Census, 1961), p. 68.

of city boundaries; in the Pacific states, 45 percent of the change was due to such extension. The Middle Atlantic cities, as a group, lost population. The gain and loss of population by cities of 10,000 inhabitants or more is shown in Table IX.

## TABLE IX

Population change according to size of city, in geographic divisions of the United States, 1950 to 1960

| Geographic division: | Cities classified by size of population in 1950 | | | | | |
|---|---|---|---|---|---|---|
| | 10,000 and over | 10,000–14,999 | 15,000–24,999 | 25,000–49,999 | 50,000–99,999 | 100,000 and over |
| | Percent increase * in population, 1950 to 1960 | | | | | |
| United States—Total | 13.5 | 35.2 | 30.7 | 23.6 | 17.2 | 6.9 |
| New England | .4 | 9.0 | 14.3 | 12.5 | 3.1 | -8.8 |
| Middle Atlantic | -2.2 | 4.9 | 2.5 | -.1 | -2.2 | -2.7 |
| East North Central | 8.3 | 21.1 | 28.1 | 18.7 | 15.8 | 1.2 |
| West North Central | 10.0 | 18.0 | 17.5 | 22.1 | 23.7 | 1.3 |
| South Atlantic | 21.4 | 39.5 | 33.2 | 25.6 | 27.0 | 13.3 |
| East South Central | 19.4 | 33.3 | 50.5 | 15.8 | 18.9 | 12.6 |
| West South Central | 38.4 | 31.2 | 35.8 | 38.0 | 35.1 | 40.4 |
| Mountain | 61.2 | 50.4 | 55.3 | 70.3 | 66.6 | 59.3 |
| Pacific | 30.8 | 85.2 | 61.1 | 48.1 | 26.4 | 18.5 |
| | Number of cities with population change, 1950 to 1960 | | | | | |
| United States—Total | 1,086 | 316 | 302 | 236 | 125 | 107 |
| Increase | 863 | 272 | 251 | 192 | 88 | 60 |
| Decrease | 223 | 44 | 51 | 44 | 37 | 47 |

SOURCE:: Computed by the Statistical Bureau of the Metropolitan Life Insurance Company from 1960 Census, Series PC(1)-A and 1950 Census, Series P-A. *Statistical Bulletin*, 43 (May 1962), pp. 3–5.
* Minus sign (–) denotes decrease.

# NOTES

1. Chauncy D. Harris and Edward L. Ullman, "The Nature of Cities," *Annals of the American Academy of Political and Social Sciences*, 242 (November 1945), pp. 7–17.

2. Richard C. Wade, *The Urban Frontier* (Cambridge: Harvard University Press, 1959), p. 1.

3. R. D. McKenzie, *The Metropolitan Community* (New York: McGraw-Hill, 1933), pp. 4–5.

4. Charles H. Cooley, *Theory of Transportation*. Reprinted in *Sociological Theory and Social Research*, ed. R. C. Angell (New York: Holt, 1930, pp. 75–83.

5. Richard C. Wade, *The Urban Frontier*, pp. 30–35.

6. R. D. McKenzie, *The Metropolitan Community*, pp. 3–6.

7. R. M. Tryon, *Household Manufactures in the United States, 1640–1860* (Chicago, 1917), pp. 81–84, 169–182.

8. Eric E. Lampard, in *Regions, Resources, and Economic Growth*, by Harvey S. Perloff and others (Baltimore: Johns Hopkins Press, 1960), pp. 109–110.

9. Chester Whitney Wright, *Economic History of the United States* (New York: McGraw-Hill, 1949), 2nd ed., p. 319.

10. Ernest S. Griffith, *History of American Government, the Colonial Period* (New York: Oxford University Press, 1938), pp. 418–423.

11. Carl Bridenbaugh, *Cities in the Wilderness* (New York: Ronald Press, 1938); and *Cities in Revolt* (New York: Knopf, 1955).

12. Carl Bridenbaugh, *Cities in Revolt*, pp. 136–138, 282–284, 420–421.

13. *Cf.* James Bryce, *The American Commonwealth* (New York: Macmillan, 1896), 3rd ed., I, pp. 623–625.

14. James Bryce, *American Commonwealth*, I, p. 637.

15. "The Government of Cities," *Forum*, 10 (1890–1891), p. 357.

16. James Bryce, *American Commonwealth*, I, pp. 628–629.

17. Lincoln Steffens, *The Shame of Cities* (New York: P. Smith, 1904).

18. Jefferson, *Writings*, Vol. 4, p. 88, and Vol. 7, p. 459.

19. Arthur M. Schlesinger, *The Rise of the City: 1878–1898* (New York: Macmillan, 1933), pp. 53–77.

20. For an extended discussion, see Anselm Strauss, *Images of the American City* (New York: The Free Press of Glencoe, 1961).

# · VII ·

# *Economic Classes of Cities*

### Urban Division of Labor

The United States is a nation of cities today. Its people live in more than 6,000 urban places, which range from small trade centers to great metropolises. Many urban places coalesce to form metropolitan areas; metropolitan areas, in turn, combine to create megalopolitan areas. Urban places are distributed throughout the entire country and in all its sections.

These cities and metropolitan areas contain the nation's business and industrial activities, its stores, markets, and financial institutions, and its facilities of transportation and communication. They are places of enormous economic productivity, and provide employment for a large majority of the American people. Urban dwellers compose large, highly skilled, and diversified labor forces which work in many different occupations and economic pursuits. With their earned incomes they possess a huge purchasing power, and use it to maintain their families and homes and to improve their standards of living. Thus the vast economic activities of American cities profoundly affect the social life and cultural activities of their populations and the character of the cities as well.

For these reasons, American cities are designated, in ideal type, as commercial-industrial cities, with economic institutions paramount in their social order. An analysis of their economic organization, as well as of urban and metropolitan economies in the country, should therefore precede that of their social organization. This will assist a social analysis of cities, and contribute to an understanding of urban communities and their place in the national community of the United States.

To investigate urban economic organization, a classification of cities into categories which identify their important traits and permit valid comparisons among them is necessary. American cities differ not only in number of inhabitants and in geographical location but also in the number, kind, and scale of their economic activities and in their position in or outside metropolitan areas. They share in an urban division of labor, as it were, in the national economy, and classifications of them commonly rest on the important economic tasks which they fulfill.

Cities perform two types of economic activities: one, varied, specialized activities which provide economic goods and services for regional or national markets; and two, maintenance activities which they provide for their own populations. The first type of activities constitutes the specialized activities of cities in the national economy and provides a basis for the classification of cities into economic types. The latter activities supply urban dwellers with the daily necessities of life, and all cities engage in them.

There are several factors which affect the economic specialization of cities. First, cities have basic industries which have made their growth possible and whose influence permeates their social and economic life. These industries are basic in that they provide the principal sources of livelihood, and therefore employ a large part of the cities' labor forces. Moreover, subsidiary industries are attracted to cities because of major industries, on which they depend for existence.

Obviously basic industries affect the number, composition, and characteristics of urban inhabitants by the technical, educational, and other skills they require from workers. Furthermore, employees expend their earned incomes to buy the necessities of life, thereby supporting many tertiary businesses in cities: stores, shops, professional offices, and service industries of many kinds. The effect of basic industries is plain to see in cities which have only one industry—a mining town, for example—but they determine the character of even great cities such as Detroit and Pittsburgh.

A second factor affecting the economic specialization of many cities is the metropolitan area in whose economy they are incorporated. The specialized activities of such cities are affected by their position as central or suburban cities in their areas, by the size of their population, and by the character of their economic areas. Surrounding areas may differ in raw materials, food commodities, labor force, industrial power, shipping facilities, and other resources. With 212 SMSA's now in the United States (see Chapter VI), the metropolitan organization of the American economy has become enormously important.

Metropolitan economies arise through the economic expansion of large cities into their surrounding territories. As these cities grow, their interior sections become overcrowded with people and buildings. Their streets and facilties are congested with traffic. To overcome the resulting costs and inconveniences, some business and industrial firms relocate their plants or operations in more favorable surroundings: they move to other locations in central business districts, remove to sub-business districts or industrial zones, or migrate to suburban cities and villages.

They do not decentralize further than the metropolitan area because, while continuing to utilize the market and other facilities of central cities, they find ample land, specialized labor forces, and other economic advantages in suburban places. Similarly urban populations resettle as central cities grow, either moving to other localities within cities or to suburban cities and villages. They also do not decentralize further because they continue to work in central cities and to enjoy a social and cultural life there, and they want to live within commuting distance. As suburbs grow, their populations attract businesses and service industries from central cities which seek the suburban markets they constitute.

In this process, central and suburban cities become specialized in their economic activities, as well as mutually interdependent. Central cities tend, in general, to intensify their commercial and reduce their industrial character. They retain the business enterprises which require a  central location for access to local, metropolitan, and national markets and the other economic facilities which central cities provide. Thus department stores, specialty shops, hotels, commercial banks, administrative offices, communication agencies, public entertainment, and light industries locate in central cities and ordinarily do not quit them. But other enterprises, heavy industries for example, are seriously disaffected by the internal congestion of such cities. Moreover, they do not require close contact with their markets, and are likely, therefore, to settle outside the cities. The economic specialization of central cities within metropolitan economies is therefore in commerce, finance, communication, business management, transportation, professional, and public services, and in light industries.[1]

Most suburban cities, in turn, are specialized as residential cities, with stores, shops, and offices to meet the economic needs of residents. Other suburbs, however, are industrial cities with manufacturing or other industries. With the exception of exclusive suburbs, many suburban cities solicit business and industrial enterprises to settle in them, hoping to widen their economic base and to gain large taxpayers. The business firms which suburbanize are commonly in retail and wholesale trade, manufacturing, electronic and other industries, warehousing, trucking, and comparable enterprises. In megalopolitan areas the exodus of business firms from central cities sometimes includes the offices and factories of industrial corporations, administrative offices of companies, insurance companies, research organizations, and many kinds of branch stores and other outlets of city firms. Some suburban cities come to resemble central cities in their economic activities and even to acquire suburbs of their own.

Today metropolitan areas contain the bulk of the commerce and industries of the entire United States; indeed, a third of the national economic activity occurs in the ten largest SMSA's.[2] Their metropolitan economies, as a result, are highly diversified in their mixture of economic activities: they have major industries, many lesser ones, light and heavy manufacturing, food processing industries, public utilities, railroad lines, and other enterprises. One or more basic industries, with the subsidiary industries which serve as sub-processors, suppliers, or distributors, sometimes dominate them. They contain large, highly specialized labor forces which work in both central and suburban cities and commute from work to residence by private and public transportation. These populations, with large total incomes and hence great purchasing power, constitute vast markets of consumers whose numbers and patronage encourage a proliferation of tertiary businesses and industries.

Great cities expand far beyond their metropolitan areas into wider economic regions and even throughout sections of the country. As they do so they establish a specialization of economic activities and an interdependence with cities throughout their region. Such cities thus create regional as well as metropolitan economies in the United States— a third factor in the specialization of cities. By performing metropolitan functions of marketing, industrial production, transportation, and finance in regional economies, they become metropolitan cities.[3] Other cities of the region possess the businesses and industries appropriate to them in the division of labor which exists between them and the metropolitan city.

We have already touched on the process by which American cities promoted the settlement and economic development of their regions. Initially cities served as urban places of business through which settlers passed to their hinterlands; thereafter the cities provided markets for the sale or transshipment of agricultural commodities which farmers raised. These cities also became centers of industries which encouraged the exploitation of natural resources or raw materials in their territories, accelerating the growth of regional industries. The railroads and other means of transportation developed around the large cities, which meant that farm commodities and manufactured goods produced in the regions passed through them to local or national markets. Then also, these developments necessitated the rise of financial institutions in the cities, which hastened the economic growth of cities and regions. The older cities which shared in the growth of the country and established an economic ascendancy in their regions at an early time now constitute most of the metropolitan cities of the United States.

Business firms and industrial corporations also influence the specialized economic activities of cities by their decisions to expand into other cities or areas. As independent companies, active in the national economy, often with offices and plants in several cities, they are in business to make profits. As they enlarge operations, they calculate the economic advantage of placing their facilities in various cities in terms of their organization, their policies, and the city's economic attractions. They compare urban places with respect to markets, labor force, raw materials, transportation costs, or whatever other factors appear crucial. When they finally select a city, their activities strengthen its economic base and perhaps increase its economic specialties.

While the administrative decisions of business firms are enormously important in determining the location of industry in America, the government, too, affects the economic activities of cities. Congress and various public agencies may decide to locate government buildings or activities there. Agencies may also award business contracts to corporations, promote industrial and military research and development, and expand new armament or space travel facilities, all of which strengthen the economies of cities receiving such business.

## Economic Classifications

Sociologists, geographers, and economists have advanced various economic classifications of American cities.[4] While differing in details, they all sort cities into types according to their important economic activities. For the most part, two procedures are followed in deciding what these businesses are. The first procedure identifies economic functions, comparing the labor force a city employs in various specific activities with that of other cities, and with the national labor force. The specialized activities of a city employ significantly larger proportions of workers than the same activities do in other cities—the degree of significance is determined by sensible but arbitrary statistical measurements.

The second procedure classifies cities by their economic base: i.e., the industries which produce and distribute economic goods and services in markets outside cities or which attract consumers to them from outside. In either case, such industries are basic because they attract to cities a flow of new money which provides capital to maintain, expand, or diversify their economies. To determine a city's economic base in terms of an import of money smacks of mercantilist thinking and is actually hard to compute, but it is nevertheless used.[5]

But however conceived, urban classifications are quite similar and one of them may illustrate the kind of classes they all propose. American cities of 10,000 inhabitants or more are divided in this taxonomy into eight categories: manufacturing cities (two classes), retail centers, diversified cities, wholesale centers, transportation centers, mining towns, university towns, and resort and retirement towns.[6]

There is no real quarrel with these categories. They are carefully devised and are useful in indicating a city's basic industries. But as a tool for analyzing urban economies, they have several weaknesses. For one, they classify small cities more reliably than large ones. Small cities often have a single important industry, but large ones have diversified industries, which makes it harder to classify them. This contributes to a second weakness, namely, that the various classifications may classify the same city by different specialized activities.[7]

Third, since large cities are a part of metropolitan areas, their economies are metropolitan as well as urban and, realistically, should be classified according to both categories. Finally, the size of cities and their metropolitan areas is itself a factor in determining economic activity. Their size is related to the scale of their industries, labor force, markets of consumers, total income, and other competitive advantages.

We are using here a taxonomy of cities which should aid in analyzing both their economic and social organization. It retains existing classifications for small cities and reclassifies large cities in terms of their diversified economic activities, number of inhabitants, and metropolitan functions.[8]

1. *Metropolitan cities.* These are the great cities of the United States which are situated in the larger metropolitan areas that have a total combined population of 300,000 inhabitants or more. For purposes of analyses, they may be considered the central city of their metropolitan areas or the SMSA's of which they are a part. As their name suggests, they perform metropolitan functions in the regions of the country.[9]

2. *Economically diversified cities.* The middle-sized cities of the country which occur in smaller metropolitan areas that have a total combined population ranging from 50,000 to 300,000 inhabitants are classified as economically diversified cities. They are also considered to be either central cities in their metropolitan areas or the SMSA's to which they belong. As their name indicates, they have diversified economic activities and exercise some economic influence over their regions. Again, their minimal size of 50,000 inhabitants appears significant in differentiating them from small cities. This figure is convenient, moreover, because the census bureau stipulates that SMSA's have a central city with 50,000 inhabitants or more.

3. *Residential cities.* Residential cities are suburban cities which exist in metropolitan regions and are economically dependent on central cities. Their main function is to serve as places of habitation for suburban populations who work in larger cities. As such, they have no economic base which resembles that of independent cities of comparable size. While they contain stores, shops, and offices, often assembled in shopping centers, they do not perform commercial functions for their adjacent rural populations. Nor do their inhabitants ordinarily work in any large proportion in industries in their own suburbs: rather employees travel to them from central and suburban cities throughout the metropolitan region.

4. *Commercial cities.* As their name implies, commercial cities are the numerous, small trade centers which exist everywhere in the United States. They are inhabited mostly by populations which assemble, distribute, and exchange economic goods and farm commodities in their trade area and provide some personal, mechanical, and professional services in addition.

5. *Industrial cities.* Industrial cities are small, with one or two industries, or perhaps with one or several plants of large companies whose main offices are located elsewhere. The industries may be manufacturing, mining, lumbering, or some similar activity. Because of the nature or location of the industry, these cities commonly do not perform commercial functions, although they have stores and services for the maintenance of inhabitants.

6. *Other economically specialized cities.* Some economic pursuit other than commerce or industry provides an economic base for these cities, which are relatively small in size. They are variously college or university towns, state capitals, resort cities, medical centers, military installations, or other. However, their inhabitants also carry on trade and service industries. Some of these cities are sufficiently attractive in their appearance and amenities to attract businesses and industries, in which case they become economically diversified cities.

## Metropolitan Cities

Metropolitan cities are interchangeably the great cities of metropolitan areas or the larger SMSA's with total populations of 300,000 inhabitants or more. In 1960, 81 SMSA's, in 1950, 56 SMSA's, were metropolitan cities by this definition. Five cities had populations over 1,000,000 inhabitants in 1960: New York, with 7.8 millions; Chicago, 3.5 millions; Los Angeles, 2.5 millions; Philadelphia, 2 millions; and Detroit, 1.7 millions. Their combined population was 17.5 millions, or nearly one-tenth of the national population. The five largest SMSA's had even larger populations: New York, 10.7 millions; Los Angeles, 6.7 millions; Chicago, 6.2 millions; Philadelphia, 4.3 millions; and Detroit, 3.8 millions; their combined population was 31.7 millions, or one-sixth of the national population.

The 81 SMSA's are the great population and industrial centers of the United States. While a large proportion of them are located in the northeastern and middlewestern states, they are nevertheless distributed over the entire country and tend to dominate their regions economically. Of course, the SMSA's do not all perform metropolitan functions in their regions to the same extent. They differ in their ability to penetrate their regions economically, in the scale of their economic enterprises, and in the advantages and disadvantages of transportation facilities. Large cities are formidable competitors to smaller cities in their own region; older cities have dominated their regions from an early time, and resist surrender of their dominance to newer cities. Economic regions also differ in natural resources, size and distribution of populations, industries, lines of transportation, and other characteristics, which affect the efforts of great cities to dominate them. Moreover, when many large cities are concentrated in the same section of the country, economic competition among them is acute. For these reasons, these cities are variable in their metropolitan character.

A classification of metropolitan cities into sub-classes makes clear the nature of these differences. Such a taxonomy of them was made in a valuable study of the 56 SMSA's which had populations of 300,000 inhabitants or more in 1950, based on a calculation of their economic inputs and outputs in the national economy and economic relationships with their regions. It is reproduced in Table X.

As this table reveals, the five cities with 1,000,000 inhabitants or more are national cities of the United States, performing some metropolitan functions throughout the entire country; San Francisco, Boston, and Pittsburgh should per-

## TABLE X

Classification of standard metropolitan areas of 300,000 inhabitants or more according to metropolitan functions and regional relationships

*National metropolis* (N)
New York
Chicago
Los Angeles (Nd)*
Philadelphia (Nd)
Detroit (Nm)

*Diversified manufacturing with metropolitan functions* (D)
Boston (Dn)
Pittsburgh (Dn)
St. Louis
Cleveland
Buffalo
Cincinnati

*Diversified manufacturing with few metropolitan functions* (D−)
Baltimore
Milwaukee
Albany-Schenectady-Troy
Toledo
Hartford
Syracuse

*Specialized manufacturing* (M)
Providence
Youngstown
Rochester
Dayton
Allentown-Bethlehem-Easton
Akron
Springfield-Holyoke
Wheeling-Steubenville
Charleston, W. Va.

*Regional metropolis* (R)
San Francisco (Rn)*
Minneapolis–St. Paul
Kansas City
Seattle
Portland
Atlanta
Dallas
Denver

*Regional capital submetropolitan* (C)
Houston
New Orleans
Louisville (Cd)
Birmingham (Cm)
Indianapolis (Cd)
Columbus (Cd)
Memphis
Omaha
Fort Worth
Richmond (Cd)
Oklahoma City
Nashville
Jacksonville

*Special cases* (S)
Washington
San Diego
San Antonio
Miami
Norfolk-Portsmouth
Wilkes-Barre–Hazleton
Tampa–St. Petersburg
Knoxville
Phoenix

SOURCE: Duncan *et al.*, *Metropolis and Region* (Baltimore: Johns Hopkins Press, 1960), p. 271.

\* The two letters in parenthesis which follow the names of some cities mean that they belong to one category but resemble cities of another category also. Thus Los Angeles is a national metropolis with diversified manufacturing, and San Francisco is a regional metropolis with other functions, especially financial, which resemble a national metropolis.

haps be added to their number. Other cities are regional capitals of their sections, some of which—San Francisco, Minneapolis–St. Paul, and Kansas City, for example—perform important metropolitan functions in them; and others —such as Houston, New Orleans, and Louisville—somewhat less so. Some large cities with diversified manufactures—such as Boston, Pittsburgh, and St. Louis—have important metropolitan functions; and others—Baltimore, Milwaukee, and Schenectady among them—have less. But cities with specialized manufacturing tend to perform few if any metropolitan functions.

The cities classified as special cities lack the usual economic base of large cities and have few if any metropolitan functions. They are Washington, the national capital; San Diego, San Antonio, and Norfolk-Portsmouth, which have military installations; Miami, tourist trade; Wilkes-Barre–Hazleton, coal mining; and Tampa, Knoxville, and Phoenix—agricultural, fishing, and forestry industries.

As central cities of their SMSA's, metropolitan cities have specialized economic activities. To the extent that they perform metropolitan functions in their regions or throughout the United States, they have the economic organizations necessary to fulfill them. These are the great number and variety of business firms and corporations which engage in marketing, transportation, financial, and communication activities, as well as in manufacturing and other industries. In addition, these cities are places of great and highly diversified economic consumption: they are filled with stores and shops, eating establishments, places of entertainment, and cultural organizations. Finally, they have the maintenance activities which provide personal, mechanical, and public services, and other necessities of life to their residents.

A survey of their central business districts reveals the kinds of business establishments which exist in metropolitan cities. Department stores, high-priced specialty shops, retail stores, hotels, restaurants, and theatres are crowded in these districts. There are office buildings for business and industrial firms as well as for lawyers, doctors, architects, and other professional groups. Commercial banks, savings and loan banks, commodities markets and offices, securities offices, insurance companies, and loan agencies create their financial districts. Newspapers, news syndicates, radio and TV syndicates and stations, publishing houses, and printers similarly locate their office facilities in central cities. Real estate firms, public utilities companies, local, state, and federal government offices, and many voluntary organizations also settle there.

Metropolitan cities also have manufacturing, although it is by necessity specialized in character. They retain some heavy industries, often those basic industries whose growth accompanied theirs but which commonly quit the cities over the course of time, relocating in their suburbs or areas. Light industries, in contrast, persist in metropolitan cities; in many cases they could not survive outside them. Light industries stay in big cities for many reasons: to be near their markets, shipping facilities, financial agencies, or sources of supply; to stay close to industrial companies whom they serve as sub-contractors or from whom they buy industrial goods or services; or to share in facilities with other firms, for example, office and factory space in industrial buildings, or machinery or trucks. The bulk of them are small companies with limited capitalization which have relatively small labor forces. For example, the majority of such firms in New York City hired 60 employees or less in 1950.[10] In total number and productivity, however, they are highly important. Moreover, they provide a large number of jobs in diverse fields.

Many manufacturing firms and most heavy industries leave metropolitan cities to resettle in suburbs and metropolitan areas. Some of the innumerable difficulties which force them to move out of the cities are: high costs of oper-

ation, internal congestion, old or obsolescent buildings, in-
efficiently designed and equipped factories, traffic congestion, restricted space for loading, parking, or expansion,
confining gridiron street systems, and, in general, overcrowding of people and buildings alike. In some cases these
firms remove their entire plant facilities and office forces
into suburbs; in other cases and more frequently they keep
their offices and older factories in cities, but when they expand build new factories in the suburbs. The factories are
groups of one-story buildings built to conform to work-flow
processes of production, equipped with modern technological machinery, including electronic controls, which maintain high levels of output. The suburbs provide adequate
mechanical power, transportation facilities, land for buildings, storage, and parking; and, in addition, employees can
commute to such factories with little inconvenience from
wherever they live in metropolitan or suburban cities.

Many business firms leave metropolitan cities to relocate
in expanding suburbs which offer new markets, for example, department stores and specialty shops which establish
branch stores in suburbs. But independent stores, offices,
and shops engaged in retail trades may move, too, as well
as firms which offer personal, public, and professional services. For certain other business firms, economic or technological changes in their activities may diminish the advantages of a metropolitan locality. They too remove to suburbs
or metropolitan areas. Their numbers and kinds multiply,
especially in megalopolitan regions, and now include,
among others, the offices of industrial corporations, insurance companies, electronics firms, construction companies,
trucking firms, and research laboratories.

Despite the exodus of these firms, metropolitan cities still
retain those specialized businesses and industries whose
activities are metropolitan in character and whose personnel requirements dictate a metropolitan location. These
businesses generally employ both a great number and a

great variety of people in many occupations and belonging to all economic classes. Although a large proportion of their employees are white-collar workers, performing sales, clerical, and office functions, these businesses also employ specialists in marketing, finance, communication, transportation, and other activities. Only a metropolitan location can supply such a diversified labor force.

Both the number of employees and the number of jobs are proportionally much greater in the metropolitan cities than in their metropolitan areas. They are concentrated in central business districts.[11] As a result, great masses of workers travel to places of employment in the business district and other localities from all sections of the city and from the suburbs, causing the tides of traffic familiar to all who live in cities. This labor force comprises persons of every kind and condition: rich, powerful executives, prominent officials, important corporation figures, bureaucratic officials, people of middling status, skilled workers, unskilled workers, the poor and afflicted. The mixture and variety make metropolitan cities places of color, stimulation, excitement, achievement—and also of meanness and depravity.

Most persons who work in metropolitan cities also live there, but many commute from suburban cities and metropolitan areas. These suburbanites continue not only to work but to participate in the social and cultural life of the city. The metropolitan city does not offer many residential amenities, however; it is burdened with substandard or obsolescent buildings, deteriorated neighborhoods, extensive slums, inadequate street systems, traffic congestion, and other unattractive features.

Therefore many families flee the cities to live in their suburbs, where they buy or build houses in good neighborhoods, seek small town life, cultivate family living, and combine urban and rural modes of existence. To suburbanize, however, they must be able to afford single-family houses, the costs of commuting, and the added expenses of suburban life. This means, in effect, that only families of at least moderate and stable income can suburbanize and that suburbanization is therefore selective of middle and upper economic classes.

Not all the rich or successful forsake the cities to live in their suburbs. Many who are city born and bred cannot endure life outside them. Some have acquired cosmopolitan tastes which can be gratified only in cities. Others continue to live in them because of their specialized work or hours of employment. Finally, many others stay for reasons of family—or no family. They are variously childless couples, young married couples, single persons, divorced or separated persons, or elderly people who find housing and other accommodations more satisfactory in cities.

As middle- and upper-class families leave metropolitan cities, the working classes, who are far more populous, increase proportionally in them. While some workers' families reside in suburbs, most live in metropolitan cities where they have access to jobs or other sources of livelihood, housing, municipal services, public welfare, cultural activities, and urban amenities. They dwell in single- or multi-family buildings in these cities, often in obsolescent structures in neighborhoods which are becoming or have already become slums. At present, these seriously deteriorated localities now engulf a fifth or more of the interior areas of the cities. In many cases, people are segregated into religious or racial subcommunities and live and play separately.

Because urban populations differ vastly in employment, size of incomes, levels of education, and other distinctions and attainments, they have diverse standards of living. A variably large number of them suffer poverty, lead lives of crime, or are other casualties of the great cities.

At the turn of the century, metropolitan cities were foreign cities in the United States in the sense that European immigrants settled disproportionately in them and established ethnic colonies. Now they are becoming Negro cities in the same sense: that Negro migrants, on leaving the southern for the northern and western states, tend to settle in metropolitan cities, not in the smaller cities and seldom in rural areas. They choose to settle in metropolitan cities because they have better opportunities to find work and housing there and because they are more often helped by public welfare agencies in their transition to the metropolis. In these cities they live in racially segregated areas, creating large Negro subcommunities. But, in another generation or two, like the second- and third-immigrant generations now, they too will relocate in other sections of the cities and some will find their way into the suburbs.

Nonwhite populations comprise a large and increasing proportion of the inhabitants of metropolitan cities. In 1960, they were 15 percent of New York's population; 24 percent of Chicago's; 27 percent of Philadelphia's; 30 percent of Detroit's; and over 50 percent of Washington, D. C.'s. These same cities however lost in total population in the decade 1950–1960, despite an increase in their Negro inhabitants, because white families migrated to their suburbs and metropolitan areas.

## Economically Diversified Cities

These cities and their metropolitan areas constitute the smaller SMSA's of the United States as reported by the census bureau. In 1960, there were 132 middle-sized cities with their suburbs distributed over the country. At their upper limit, with populations approaching 300,000 inhabitants, they are nearly metropolitan cities; at their lower limit, with 50,000 inhabitants or more, they are no longer small cities.

With this variation in size of population, these cities obviously differ among themselves and could, if necessary, be further subcategorized. But in the main, they do not perform many metropolitan functions in their areas and cannot compete with greater cities that are able to perform them far more effectively. Indeed, some of these economically diversified cities are often enclosed in the metropolitan areas of the greater cities, within which they are subdominant urban centers.

In many respects, these cities resemble metropolitan cities, but in modest scale. As their name implies, they have diversified economic activities, often one or several basic industries, and a mixture of other commercial and manufacturing enterprises. With populations of 50,000 inhabitants and more, they clearly need adequate economic bases to maintain them. Only the larger cities among them and perhaps cities with heavy manufacturing have experienced a major loss of population and industry to their suburbs and metropolitan areas.

The specific diversification of their economies is important to these cities. If they are predominantly commercial cities and have other attractions of location and residence, they often have social and cultural organizations which enrich them: state governments, colleges and universities, military establishments, or non-profit organizations. But if they are manufacturing cities, they repel these other organizations and sometimes have trade zones which scarcely extend beyond their municipal boundaries.[12] In all these cities, their industries affect the size and composition of the labor force, the employment and income levels, the social and cultural characteristics of workers, and determine to a large extent the different economic classes.

## Residential Cities

The suburbs of metropolitan cities are cities in their own right, usually incorporated as such, and with populations which in some cases approach and even exceed 50,000 inhabitants. They possess no basic industries but are suburban places of residence for inhabitants who work in metropolitan cities or areas. While they have business and industrial establishments, they are not commercial cities in the sense that merchants perform functions of assembly and exchange of commodities in their hinterlands, nor are they industrial cities the bulk of whose inhabitants are employed in manufacturing. They are residential cities whose existence depends on the metropolitan cities to which they are attached.

As residential cities, suburban settlements are not novel. They appeared as early as the Mesopotamian cities, where they served as residences of the servile classes. But their number, size, and residential specialization in metropolitan areas is unique: the wealthy now seek them out; the poor cannot afford to live in them.

Suburban settlements existed outside New York, Boston, Philadelphia, and other eastern cities by the turn of the century. Often wealthy families established summer homes, then later permanent homes, in small cities and villages lying along railroad lines and having amenities of residence and commuted between them and the large cities. Many suburban dwellers still commute by train, especially to the older great cities, but today most live in suburban cities located closer to metropolitan cities and travel to them by car or bus.

The growth of suburbs has been so extensive that urban populations have tended to fill the suburbs close to metropolitan cities and now are moving into more distant ones. In this outward expansion, they have inundated independent cities, villages, rural townships, counties, and unincorporated places. They have also occupied new suburban cities and villages developed after World War II by large-scale house builders and construction firms. Therefore suburban cities now differ in their ecological distribution. Some are attached to metropolitan cities and often to each other; others stand apart from metropolitan cities at distances

from a few to 50 miles. There are even some faraway suburbs for persons who commute infrequently to metropolitan cities. Nearby suburbs contain the bulk of suburban
populations because they reduce the costs, time, and inconveniences of commuting.

Suburban cities have been differentiated ideal-typically
into residential and industrial suburbs.[13] This is generally
a helpful classification in analyzing them, but it should be
further expanded to include the present variety of suburban sub-types, which is likely to increase as they diversify
their economic activities. Several such suburban typologies
have been attempted, based on their economic functions.
But since suburbs are residential cities, the social and cultural traits of their inhabitants and not the business activity
in them should properly provide the identifying criteria.

We have already noted some characteristics of suburban
cities: the predominance of middle- and upper-class families; the virtual absence of Negroes; the anticipation by
some suburban families of small town living; and the combinations of urban and rural living. Equally important, suburbs are places of family living. Most suburban dwelling
units consist of single-family houses, and most families own
the home which they occupy. Therefore they have been
called residential cities.

Children are one of the most commonly cited reasons for
moving to the suburbs. When their children reach preschool
age, parents often become concerned with the quality of the
neighborhood in which they live and the character of neighborhood schools and other organizations. At this time, if
they are living in metropolitan cities and have the financial
means to leave them, they may be attracted to suburban
cities. They are likely to consider them as better places in
which to rear children and to cultivate family living. At any
rate, most suburban dwellers are family members and
family-minded, and they reside in the suburbs at least during the time that their families are intact and their children

are growing up. When families are broken by death or divorce, or children grow up and leave home, or when parents are elderly, some suburban residents return to cities to live, often in apartments.

After 1935 the federal government contributed enormously to the growth of suburbs as residential places through its FHA housing program. The FHA (Federal Housing Administration) established a system of federal insurance for home mortgages, enabling middle-income families to borrow money from banks to buy their own homes. In the administration of the act, the FHA encouraged families to purchase homes in suburban neighborhoods. At the same time, it assisted house builders, by provisions which made their houses conditionally eligible for mortgage insurance, to build vast tracts of new houses. Since tracts of available land existed only in suburbs, builders located their houses there and they are the homes of mass suburbia today. But FHA, by its success, also stimulated commercial banks and private builders to develop new housing in suburbs. In consequence, there has been a virtual revolution in home ownership in the United States. About 60 percent of American families owned their homes in 1960, in contrast with 40 percent in 1940 and 25 percent in 1900.

In new or rapidly growing suburban cities, the concentration of families with children has overburdened their public schools and increased demands on their governments for improved municipal services. These include the construction of more and larger school buildings, the expansion of municipal water and sewage disposal systems to replace the use of private wells and septic tanks, the building and paving of streets and roads, and enlarged police and fire protection. To pay for these services, suburban governments levy taxes mainly on houses and land, which their own home-owners pay and which they often find onerous. To widen the tax base of their cities, public officials therefore

solicit business firms and industrial companies to settle
in them, either in shopping centers or in industrial parks.
At the same time, they try, through zoning regulations,
restrictive covenants, and building codes, to keep the
prices of houses at some desired level in order to maintain tax valuations and to prevent the settlement of lower-
income families who might conceivably become public
charges.

Since suburban cities are selective of the middle and upper classes, they have prestige as places of residence and
are ranked among themselves in terms of their relative degrees of status. For the most part, resident families impart
their own social prominence to their suburbs. Wealthy, important families establish suburbs of high social standing
which they enhance through the elegance of their homes
and neighborhoods and through pretensions to exclusive-
ness. Similarly, middle-class families confer their status on
their suburbs. Status and occupational subcommunities also
create suburbs which reflect their social position in metropolitan society. Suburban populations, mindful of these distinctions, tend to segregate in suburbs which contain social
and cultural groups of their own kind.[14]

There is some indication that suburban dwellers have
now attained a relative stability and permanence as suburban populations. Since 1920, suburban cities have outgrown
central cities in their rate of increase; in the decade 1950–
1960, their increase was 48.6 percent, and central cities,
10.7 percent.[15] This growth is so large as to suggest that the
suburbs expanded more by the movement of populations
into them from other suburbs and by their own natural increase than by the migration of families from metropolitan
cities. More and more, families who move to large metropolitan areas settle directly in their suburbs, having had
previous suburban experience, or live in central cities only
long enough to find a suburban place of residence. Thus, an
increasing proportion of the suburban dwellers are subur-

ban born and bred and accustomed to suburban lives and activities. They are people who work in and visit metropolitan cities but avoid living in them.

## Commercial Cities

American cities developed originally as commercial cities, serving as urban places for the assembly and exchange of farm commodities and raw materials and for the distribution of manufactured goods and services. These cities still preponderate numerically in the United States and are widely distributed in all its regions. They vary in size from 2,500 to 50,000 inhabitants, but most of them have populations of half or less than half of 50,000. Their inhabitants are employed mainly in retail trades and in personal, mechanical, and professional services.

Since these cities function as trade centers for rural populations, they depend for survival on the productivity of agriculture and other rural industries in their localities and on their patronage by nearby farm and village families. They are favorably situated, of course, if they stand in rich rural territories and their trade zones encompass relatively affluent rural populations. In this event, they are likely to have a large number and variety of stores and services: specialty stores, hotels, restaurants, theaters, professional offices, and shops. Some cities serve as seats of county government or have state government facilities located in them. Occasionally colleges are located there. But if they are in areas of marginal agricultural activity or are too near metropolitan areas, they lack any large number of commercial enterprises.

When they are favorably located or have other competitive advantages, some cities acquire manufacturing or other industries. Some of these are locally owned factories which utilize available raw materials and others are factories located there by national corporations. The officials and merchants of commercial cities often solicit business firms to establish plants in these cities in order to diversify their economies.

## Industrial Cities

Industrial cities have heavy industries as their economic base. They manufacture durable economic goods, such as textiles, leather goods, paper products, or chemicals; or they are primary metal producers, having blast furnaces or steel mills; or they have mining or lumbering industries. For reasons related to the character of industry—their massive size, noxious by-products, resource orientation, or other traits—industrial cities seldom have the advantages of business locations, and commercial enterprises do not flourish in them. Without economic diversification, only a few industrial cities ever attain a population of 50,000 inhabitants or more, and most of them are smaller than this.

Since basic industries vary, so do industrial cities. Manufacturing cities, especially when they contain factories which produce a variety of industrial products, are economically more stable than the others. Not only do industrial firms employ large numbers of factory workers, but ordinarily they pay them better than other industries do. However they also concentrate lower economic classes in these cities because the bulk of the jobs they provide are in semi-skilled or unskilled labor. One or more ethnic groups often provide much of the labor force, and their presence is conspicuous in the cities, but the companies sometimes show scant interest in them. The company which manufactures goods for sale in national markets is often not concerned with local populations. Frequently, their managerial and office personnel reside in other cities or suburbs. For these reasons, manufacturing cities have relatively few social and residential amenities.

Mining and lumbering cities are based on a single industry and are located wherever the necessary natural resources exist, sometimes in remote areas of the country. The life of these cities is bound up with the prosperity of their industry. Its business fluctuations and seasonal swings of employment determine their civic enterprises and affect their social and cultural activities. In single industries there are few occupations, many of them involving semi-skilled or unskilled work. Again, one or a few ethnic groups may dominate the labor force, establishing their subculture as a feature of the cities.

In industrial suburbs, these various effects of manufacturing and other industry on cities are mitigated in part. At least the newer suburbs contain attractive modern factory buildings which enhance the area and control manufacturing's possible injurious effects on surroundings by modern technological means. Many factories are also relatively small and are devoted to manufacturing articles of high quality. Workers often commute to them from metropolitan cities or suburbs and are not controlled by employers or influenced by the industry as much as the populations of other industrial cities.

## Other Specialized Cities

Originating as commercial cities in most cases, specialized cities added other activities to trade because of their location or for other reasons, thus altering their economic bases. Specialized cities may be state capitals, college and university towns, medical centers, religious cities, military posts, resort towns, gambling towns, and so on. With their continued growth, some of them attract still different enterprises and diversify their economies even more. Rochester, Minnesota, is a medical center, with important commercial and industrial activities; such university cities as Ann Arbor and Princeton contain business enterprises drawn to them by their amenities; and Madison, state capital and university city, contains a significant amount of business and industry.

These cities show the impress of their specialized activities in various ways. Capital cities benefit in increased trade and prestige from having state governments located in them. Not only do governments employ large numbers of workers, but they purchase vast quantities of consumer and industrial goods to carry on the multitude of their activities. Hotels, restaurants, and similar businesses exist in these cities to accommodate those who have business with the state. College and university cities contain large numbers of faculty, students, and school employees who are important consumers of local goods and services and affect the cities through their social and cultural activities. Similarly, medical centers have large staffs of medical and hospital personnel and, of course, patients and their families. Much of their social and cultural life, as well as the business of hotels, transportation companies, and service industries, revolves about medical activities. Military posts, penitentiaries, state hospitals, and other institutions have their own peculiar effects on cities. Salt Lake City demonstrates the importance of a church on the life of a city.

Resort and gambling cities attract people on vacation or, it may be, on moral holiday, and contain the business establishments which cater to their pleasures. The former fill with visitors seasonally, when the commercialization of eating and drinking, entertainment, and recreation becomes intense and shrink to a small number of permanent residents during the off-seasons. In gambling cities, of which Reno and Las Vegas are examples, some activities border upon or are openly illegal; but since these are important sources of income, local law officers tolerate them. Without the permission of the police, such gambling cities could not exist. Therefore they are located well outside the jurisdiction of large cities and in states which welcome them for their own reasons.

# NOTES

1. R. D. McKenzie, *The Metropolitan Community* (New York: McGraw-Hill, 1933), p. 71.

2. Ezra Solomon and Zarko G. Bilbija, *Metropolitan Chicago* (New York: The Free Press of Glencoe, Ill., 1959), p. 1.

3. N. S. B. Gras, *An Introduction to Economic History* (New York: Harpers, 1922), pp. 187, 292–316.

4. Otis Dudley Duncan and Albert J. Reiss, Jr., *Social Characteristics of Urban and Rural Communities*, 1950 (New York: Wiley, 1956); Gunnar Alexandersson, *The Industrial Structure of American Cities* (Lincoln, Neb.: University of Nebraska Press, 1956); Chauncy D. Harris, "A Functional Classification of Cities in the United States," *Geographical Review*, 33 (January 1943), 86–99; Grace M. Kneedler, "Functional Types of Cities," *Public Management*, 27 (July, 1945), 197–203; Victor Jones, "Economic Classification of Cities and Metropolitan Areas," *Municipal Yearbook*, 1953, 49–57; and Howard J. Nelson, "A Service Classification of American Cities," *Economic Geography*, 31 (July, 1955), pp. 189–210.

5. Richard B. Andrews, "Mechanics of the Urban Economic Base," *Land Economics*, 30 (Feb., May, Aug., Nov., 1954), 52–60, 164–172, 260–270, 309–319); Arthur M. Weimer and Homer Hoyt, *Principles of Real Estate* (New York: Ronald Press, 1954); Homer Hoyt, *Economic Status of New York Metropolitan Region in 1944* (New York: Regional Plan Association, 1944); and Duncan and Reiss, *Social Characteristics of Urban and Rural Communities*, pp. 215–217.

6. Chauncy D. Harris, "A Functional Classification of Cities in the United States."

7. Otis Dudley Duncan, *et al.*, *Metropolis and Region* (Baltimore: Johns Hopkins Press, 1960), pp. 34–35.

8. *Cf.* William B. Munro, "City," *Encyclopedia of the Social Sciences*, III, 1930, p. 478.

9. "Perhaps it is not too wild an extrapolation to suggest that in the United States of 1950 an SMA size of roughly 300,000 inhabitants marked a transition point where distinctively 'metropolitan' characteristics first begin to appear." Duncan, *et al.*, *Metropolis and Region*, p. 275.

10. Edgar M. Hoover and Raymond Vernon, *Anatomy of a Metropolis* (Cambridge: Harvard University Press, 1959), p. 50.

11. *Cf.* Edgar M. Hoover and Raymond Vernon, *Anatomy of a Metropolis*, p. 13.

12. Otis D. Duncan and Albert J. Reiss, Jr., *Social Characteristics of Urban and Rural Communities*, pp. 260–265, 344–345.

13. Harland Paul Douglass, *The Suburban Trend* (New York: Century, 1925), pp. 74–92.

14. A. C. Spectorsky, *Exurbanites* (Philadelphia: Lippincott, 1955); and Bennett M. Berger, *Working Class Suburb* (Berkeley and Los Angeles: University of California Press, 1960).

15. *Census of Population, U. S. Summary,* I, p. 106.

# · VIII ·

## *Cities and the*
## *American Economy*

### Business Organization

The typology established in Chapter VII classifies American cities by their specialized economic activities in the national economy. It identifies their basic industries, hence their principal sources of livelihood, and reveals something of the social and economic life of urban dwellers. But it does not deal adequately with the economic organization of cities or with the institutionalization of economic behavior in them. To understand these, an analysis of the national economy, whose organization and institutions are predominant over the economies of cities, is necessary. Therefore the national economy, although only a sketch of it is possible, is discussed in this chapter. The analysis of the American economy is made in terms of four institutions: business, government, labor, and the family.[1]

Business and industrial firms, adhering to the institutions of capitalism, provide an organization of economic activities in the United States. Federal and state governments intervene actively to maintain and regulate the economy and to ensure the general welfare, and have helped to establish a mixed private-public enterprise system. America has a gross national product of economic goods and services which exceeds $550 billions annually and continues to grow. There are over 67 million men and women in the national labor force working to produce this tremendous output of commodities and wealth. As individuals and members of families, they expend their earned incomes to buy the economic goods and services which the economy provides in such abundance. These institutions determine the distinctive character of the American economy.

As a mixed private-public enterprise system, American capitalism differs significantly from its earlier forms. Though today's capitalism is also based on the institutions of private property, individual initiative, free enterprise, economic competition, and the profit system, business regards them in a different spirit today than it did in the past. Often economic initiative is due to corporation or government action; much property consists of legal claims to economic and political rights and privileges rather than tangible goods and services; and public controls over the economy restrict the freedom of private enterprise. While the end of production is still profit, other considerations also determine the volume of output of goods and services.

The determination of prices by supply and demand persists, but corporations also set many prices by administrative decisions. The principles of self-regulation of economic activity through the market and the laissez-faire policies of government, so revered in the nineteenth century, are no longer part of our thinking. Even corporations want the government to support their enterprises when foreign competition becomes too formidable or when intervention benefits them.

In this sense the economy is politicized; it is no longer an autonomous economic system capable of sustaining itself. Many other institutionalized practices characterize the

American economy: its capital accumulations; system of money; commercial credit; business contracts; commodity, money, labor, and other markets; business corporations; trade unions; industrial technology; mass production; and applications of science.

Based on these institutions of capitalism, some 4.5 million business enterprises exist in the United States. The great bulk of them are small proprietorships or partnerships in retail trade and services. Large numbers of these are founded each year and have an average existence of six to eight years. Only 13 percent of all business enterprises are corporations. However, corporations predominate in the affluent sectors of the economy: manufacturing, mining, public utilities, transportation, and finance. Through large-scale organization, vast capitalization, mass production, and scientific technology, these corporations produce a major share of the total national product each year. Their enterprise in these sectors accounted, in 1955, for 51 percent of the total national income and for 57 percent of the privately-produced national income.[2]

## The Dominant Corporation

A few giant corporations dominate the economic activity in the affluent sectors and produce most of their goods and services. This concentration of power, wealth, and control in a small number of large corporations—becoming monopolistic in some areas, such as in electric and gas utilities and telephone communication, and almost oligopolistic in others, such as transportation, finance, some durable and capital equipment fields in manufacturing—is a significant characteristic of the economy today. Several studies have testified to their size and dominance.[3]

Today 200 largest non-financial corporations own more than one half of the assets of all such corporations and more than a third of the banking assets; more than 56 of them had total assets over one billion dollars in 1950. Moreover, these

200 corporations employ about one fourth of the national labor force and, through their suppliers, subcontractors, dealers, and distributors, affect the employment of another one fourth or more. Twenty-eight giant corporations with 50,000 employees or more account for about 10 percent of the total employment in the country. Some 130 corporations produce one half of the entire output in manufacturing. A small number of corporations receives the major proportion of government defense contracts and employs the majority of technical and scientific personnel in industrial research.

This dominance of corporations in the economy—although not their monopoly of production and power—is perhaps inevitable. Large-scale organizations with the economic and legal advantages of corporations are necessary to mass produce economic goods and services, to distribute them in mass markets, and to support a population of more than 180 million Americans. As a form of business organization, corporations accumulate huge capital resources, centralize leadership, provide professional management, hire specialized labor forces, pursue diversified economic activities, and carry on industrial research and development. They are mostly publicly owned business firms, incorporated by states, which afford limited liability to stockholders and which are treated as legally fictitious persons by the courts and in the law. Corporations are independent business companies which compete with other corporations to increase their economic productivity and control of resources and to sell their commodities in domestic and world markets.

Corporations have brought the American economy to its high stage of development. In acquiring economic ascendancy, they have also won enormous social and political power in the society. The policies and practices which determine their production, plant expansion, and other activities, affect the stability and prosperity of the economy. Their authority to determine these matters gives them the means to acquire other forms of power or to exact political privileges for the economic services they perform.

Corporations are consciously political in their efforts to legalize their immense power and wealth, which they exercise as private companies for essentially privately determined goals. The government treats them as semipublic agencies when it makes them responsible for researching and developing military armaments, defense projects, and other activities, and even uses them to carry out American aid programs and policies in foreign countries. As business organizations, they resemble industrial empires in their resources, power, scale of operations, and number of employees. In a political sense, they may be likened to cities [4] and even to nations.[5]

The diversification of ownership among many thousands of small stockholders is an important aspect of corporations. Stockholders commonly buy securities for investment and do not participate in the operation of the corporations. Thus corporation ownership is separated from its management. On the other hand, the control of corporations is highly concentrated in a small owner-management group of stockholders, who seldom own more than one fifth, or, more likely, one tenth of the outstanding stock. This minority group elects the directors of the corporation who appoint its president and other officials. While there are exceptions, the president and officials administer the corporation and its affairs without much intervention by the directors if they do their work well.

These people constitute a class of professional executives or managers, trained and experienced in the leadership and operation of business firms. By right of office and other acquisition of power, they have enormous influence over policy. A few thousand such men control and administer the great corporations of the United States.[6] Yet they are employees of corporations, seldom owning—even with generous stock options—so much as 3 or 5 percent of their stock.

These officials manage corporations by a bureaucratic administration of their offices and activities. (Bureaucracy is the modern system of administering organizations consisting of hierarchies of offices, with each office having an assigned set of activities and a specialized staff to perform them. Thus it is a government of organizations carried on by administrative officials, whose leadership and control is centralized in executive offices; with limited and specified authority delegated to lesser offices; and with ownership of property by organizations and not employees.[7]) All corporations have plans of organization which conform to bureaucratic principles of administration; they are, indeed, great private bureaucracies. In recent decades, many corporations have made increasing use of committees at all administrative levels to share in making decisions. To some extent, this means government of corporations by committees, although directors and executives retain responsibility for making some decisions and acting on those recommended to them by committees.

In their conduct of the business of corporations, company officials strive to meet the goals of production and such other objectives as they have formulated. Their paramount criterion of success is the profit brought in by their enterprises. Small companies have no other measure than the test of profit. But large corporations, capable of earning profits and having financial resources to offset occasional unprofitable ventures, have other considerations too. To prevent government intervention in their activities, they may be content with the share of the market they already have. They may look for stability or moderate growth. They may want, also, to eliminate competitors, influence prices, consolidate power, secure tax advantages, maintain good public relations, or avoid labor strife.

Most corporations own and operate plants in several cities (some of them abroad) and all of them buy and sell in many markets. They are usually specialized in some one industry and are principally located in the city and section of the country in which they arose. They expand by increasing the scale of their operations and by acquiring other companies, some of them competing firms, others in industries which supply raw materials or subcontract services to them. In recent decades, corporations have also entered new industries in order to diversify their economic activities, either by acquiring active companies or establishing new ones. They also manufacture new products which result from their industrial research and development or from that of another company. Through vertical and horizontal expansion, corporations continue to grow and absorb other companies which hitherto have been independent firms.

To control their operations, corporations commonly have main offices and various additional clerical, technical, and research facilities in one city and branch offices, factories, sales outlets, and other facilities in other cities. Thus they centralize the top executive and management activities in one place, but decentralize lesser management activities throughout their corporate empire by delegating authority to branch office managers, plant supervisors, sales officials, and other supervisory officials. They employ large administrative and technical staffs of highly specialized persons to manage these activities, transferring them from one office or factory to another as necessity arises and rewarding some of them by elevating them to the headquarters office. These persons pursue their careers in the corporation, advancing through its hierarchies in rank and salary. They are the "organization men." They are also "modern transients," whom corporations move from one city to another in the course of employment.[8]

In the cities where their offices and factories are located, corporations have an important, even a dominant, economic role. They often occupy large office buildings and employ considerable office and clerical personnel who live in these cities. Their factories commonly are among the larger, more modern industrial plants in these cities and employ large labor forces of skilled and semi-skilled workers at relatively high wages. Thus they are important basic industries which bring money to the cities through capital investments, pay-rolls, local purchases, payment of taxes, and, in some cases, the development of subsidiary industries. As secondary in-dustries, they provide an economic base for the tertiary in-dustries which exist in cities, and which, for the most part, are smaller, locally owned enterprises.[9] The scale of their activities thus affects the entire economy of cities and de-termines their prosperity. When corporations reduce their operations, or close their facilities or transfer them else-where,[10] the consequences for cities may be disastrous.

While corporations are significant to cities which contain their facilities, company officials do not return the interest except insofar as local conditions affect operations. Even local companies which have grown into national corpora-tions take this attitude toward their home cities, although they may retain their offices and some factories and facili-ties in them. At headquarters offices, corporation officials preside over industrial empires and give orders to their branch managers and plant supervisors, who, scattered in many cities, put into effect locally the companies' policies. In such cities the important industries are thus governed by absentee managers who are non-owners.[11]

The economic center of such cities exists in the national economy where corporations have a major influence. Hav-ing resources and influence, corporation officials use them when necessary to persuade cities to grant them special privileges for their businesses. These involve concessions in zoning ordinances, taxes, road and street improvements, and other matters which concern them. In locating new plants, corporation officials search for cities with advantages of location, markets, transportation, wage levels, housing, or amenities,[12] and then consult with city officials for the

accommodations they want. They bargain not as citizens or
as business firms but virtually as quasi-sovereign powers.[13]
They also negotiate with state officials concerning legislation,
taxes, and policies which affect their businesses. Sometimes
corporations, by threatening to leave a city in which they
have a plant, force city officials to concede certain advantages to them. At other times, despite the pleadings of
officials for them to stay, they quit a city for reasons of
their own and relocate somewhere else.

Public officials often solicit corporations to establish plants
or facilities in their cities and offer them inducements,
when necessary, to do so. City and state economic commissions exist to attract business firms to their jurisdictions;
they are aided by chambers of commerce and businessmen's
associations. Local companies sometimes oppose the entry
of outside corporations into cities because their own dominance and wage and labor policies are threatened but few of
them resist for long.

## Government in the Economy

Private enterprise continues to produce the bulk of economic goods and services which Americans consume. But
the federal government controls and directs many areas of
private enterprise and also engages in the public production
of some kinds of goods and services. The federal government
has ascendancy over state and local governments and over
the national economy as well. It is itself the biggest business
in the United States: no corporation matches it in size,
power, expenditures, number of employees, and diversification of activities.

In its public economic policies, the federal government
assumes responsibility for the stability and prosperity of the
economy and for the economic security of the nation. It not
only performs the usual duties of government in maintain-

ing the public order necessary to economic enterprise, but it
also uses its political power to regulate and guide the economy in achieving social and economic objectives which promote the general welfare. Thus it strives to assure maximum
production of goods and services, enforce competition among
business firms, keep prices and income in some relation to
each other, promote full employment, control inflation, fight
depressions, conserve natural resources, and protect minority economic groups, including small business, labor, farmers, and consumers.[14]

Government's economic objectives are still being formulated. There is no consensus about what they are or how to
achieve them. In fact, only since 1934, when the depression was at its nadir, has the government used its political
and financial resources to help the economy to recover and
to relieve the distress of millions of unemployed persons. At
that time it established public agencies and institutionalized
certain practices which have since determined its further
intervention in the economy. With World War II, the government mobilized the entire economy to produce economic
goods and military armaments, imposing the most thoroughgoing controls to date. Since then, it has only partially re-
laxed these restrictions. Other new or recurring events,
postwar world recovery, the Korean war, the cold war, and
foreign economic competition have compelled its continued
activity in the economy. Each administration in Washington
accepts the public economic policy which has evolved and
amends it as necessary during its incumbency in office.

In earlier times, the government's participation in the
economy was restricted, for the most part, to its "police
powers" to regulate interstate commerce, its power to control business "affected with a public interest," and its war
powers over the economy. Initially public policy was largely
determined by Jefferson's conception of a government with
powers limited to regulating the trade relations of city mer-

chants, artisans, and farmers, and devoted to nurturing individual freedom. In the nineteenth century, government espoused the principles of laissez faire and the market regulation of business competition. When corporations attempted, in the 1880's, to create monopolies in their fields, the government acted to destroy their trusts and to enforce competition among them. Thereafter it instituted public controls, initially over utilities and railroads, then over other industries. In the following years, state legislatures, motivated by humanitarian impulses as well as economic considerations, enacted laws intended to curb excesses in factory labor, food distribution, women's and children's work, and other activities. But the Supreme Court, zealous in protecting property rights during these years, weakened or nullified these measures by its adverse decisions on them. After 1935, however, with different justices and in different times, the Supreme Court reversed many previous rulings and sanctioned the government's increasing authority over the economy.

To fulfill its economic policies, the government controls the economy through its various departments and bureaus, regulatory commissions, and other public bodies. But the government has become so powerful and enormous, with total annual expenditures of funds more than double that of state and local governments combined, and with more than two million employees, that all its actions affect the nation's economic life. Its annual budget—over ninety billion dollars —indicates the magnitude of its expenditures and the extent of its involvement in the economy. To be sure, nearly 80 percent of the budget is devoted to the national defense, veterans' services and benefits, interest on the national debt, and international affairs and finance,[15] but the government pays much of this money to American business firms for goods and services or spends it in the American economy; some appropriations to foreign countries are also indirect subsidies of American businesses and industries. In handling its expenditures, the government is concerned with making a favorable impact on the economy.

## Areas of Government Activity

The government acts in the economy by regulating and promoting business, by providing welfare services, by ownership and enterprise, and sundry other acts and policies. It asserts its authority through a great number and variety of statutes, executive orders, administrative rules and regulations, and other edicts which are intended to regulate private enterprise and safeguard the institutions of capitalism. But it also aids and abets the economy through services and subsidies which its departments and agencies provide to business and industry, protecting their interests abroad also. Finally, as exigencies arise which compel its action, the government intervenes in the economy in still other ways, and to an extent determined by circumstances.

In the public interest and to keep the economy free and competitive, the government regulates the enterprise of business and industrial companies extensively. Through the imposition of rules and regulations, its regulatory commissions strive to enforce fair business practices and to maintain order and stability in the economy. Thus they forbid monopolies, restrict oligopolies, prohibit price fixing, prevent manipulation of markets, protect consumers from excessive exploitation, and interdict other practices which violate the tenets of capitalism. But they also endeavor, more positively, to help business firms to function by publishing new regulations as need for them arises, determining public rates for services, and recommending new legislation to the Congress. The commissions have some power to enforce their edicts, but when this does not suffice, they appeal to the courts.

To enumerate the major regulatory commissions and their fields reveals how much the government controls the economy. These commissions include the Interstate Commerce

Commission, which has jurisdiction over all forms of interstate public transportation except air carriers and pipe lines
for gas and water; the Federal Trade Commission, which
enforces competitive and fair trade practices in all interstate and foreign commerce, except banks and some other
businesses controlled by other agencies; the Commodity Exchange Authority, which regulates all commodity exchanges;
the Securities and Exchange Commission, which controls
national securities exchanges, and all brokers and dealers
using the mails or other instrumentalities in interstate commerce; the National Labor Board, which regulates labor
organizations and collective bargaining; the Federal Power
Commission, which regulates hydroelectric projects and the
transmission of electrical power and of gas in interstate
commerce; the Federal Communications Commission, which
has jurisdiction over interstate and foreign communications
by telephone, telegraph, and radio; the Civil Aeronautics
Board, which regulates interstate air commerce; the Packers
and Stockyards Act (U.S.D.A.), which establishes jurisdiction over meat packers and market agencies for livestock;
the Federal Maritime Board, which has broad powers over
American ships in foreign commerce and foreign ships
which serve American territories; and the Anti-Trust Division (Department of Justice), which undertakes litigation
against business and industrial firms which violate the
anti-trust laws against monopolies.

The government also acts to promote American business
and to protect and advance its interests both in domestic
and foreign fields. Indispensable to the economy, it supports
sound money, establishes standards of weight, measure, and
quality of goods, collects and distributes market and other
information nationally and internationally, and enacts
statutes which regulate the incorporation of business firms,
their bankruptcies, and the protection of property rights
in ideas through patents, copyrights, and trade marks.
Through tariffs, it protects and indirectly subsidizes domes-

tic businesses against foreign competition. Other help is provided through loans or extension of financial credit and sometimes outright grants and subsidies. Thus it has come to the aid of the railroads, airlines, small business, and agriculture, to name only a few industries which have received its largesse.

The government helps cities, too, and supports their industries by similar grants of funds or through financial credits. It provides most of the financing for urban renewal projects and public housing. Through FHA, it enables families to buy or build their homes and also invigorates the housebuilding industry; its role in accelerating the growth of suburbs was noticed before. In addition, it finances public projects such as the federal interstate highway program, public buildings, and harbor and river improvements. By its loans to small business, defense contracts to corporations, purchases of supplies and services, and its subsidies of industrial research and development, the government aids many business firms, and stabilizes the economies of cities. It thus helps cities as large as Los Angeles, whose vast aircraft industry could scarcely survive without government contracts and subsidies.

Since 1934, the federal government has expanded its social services and expenditures for social welfare, and taken on the functions of a welfare state. It assumed responsibility for the relief of the millions of unemployed persons in the depression of the 1930's, initially by putting them to work on public projects and later by establishing a national system of social security which provides for old age pensions and survivors' insurance for persons employed in the labor force. In addition, it assists the states, through matched federal funds, in the care of categories of distressed persons, such as the blind, deaf, and mentally ill. By such grants of money, it attempts to establish minimal standards for the health, nutrition, and security of the American people.

In addition to their humanitarian value, these welfare

expenditures are economically important because they give purchasing power to those who receive them—veterans, old people, the unemployed, widows with dependent children, and others—at a time when they earn little if any income. Retired persons with pensions can resettle in cities which appeal to them: increasing numbers of them are migrating to southern states with pleasant climates, forming blocs of elderly persons in some southern cities. Wherever they live, however, they consume goods and services, and their purchases aid urban economies.

To pay for welfare expenditures, the government levies taxes, mainly personal income taxes and corporate income and profit taxes, which are assessed progressively by size of income or earnings. Thus, the rich pay these taxes to help the poor. In effect, these taxes transfer wealth from upper to lower economic classes and tend to level income distribution among the American people. Again, the effect of this on cities and their economies is evident.

In some activities strongly imbued with a public interest, notably the post office and parcel post delivery, the federal government is itself active, and does not hire business firms to perform these services. Otherwise its ownership of business is limited to such projects as TVA, some other public power and irrigation projects, and its operation of the national parks and forests. But cities often own public utilities and other public enterprises. Among the latter are airports, indispensable to their existence, to whose costs the federal government contributes through subsidies.

When the government embarked on its welfare activities, public officials and agencies encountered many economic groups and subcommunities which needed its assistance. To facilitate its dealings with them and to enable them to represent their economic interests more effectively, it encouraged them, as another part of its public policies, to organize into associations. Thus, it aided labor, farmers, consumers, and other groups to form organizations, as well as groups in the business community which lacked them. Similarly it compelled cities to establish municipal planning, zoning, housing, urban renewal, and other commissions to carry on public projects for which the government paid much of the costs.

Not only federal but state and city governments promote and regulate private enterprise. The larger states impose public controls over business and industrial firms which resemble federal controls. Thus, they regulate corporations through anti-trust laws, charter and regulate banks, supervise railroads and other public carriers, determine rates for consumer services of public utilities, and enforce labor laws. Also, they have state systems of unemployment insurance, maintain employment offices, administer industrial accident compensation, inspect factories, protect the public health, license professions and trades, and control still other economic activities. The smaller states have less elaborate means of regulation, but none of them lacks them entirely.

State governments levy taxes with some concern for their burden on business corporations, which may enter or leave a state because of the "tax climate." But their expenditures, like those of the federal government, increase steadily. Their funds go principally to provide four types of public service: education, highways, public welfare, and health and hospitals.[16] In some cases, states perform these services directly; in other cases, they subsidize cities and other legal subdivisions to provide them. Thus, states undertake highway construction, maintain mental hospitals, and support universities, but assist local governments to finance public schools and other services.

City governments regulate business activities by public agencies and offices which enforce municipal ordinances concerned with zoning, building codes, city planning, health regulations, industrial safety, the licensing of businesses and trades, and other matters. Their principal expenditures, similar to those of states, are for schools, highways, public welfare, and health and hospitals, with schools the most costly.[17] To pay for these services, municipal governments levy taxes disproportionately on homes and real estate.

## Labor in the Economy

The organization of labor into unions and the institutionalization of collective bargaining are part of the American economy. Some fourteen million workers belong to 180-odd national (or international) craft, industrial, and white-collar unions. They constitute nearly the entire labor force in some industries, notably railroads, water transportation, trucking, basic steel, automobiles, construction, mining, and printing, and smaller proportions of employees in other industries, with the exception of farming, finance, personal and public service, and government. Other millions of workers who have not joined unions nevertheless are covered by union contracts which determine hours, wages, and conditions of work in their employment. Only unskilled workers, for the most part, are neglected by unions. They lack skills, steady employment, and the motivation to organize. As a result, unions sometimes discriminate against them. Many such workers are members of racial subcommunities, whose numbers increase in metropolitan cities.

Most unions are strong enough today to stop the operations of even the giant corporations and to cripple important segments of the economy when they go out on strike. But they do perform other major roles in the economy. Through collective bargaining with management, they affect the income, job opportunities, work discipline, leisure, and retirement of members and of other workers. While their part in raising wages in American industry is hard to determine, their ability to wrest the fringe benefits from management which have added to the real income of workers is not: these include improved pension, sickness, accident, and unemployment supplemental benefits, added holidays, and

longer vacations.[18] Moreover, they protect the economic interests of members at their places of employment through
grievance procedures which they help to administer. In
addition, unions constitute groups of workers who maintain
a social and cultural life, cultivating a sense of community
among themselves. Many unions are also politically active,
engage in lobbying, and attempt to influence the nomina-
tion and election of candidates in both political parties who
are friendly to labor.

Having to contend with big business and big government,
the unions have themselves grown to great size and have
acquired considerable economic and political power. But
with their present success after many years of bitter struggle, they have also become conservative. They are no longer
the fighting organizations they once were.[19] Never class-
conscious in a Marxian sense, they are largely accommodated to modern capitalism, content for the most part to
win limited economic gains for members. To realize these
objectives they strive to bargain responsibly with management, cooperate with government in its public economic
policies and programs, and administer their offices and
activities efficiently. As a result, union officials are professional leaders who resemble corporation executives in some
respects, and their administrative staffs are in process of
bureaucratization.[20]

But this development is partly forced on unions by the
government which increasingly regulates them. In the National Labor Relations Act of 1935, the government undertook to aid the unions in organizing industries and accepted
collective bargaining as a public policy. But with the Taft-
Hartley Act of 1947 and subsequent legislation, it imposed
controls over them and restricted some of their activities.
In the future, it will most likely restrain management-labor
disputes and limit collective bargaining in industries invested with a public interest.

Unions are not the only form of work organization in the

economy. Persons employed in occupations which require prolonged intellectual training and experience and offer specialized services to the public are likely to organize into professional associations. Through such bodies they attempt to control their occupation and to protect their economic interests in it. Among other things, they have to regulate the methods of recruitment into professions, determine necessary education and practices, set standards in performance and in behavior, and enforce codes of ethics which safeguard the public interest by their services. The members of professions comprise occupational subcommunities which tend to develop a unifying social and cultural life.

Some millions of persons belong to associations in such established professions as law, medicine, theology, education, and architecture, and in newer professions such as city planning, city management, and corporate management. Other persons are affiliated in semi-professional bodies in such occupations as welfare work, nursing, advertising, library work, and real estate. Still others form trade associations when their occupations lack unique skills and intellectual training to become professions. Some of these also organize into unions.

Workers organize into unions and professional associations to protect their economic interests by safeguarding their employment and controlling their occupations. In cities there seems to be a historical necessity to organize into economic associations—whether ancient guilds or modern unions. The impulse is intensified perhaps in the modern economy. Members of labor forces work for hire at jobs which determine their sources and size of income. They do not own the instruments of production and have no alternate means of making their livelihood. Their employment provides them with access to wealth, prestige, and power, and hence to the achievement of their goals. The corporations which employ them determine their conditions of work, job tenure, and wage rates, and have largely organized their employment practices by bureaucratic procedures. Now too, the government affects the economic interests of workers through its public economic policies and programs, and workers are impelled to become politically active through their unions. Without organization for collective action, individuals are helpless in the modern society. Hence workers have created industrial unions in response to the emergence of giant corporations,[21] and they organize or professionalize every occupation, even the meanest.

America now enjoys a general prosperity. Not only the upper, but middle and lower classes enjoy a standard of living made possible by the productivity of the economy. While the rich lead lives of greater comfort, the poor have many conveniences of life too, and indeed, suffer less economic penalty for their inferior status than ever before. At their different income levels, the people consume an economic abundance in material goods and services: food, clothing, shelter, and other necessities of life. They also have cars, TV's, home appliances, and other articles which they regard as ordinary rather than luxury goods. To attain a standard of living, not merely to survive, is the economic problem for most of them.

Despite the affluence of the economy, some economic groups experience hardships, if not dire poverty, in their struggle to exist. About one fourth of all workers are unskilled or semi-skilled laborers. Their employment is unsteady and their incomes relatively low. They include many ethnic and racial subcommunities, as well as some white migrants to cities. They often find jobs hard to get because they lack education, work experience, vocational training, or other aptitudes necessary for industrial employment; or they suffer from discrimination by employers and unions.

The uneven distribution of economic abundance among Americans is shown in the disparities in annual income which they receive. In 1960, the median income of the nation's 45,500,000 families was $5,600, but 22 percent of these families had incomes under $3,000, and another 20 percent from $3,000 to $5,000. In contrast, 14 percent of families received incomes of $10,000 or more, and 20 percent from $7,000 to $10,000. White families had a median income of $5,835, but non-white families only $3,233.[22]

Since most Americans earn their income from work, they are concerned with economic changes which affect their occupations and jobs and hence the size and sources of their income. The economy has advanced to its present stage with consequences of vast importance for their employment. The United States has a labor force of more than 67 million gainfully employed persons; it has become a nation of employees rather than of self-employed persons. The huge increase in employment has been in maintenance, or tertiary, industries. One estimate, for 1940, was that four fifths of urban employment is in maintenance activities.[23]

Another result of economic change has been a shift in the occupations which employ great numbers of workers to those which corporations, government, and other large-scale organizations need in their activities. These occupations are concerned with specialized tasks in administration, technical and scientific pursuits, professional and semi-professional services, office management, sales, and communication. These occupations, in the main, deal with people and ideas rather than with material things. They emphasize mental and verbal rather than manual skills. Therefore they require education, technical training, social aptitudes, and relative sophistication. Such occupations comprise the specialized vocations which occur in administration, office and plant supervision, professional specialties, scientific and engineering technologies, finance, publicity, and office, sales, and clerical work. The major occupations and industries which employ urban, suburban, and farm populations are summarized in Table XI.

There have also been important changes in industrial

## TABLE XI

### Composition of the employed labor force by major occupational group, major industry group, and residence, 1950

| Major occupation and industry group | Percent distribution 1950 | | | Estimated percent change, 1940–1950 | | |
|---|---|---|---|---|---|---|
| | Urban | Rural non-farm | Rural farm | Urban | Rural non-farm | Rural farm |
| Occupation group, total | 100.0 | 100.0 | 100.0 | 27.6 | 49.6 | −19.8 |
| Professional, technical, and kindred workers | 9.3 | 6.1 | 1.2 | 44.9 | 35.5 | 0.5 |
| Farmers and farm managers | 0.4 | 3.0 | 56.3 | — | — | −19.6 |
| Managers, officials, and proprietors | 13.0 | 10.7 | 2.0 | 35.9 | 33.0 | − 0.9 |
| Clerical and kindred workers | 8.4 | 4.3 | 1.0 | 21.7 | 45.4 | 28.1 |
| Sales workers | 8.2 | 5.1 | 1.1 | 6.1 | 40.0 | 5.3 |
| Craftsmen, foremen and kindred | 21.2 | 21.6 | 5.5 | 42.7 | 74.6 | 31.3 |
| Operatives and kindred workers | 21.8 | 25.0 | 7.8 | 28.5 | 52.4 | 33.5 |
| Private household workers | 0.2 | 0.2 | 0.1 | — | — | — |
| Service workers except private household | 7.6 | 4.3 | 0.8 | 13.6 | 38.7 | 5.4 |
| Farm laborers and foremen | 0.6 | 6.5 | 19.1 | — | 56.0 | −44.9 |
| Laborers, except farm and mine | 8.2 | 11.8 | 4.0 | 8.2 | 28.2 | −15.3 |
| Industry group, total | 100.0 | 100.0 | 100.0 | — | — | — |
| Agriculture | 1.1 | 9.1 | 71.0 | — | 72.7 | −25.1 |
| Mining | 0.9 | 4.9 | 1.3 | — | 19.5 | — |
| Construction | 6.0 | 8.9 | 3.1 | 63.3 | 89.6 | 28.7 |
| Manufacturing | 29.4 | 25.6 | 9.4 | 31.4 | 57.1 | 30.0 |
| Transportation | 9.0 | 7.4 | 2.1 | 35.5 | 54.5 | 24.9 |

TABLE XI (Continued)

| | Urban | Rural non-farm | Rural farm | Urban | Rural non-farm | Rural farm |
|---|---|---|---|---|---|---|
| Trade | 21.9 | 18.0 | 4.3 | 33.7 | 57.3 | 23.6 |
| Finance | 4.4 | 1.9 | 0.5 | 22.8 | — | — |
| Business services | 2.7 | 3.1 | 0.8 | 55.1 | 74.8 | — |
| Personal services | 7.2 | 5.9 | 1.7 | -15.5 | 6.3 | — |
| Entertainment services | 1.2 | 0.8 | 0.1 | — | — | — |
| Professional services | 9.5 | 8.4 | 2.7 | 44.8 | 47.8 | -12.0 |
| Public administration | 5.2 | 4.0 | 1.2 | 74.8 | 81.4 | — |

SOURCE: Donald J. Bogue, *The Population of the United States* (New York: The Free Press of Glencoe, 1959), p. 519; and "Urbanism in the United States, 1950," *American Journal of Sociology*, 60 (March, 1955), p. 483.

employment. As corporations adopt new technologies or forms of mechanical power, they hire skilled workers capable of operating and maintaining the costly, complex machinery which these entail. They create, moreover, new kinds of jobs which require technical ability and intelligence. This is reflected in the detailed description of jobs and the titles assigned to them. In general, an upgrading of occupations and jobs, a substitution of new skills for traditional ones, elimination of hard, routine work through continued mechanization, and more specialization of tasks are evident in industry. Indeed, all Americans have progressed in their basic knowledge, or "know how," of industrial technology in its contemporary stage.[24]

As their occupations and hence sources of livelihood alter, workers undergo still other changes in their lives and circumstances. One is their need for more or higher education and technical training to become specialized in occupations and to qualify for the better jobs in the economy. Managerial, professional, and technical workers obviously require a college education and some additional professional training, but skilled and even semi-skilled workers need a high school education. Thus the economy places a high value on education. Colleges and universities provide a means of advancement for educated persons; the lack of education keeps semi-literate persons in the lower classes.

Consequently there has been an upsurge in student enrollment in American schools and it continues to accelerate. Thus in 1961, the total number of persons attending schools and colleges in the United States was 47.7 million. Of these, 2.3 million were in kindergartens, 30.7 million in elementary schools, 11 million in high schools, and 3.7 million in colleges and professional schools. Of college age students, 38 percent of those who were 18 and 19 years old, and 13.7 percent of those 20 through 24 years of age were enrolled in school.[25] By 1970, the number of high school graduates is expected to be about 70,341,000 persons, or 48 percent of the population that is 15 years of age and over; and college graduates are expected to be 10,810,000, or 8.5 percent of the population 15 years of age and over. The estimates for 1980 are 95,115,000 high school graduates, or 54.7 percent of the population 15 years of age and over, and 14,895,000 college graduates, or 9.8 percent of the population 15 years of age and over.[26]

Because of occupational and educational advances, workers experience some amount of social mobility in the society. For the most part, their mobility is horizontal in direction; that is, they change without improving their social situations. At various times, they shift from one employer to another in the same or another industry, attain better jobs as they acquire technical skills and experience, or are upgraded on their jobs because technological advances raise the pay and prestige. In some of these cases, they advance from unskilled to skilled work, or from workmen to foremen or supervisors. As these advances occur, and depending on what they are, workers make other changes in their lives, perhaps acquire a home of their own, and raise their standards of living. Nevertheless they rise socially only within their class.

But some persons undergo vertical mobility; that is, they move into a higher status class through large improvements in their economic status. In various cases, they transfer from one occupation to another with some change in their social position—as does a worker who becomes a businessman; or they advance in the administrative hierarchy of the business organization which employs them; or, in their professional careers, they attain status, influence, and wealth as they become older and gain a reputation.

Finally, as a legacy of the economy, workers toil through a shorter work day and a shorter work week and enjoy more holidays from work, including some long week-ends, than ever before. Most of them now have a five-day, forty-hour work week, with exceptions above or below these hours in some industries. In the future, if automation and other factors augment technological unemployment, they are likely to have 35- or 32-hour work weeks. In that event, higher economic groups, it may be, will work more hours a week than the working classes do.

At all events, workers have leisure time now—time free from work and family obligations—and some income with which to enjoy it. They engage in both private and public recreation, some of it informal and pursued on their own initiative, but much of it organized and provided by schools, business firms, government agencies, and private enterprise. A vast recreational industry has risen to divert them; it comprises professional sports, public entertainment, outdoor sports, public parks, and other forms of amusement; it includes activities for spectators and participants. Today this industry has become big business; it is also mass culture.

## Families in the Economy

The men and women who work at jobs in the economy live in families and work to support them and to maintain their homes. In their economic roles, they were, in 1961, a labor force of over 67 million gainfully employed persons; In a social sense, they were members of 45.4 million families and 53.3 million households. (Household denotes a person or group of persons who occupy a dwelling unit.) Of the total population 14 years and older in that year, 66.1 percent were married, 12.2 percent were widowed, and 2.2 percent divorced; the average size of their families was 3.71 members, and of their households, 3.36 members.[27]

There are close ties between the economy and families. The economy functions to produce commodities and services which persons and families consume; and families prepare individuals to work in the economy. But families have their own organization and institutions which provide biological and cultural continuity to the succession of human generations. In the modern society, economic and family institutions are accommodated and opposed to each other. Their relations are, therefore, complex, and need careful scrutiny.

The small nuclear family which prevails in the United States is part of the Judeo-Christian tradition as mediated by England. Its institutionalized practices include monogamous marriage, marriage by civil contract, free mate selection, bilateral descent, free choice of residence (neolocal residence) after marriage, civil divorce, romantic love, limited kinship system, weak kinship groups, equality of sexes in inheritance, high status of women, and high evaluation of children. In general, the family created by these institutions is autonomous, centered on its immediate members, segregated from kindred except for closely connected relatives, settled neolocally, and more concerned with marital and parental ties than with kinship obligations; its members are individualized as persons in their families, and strive for high standards in family living.[28] While most Americans hold to these family institutions, subcommunities diverge from them in some practices or abide by them with different degrees of conviction.

In families Americans pursue their domestic lives, and carry on the daily routine of activities which revolve about the home. They manage their household economies with such income and business acumen as they have and at levels of consumption which they can afford. For the most part, they buy nearly all the commodities and services which they consume: food, clothing, and shelter; household furnishings and appliances; personal, mechanical, professional, and public services; the education of the children; family recreation; and luxury goods, some of them accounted necessities now. In most homes adult members undertake some tasks of production or make their own mechanical repairs. On the whole, they attain a standard of living which reflects the prosperity of the economy but there are still many poor families.

Families affect the economy through the production and consumption activities of their members. As families they are largely removed from participating in the economy, whether as work groups or as family enterprises. Even the farm family is declining as a labor force in agriculture. While family-owned, family-operated businesses exist in cities, they are concentrated in retail trades and in service industries and are often small, marginal firms which survive in some cases only by exploiting the labor of family members. Some family-owned corporations also exist, but most have been transformed into publicly owned corporations, eliminating the last vestiges of family capitalism from the economy.

However, some wealthy families still act as families, or, more accurately, as extended family and kinship groups, in their control and management of major corporations. Over the course of time, their members have developed their business firms into large corporations and accumulated great fortunes. As family dynasties they have extended their power over other corporations and industries in the country. The Ford, DuPont, Mellon, and Rockefeller families are examples.[29] They have considerable importance throughout the country. It may even be excessive in some states and cities.[30]

At their places of employment, family wage-earners, whether male family heads, married women, or adult children—some of whom live at home—work as individuals, never as families. This variety among family workers is common now. Women, for example, comprise 35 percent of the labor force, and more than a half of women workers are wives living with husbands.[31] Wives work to support their families and, in some cases, to earn a second income to attain a higher standard of living in the home. When two or more persons in the same family are employed, they commonly work at different places of employment and perhaps commute separately to their jobs. Should the same firm employ them, however, they work in different offices or departments and at jobs which involve different tasks and skills. Their employers thus avoid awkward entanglements of work and family relationships.

Otherwise employers are seldom interested in families of workers, except in those of higher officials; but they bear them in mind, of course, when they decide on wage rates, pension and insurance benefits, and fringe benefits. Nor do they consider families when they hire labor forces, except, again, the families of officials, whose promotion to higher office depends partially on the status of subcommunities to which they belong. Conversely, families of workers are often remote from the business firms which employ their husbands or fathers. They live in residential areas removed from places of employment and may not know the precise nature of the work they do.

But families as consumers and homes as places of consumption arouse the passionate concern of business and industrial firms and are of vital importance to the economy. At present, Americans purchase about 95 percent of the national output of goods and services in the domestic market. Of this amount, the expenditures which families make for economic goods and services are enormous, and even slight changes in their expenditures affect the prosperity of the economy. For example, the estimated total cost of houses in the United States is many hundreds of billions; the mortgages which encumber them, over 200 billion; [32] no other product cost so much as houses. But, in addition, the expenditures needed to furnish homes and the food and clothing which families consume in their normal existence, run to many billions of dollars annually.

This volume of expenditures suggests the magnitude of

the mass market in which the mass-produced goods and services of the economy are distributed and exchanged. A multitude of mercantile firms are active in it: national retail corporations, department stores, retail stores, wholesale dealers and firms, jobbers and other middlemen, trucking firms, financial agencies, warehouse and storage firms, and still others. These firms employ huge labor forces which devote vast time, energy, and expense to the business of buying and selling. Their efforts have culminated in methods of supermerchandising which suit the mass market and are characterized by supermarkets and discount houses, a vast advertising industry, urban and national systems of commercial credit, improved sales services, and automated methods of handling bulk goods, keeping records, and performing other chores.

As persons and as families, Americans shop in this highly efficient and impersonal market, following its institutionalized practices in buying goods and services and in managing their personal finances. They purchase necessary commodities by cash or credit; in the latter case, they utilize available systems of commercial credit, such as charge accounts, budget and installment purchases, credit cards, and other promises to pay. On other occasions, they borrow money from banks or loan agencies through their personal credit, deposit of collateral securities, through mortgages of homes, or other sources of credit. They also save some part of their incomes through savings deposits in banks, purchase of real or other property, purchases of insurance annuities, investments in stocks and securities, and acquisition of retirement policies.

Not all Americans handle their personal and family finances or tread the mass market equally well and skillfully. The measure of their competence in doing so is attested to by their commercial credit rating. This is decided by commercial accrediting agencies which exist in most cities and assemble information on incomes, savings, indebtedness, or other financial resources of individuals and families to determine whether they are solvent. A good commercial rating attests that they are willing and able to pay their bills promptly. It is an identity they need in order to survive in the mass market.

## NOTES

1. *Cf.* Walton Hamilton, "Economic Organization," *Encyclopedia of the Social Sciences,* XI (1933), pp. 484–490.

2. Carl Kaysen, "The Corporation: How Much Power? What Scope?," in *The Corporation in Modern Society,* edited by Edward S. Mason (Cambridge: Harvard University Press, 1959), p. 87.

3. Adolph A. Berle, Jr., and Gardiner C. Means, *The Modern Corporation and Private Property* (New York: Macmillan, 1932); Robert Aaron Gordon, *Business Leadership in the Large Corporation* (Washington: The Brookings Institution, 1945); David Lynch, *The Concentration of Economic Power* (New York: Columbia University Press, 1945); Editors of *Fortune,* with the collaboration of Russell W. Davenport, *U.S.A.: The Permanent Revolution* (New York: 1954); and Carl Kaysen, "The Corporation: How Much Power? What Scope?" in *The Corporation in Modern Society,* edited by Edward S. Mason, pp. 85–105.

4. Peter F. Drucker, *The Future of Industrial Man* (New York: Day, 1942), p. 92.

5. Adolph A. Berle, *Economic Power and the Free Society* (New York, 1952), p. 15.

6. Edward S. Mason, "Introduction," in *The Corporation in Modern Society,* p. 5.

7. Robert A. Dahl and Charles Edward Lindblom, *Politics, Economics and Welfare* (New York: Harpers, 1953), pp. 235–236.

8. William H. Whyte, *The Organization Man* (New York: Simon and Schuster, 1956).

9. William H. Form and Delbert C. Miller, *Industry, Labor, and Community* (New York: Harpers, 1960), pp. 25–31.

10. For case studies, see Leonard P. Adams and Robert L. Aronson, *Workers and Industrial Change* (New York: Cornell University Press, 1957); and Charles R. Walker, *Steeltown* (New York: Harpers, 1950).

11. Norton E. Long, "The Corporation, Its Satellites, and the Local Community," in *The Corporation in Modern Society,"* p. 204.

12. A considerable literature on the economics of industrial location exists; among its representatives are Alfred Weber, *Alfred*

*Weber's Theory of the Location of Industries* (Chicago: University of Chicago Press, 1929); Edgar M. Hoover, *The Location of Economic Activity* (New York: McGraw-Hill, 1948); Augustus Lösch, *The Economics of Location* (New Haven: Yale University Press, 1955); and Walter Isard, *A General Theory Relating to Industrial Location, Market Areas, Land Use, Trade, and Urban Structure* (New York: Wiley, 1956).

13. Karl Kaysen, "The Corporation: How Much Power? What Scope?" in *The Corporation in Modern Society,* p. 100.

14. Vernon A. Mund, *Government and Business* (New York: Harpers, 1955), 2nd ed., pp. 599–620.

15. *Economic Almanac,* 1960, p. 423.

16. *Economic Almanac,* 1960, p. 444.

17. *Economic Almanac,* 1960, p. 451.

18. Neil Chamberlain, "The Corporation and the Trade Union," in *The Corporation in Modern Society,* pp. 132–133.

19. Clark Kerr, *Unions and Union Leaders of Their Own Choosing* (New York: The Fund for the Republic, 1957), p. 21.

20. Harold L. Wilensky, *Intellectuals in Trade Unions* (New York: The Free Press of Glencoe, 1956), pp. 244 ff.

21. Clark Kerr, *Industrial Peace and the Collective Bargaining Environment* (Berkeley: University of California Press, 1954), p. 48.

22. *Current Population Reports, Consumer Income. Income of Families and Persons in the United States: 1960.* Series P–60, No. 37 (Washington: Bureau of the Census, 1962), pp. 1–4, 25.

23. Otis Dudley Duncan and Albert J. Reiss, Jr., *Social Characteristics of Urban and Rural Communities* (New York: Wiley, 1956), pp. 216–217.

24. Harold L. Wilensky and Charles N. Lebeaux, *Industrial Society and Social Welfare* (New York: Russell Sage Foundation, 1958), p. 94.

25. *Current Population Reports, Population Characteristics, School Enrollment,* Series P–20, No. 117 (Washington: Bureau of the Census, 1962), pp. 1–2.

26. *Current Population Reports, Population Characteristics, Projections of Education Attainment in the United States: 1960 to 1980.* Series P–20, No. 91 (Washington: Bureau of the Census, 1959), p. 1.

27. *Current Population Reports, Population Characteristics, Marital Status and Family Status,* Series P–20, No. 114 (Washington: Bureau of the Census, 1962), pp. 7, 11.

28. *Cf.* Talcott Parsons, "The Kinship System of the Contemporary United States," *American Anthropologist,* 45 (January-March, 1943), 22–38.

29. Gustavus Myers, *History of the Great American Fortunes*

(New York: The Modern Library, 1937); Ferdinand Lundberg, *America's 60 Families* (New York: Vanguard Press, 1937); and E. Digby Baltzell, *Philadelphia Gentlemen* (New York: The Free Press of Glencoe, 1958).

30. Robert S. Lynd and Helen M. Lynd, *Middletown in Transition* (New York: Harcourt, Brace, 1939), pp. 74–101.

31. *Current Population Reports, Labor Force, Marital and Family Characteristics of Workers*, Series P–50, No. 87 (Washington: Bureau of the Census, 1959), p. 2.

32. *Statistical Abstract*, 1962, p. 763.

# · IX ·

# *The Ecology*
# *of American Cities*

## The Science of Human Ecology

The preceding chapters have dealt with the migration and
settlement of populations in cities and metropolitan areas.
Other aspects of cities are the physical and demographic—
their shape and appearance, the aggregations in them,
their patterns of growth and expansion, the location of
business, industry, and residence, the flow of human life
and activity in their buildings and on their streets. These
compose a backdrop or cityscape for urban dwellers which
affects their social order. This chapter will look at cities
from the point of view of human ecology, viewing the
impact of the social and natural environments on communities.

In its general sense, ecology refers to the study of the
mutual relations of groups of organisms and their environment. It first developed as a sub-speciality of biology
which studies the adaptation of plants and animals to
their surroundings, both living and nonliving. It investi-
gates their numbers, habitat, food supply, biotic com-

munities, commensal and symbiotic relations within and between species, and other conditions which affect their struggles for existence and hence survival. The interpretation of ecological findings rests on the postulates of organic evolution.

Sociologists borrowed the concepts of plant ecology in developing human ecology, which they envisioned as the study of human populations regarded as an animal species similarly striving to adapt itself to this earth and to survive in its mortal life. But human beings obviously differ from plant and animal organisms in their ability to create their own environments, change their conditions of life and sustenance, protect themselves from the ravages of nature, and travel about on the earth's surface. They have cultures; plants and animals do not. Therefore sociologists had to define ecology in a more restricted way, as the study of the movements and settlement of human populations as affected by their natural, social, and cultural environments. But they still conceive of man as a biological creature, and they continue to draw analogies between him and plants and animals, and to retain an evolutionary cast of mind in their conjectures about him.

Within this frame of reference, human ecologists fastened their attention on human beings as populations, never as individuals. They see them as biotic communities, settled in certain areas and in certain concentrations on the world's continents. Populations gather in such communities for reasons similar to those which seem to govern the formation of plant and animal communities: in aggregations they multiply their strength and increase their ability to survive because they can better exploit the resources of the land and mobilize their energies in a division of labor. In the human case, however, ecologists translate the struggle for existence which is paramount in the natural world into a competition for possessing and using the land. They also transform the commensal and symbiotic relations which obtain in biotic communities into relations of competition and cooperation in human communities.

Like other animals, human populations adapt to the natural world and to their own mortal existence; but in the course of living they create still other environments to which they adjust. Due to their forms of aggregation— in bands, villages, cities, and metropolitan areas—they often assemble large numbers of people in a small space. Their sheer populousness and close contact produce a human environment which is a prime condition of their lives. Unlike animals, in building cities they construct a material environment of buildings and streets, factories, railroads, highways, and other artifacts which greatly alters the face of the earth. And through the organization of their societies and cultures, they establish a social environment which differs vastly from that of animal communities.

For these reasons, human ecologists, unlike plant and animal ecologists, have to study human populations in the social and cultural world of their own making as well as in the natural world. Since their concern is with man's biological and terrestrial existence, they treat his communities and cultures as integral parts of his total environment.

Human ecologists borrowed certain technical terms from the botanists and added a few more of their own. Of these terms the paramount one is community. Ecologists concentrate on human aggregations and their forms of settlement and organization.[1] Next in importance are the movements of populations on the earth's surface, hence the ecological processes of concentration, centralization, segregation, invasion, succession, and decentralization. To some extent, the meaning of these processes is apparent in their names. Populations concentrate when they amass in certain areas, centralize when they form communities in these areas, segregate when they separate into groups in communities. Groups invade the localities of other groups by moving into them; sometimes they succeed in displacing the previous groups and take over the locality for themselves. Finally, groups decentralize by removing from the center to the periphery of communities.

Because of their leanings toward biology, ecologists employ these terms to denote the forms of human aggregation and movement, without giving them cultural content or historical meaning. Thus they define human communities much as they do biotic communities, as populations having a functional and structural organization of their lives and activities determined by adjustment to environment. Similarly they mean by ecological processes certain general types of human mobility, which occur alike in primitive wanderings, overseas colonization, modern migrations, and urbanization of societies. But these terms, lacking a social and cultural context, label rather than explain the behavior they deal with. This is true especially when ecologists use them to account for the movements of people in cities.[2]

Ecologists view competition, which they see as the human form of the struggle to survive, as supplying the motive force behind the ecological processes, providing, in effect, an economic explanation. They utilize three principal concepts to explain how economic competition operates,[3] still, at a level of generality. First is the fundamental interdependence of men: they must live in communities because they share the same human condition. Second, locality has an economic function; men locate their social, cultural, and economic activities at certain places in their communities which aid in realizing their objectives. The third concept is the friction of space: [4] human beings congest their communities by overcrowding the interior areas with people and buildings, thus constricting the spaces necessary for human movement. This congestion intensifies the competition for favorable location of activities and leads to inflation of land prices and rents, higher costs of transportation, and added time in communication and travel. People are forced to weigh these increased economic costs of congestion against the functional need of their activities for location as they continue to centralize some of their activities but to decentralize others.

Although ecological explanations of communities may become confused with economic ones in such analyses, ecologists insist that human ecology studies the impact of the natural world—mediated by human societies and civilizations—on communities in terms of such factors as area, location, aggregation, distance, space, and propinquity, and, basic to all these terms, patterns of movement and communication. It postulates that human populations occupy an area or territory in which aggregation and propinquity create physical, then social, contacts among individuals, which lead to the development of communities and the growth of cultures.

## Ecological Organization of Cities

The best known theory of ecological organization (that is, the physical structure of cities determined by patterns of settlement of populations and the location of their social and cultural activities) is the concentric circle theory of urban growth,[5] which asserts that cities expand radially from their center in a series of rings. (See Figure 4, p. 197.) At their core is a central business district (I), which is encircled by an area of transition and social deterioration invaded by business and light manufacture (II). A third ring (III) is occupied by workers' homes and a factory zone, and a fourth (IV), extending to the boundaries of the city, is a residential area comprising single-family housing and some high-rent apartment dwellings. Beyond these is the commuters' zone of suburban cities and villages (V) within a journey of thirty to sixty minutes of the central business district.

According to the proponents of the concentric circle thesis, as cities expand, each inner zone tends to extend its area by invading the next zone, causing a succession of populations or distinctive land uses. Also, populations and business concentrate in the inner zones of cities be-

FIGURE 4

Generalizations of Internal Structure of Cities

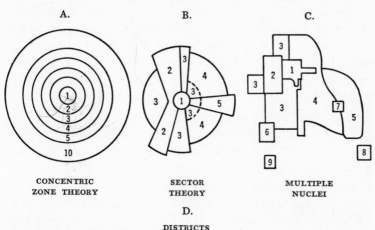

A.                              B.                              C.

CONCENTRIC          SECTOR          MULTIPLE
ZONE THEORY         THEORY          NUCLEI

D.

DISTRICTS

1. *Central business district*
2. *Wholesale light manufacturing*
3. *Low-class residential*
4. *Medium-class residential*
5. *High-class residential*

6. *Heavy manufacturing*
7. *Outlying business district*
8. *Residential suburb*
9. *Industrial suburb*
10. *Commuters' zone*

SOURCE: "The Nature of Cities" by Chauncy D. Harris and Edward L. Ullman in *The Annals of the American Academy of Political and Social Science*, CCXLII (November, 1945), 13.

cause transportation routes tend to converge there. Later, some of them decentralize to residential neighborhoods and sub-business districts in the outer zones. Thus at first ecologists explained the circular growth of cities in terms of the ecological processes which caused an organization and disorganization of communities. Later, they added the emphasis on economic competition and land function as factors behind the ecological processes.

Ecologists explained the differentiation of communities and land uses in zones in the same terms. Individuals and families, they held, are sorted and distributed by residence and occupation throughout the city. In the process, social and cultural groups segregate in areas of residence, where they compose subcommunities. Thus new immigrants and some migrants, especially those of ethnic and racial sub-communities, tend to settle in zone II, the area of disorganization, where they create ethnic colonies and ghettoes in slums. Upon assimilation and with improvement in circumstances, they resettle in zone III; this is the area of immigrant second-settlement. Here they live as working-class Americans. Still later, the more successful families among them remove to zones IV and V, to single-family houses and higher standards of living.[6]

A second theory of urban growth which applies only to the residential sections of cities maintains that cities expand in a series of sectors, somewhat resembling slices of a pie, rather than in concentric circles.[7] (See Figure 4, p. 197.) Ecologists suggest three reasons for the growth of sectors. First, each sector develops along a main transportation line, street or avenue, highway, or railroad. Its growth is axial to the outer limits of the city. It does not, however, assume the form of a radial line of houses because, with modern transportation available, urban inhabitants reside on both sides of the axial street and at increasing distances from it, at or near the periphery of the sector. Second, the quality of residence is established in the sector at or near the central business district and tends to continue to its periphery because the axial street on which it forms ordinarily passes through the center of the city.

Third, the sector which contains the upper-class residences or highest rent area exerts a pull on the central business district, which tends to grow in its direction. Wealthy families establish the better residential neighborhoods by locating their homes in areas having attractive topographical features and elevation. These areas are served by the fastest transportation lines and are farthest removed from business and industrial districts and from slums. Middle-income families then form residential neighborhoods nearby to have similar residential amenities and for reasons of prestige. Low-income families reside in areas of mixed land use in opposite directions from the better neighborhoods.

Both ecological theories utilize the same principles of reasoning and are not so much opposed to each other as they appear to be. They caused a great controversy among ecologists although most ecologists now agree that neither theory explains the growth of cities adequately. Of the two, they favor the sector theory because it takes transportation more explicitly into account than the ring hypothesis does.

In general, the concentric circle theory is useful in cross-cultural comparisons of American and other cities. It recognizes American cities as commercial-industrial cities, identifying central business districts as composing their core. It explains their structure and growth largely in economic terms and acknowledges that the poor live in interior areas of cities and the rich in the outer neighborhoods and in the suburbs.

Although the ring hypothesis does not fit other cities in the world, it nevertheless encourages different ecological explanations of their growth. The physical order of ancient cities was quite different from that of modern cities. The Mesopotamian cities, for example, had temple ovals at their centers, and mostly privileged families and their retinues lived in them; the poor lived in their suburbs. The Roman cities had forums which consisted of public buildings and temples as their centers, with market places as secondary centers. In the cities of medieval Europe, commons or squares constituted the center. They were flanked by economic, political, and religious buildings.

Modern European cities conform to the circle theory to some extent but never wholly. But Asian and African cities with their different peoples and cultures do not. They need another ecological explanation of their structures. There have been some recent studies of the patterns of growth of some African cities.[8]

An ecological, or a combined ecological and economic, explanation of urban growth is insufficient by itself. Men obviously build their cities to express their civilizations, responding to many social and cultural impulses. Some other considerations which might affect urban structure include the presence of religious, racial, and ethnic sub-communities in them and their areas of residence; the segregation of classes in neighborhoods; the location of commons, parks, cemeteries, public buildings, and land-marks which have cultural sentiment or tradition; the original plan of cities; and the events of history.[9] In addition the topographical features of the sites on which cities stand—hills, swamps, lakes, rivers, and geological faults—influence their shape. City planning commissions, zoning boards, urban renewal authorities, public housing authorities, city engineering departments, highway departments and corporations (see Chapter VIII) also determine their structures.

For these reasons, sociologists now forego ideal-typical ecological explanations of cities and instead employ ecological principles in combination with social and cultural factors to account for their growth. They have reached a consensus on the ecological organization of American cities. They believe that all cities have central business districts, irregular in size and usually rectangular in appearance, containing the activities which require central location. Commerce is located in the central and sub-business districts, as well as on radial streets, while industry is located near the means of transportation by water, rail, and highway, wherever this may be. Often the heavy industrial district is near the present or former outer edge of cities. High-grade residential districts are located on high land and away from nuisances such as noise, odor, smoke, and industrial and transportation developments; low-grade housing exists near business, industrial, and transportation developments, and is marked by a lack of residential amenities.[10]

## Local Areas in Cities

Another aspect of the ecological organization of cities is the local areas in which their populations reside. The sociologists were interested in localities in American cities long before they turned to ecological studies. At the height of mass immigration to the United States, they were concerned with the ethnic and racial groups living in cities and with their problems of assimilation. To deal with them, they had, of course, to identify these groups and their neighborhoods—to locate them in their urban habitats, as it were—and then to inquire into their social and cultural life.

To name local areas in cities, ecologists borrowed the geographical concept of "natural area" which geographers use to refer to an area of land, distinct in its boundaries and natural phenomena, that constitutes a physiographic unit. Ecologists altered the term to adapt it to cities, redefining it as an area inhabited by social and cultural groups or devoted to a specialized land use. They thought of these areas as natural in the sense that they developed naturally in the growth of cities and were not consciously planned or contrived. Comparing natural areas to ecological formations of plants and animals, ecologists suggested that they came into existence through the competition and selection of populations for possession of urban localities.

As habitats of social groups, natural areas result from the segregation of populations in areas of urban residence.

According to the ecologists, such segregation is both voluntary and involuntary. Some groups choose to reside in certain neighborhoods because of social, economic, religious, prestige, or other reasons; others must live in neighborhoods because they are forced to by custom, laws, or their own poverty. In either case, the groups have subcultures, speak a common language, have organizations, and are aware of their identity as groups. Thus they are subcommunities and not merely the populations contained in political wards or administrative areas.

Prime examples of this kind of natural area were immigrant colonies in cities. As we have noted, ecologists located these groups and their areas of immigrant first settlement in zone II, where they were known by various local names—Jewish ghettoes, Negro Harlems, Bronzevilles, Black Belts, Little Italy, Greektown, Chinatown, Swedetown. In zone II they also located other specialized areas, such as Hobohemia, the Latin Quarter, and the underworld of crime. In zone III they identified natural areas of immigrant second settlement, thus, Jewish, German, Irish, and other neighborhoods. Ecologists were not so concerned with locating the communities of native white Americans, but presumably the latter lived in all zones but more largely in zones IV and V.

In their second meaning as areas of distinctive urban land use, natural areas are formed by economic processes which fix the utility and value of land, determine its rent, and assign to it commercial, industrial, residential, transportation, or other functions. As examples of natural areas in this sense, ecologists identified the central business district and sub-business districts of cities, their industrial zones, apartment house areas, areas of single-family housing, rooming house districts, slums, and "gold coasts" of high-rent apartments near central business districts.

Using these distinctions, ecologists proceeded to make

field studies of social and cultural groups in cities. They published a number of monographs, largely based on Chicago, which reported their findings. Only a few of these books, in point of fact, actually made much use of ecological principles, and only two attempted to apply them to selected problems of city life.[11] Most of the others, once locating certain groups in local areas, dealt with them by sociological rather than ecological analysis—Wirth, among them, brilliantly.[12]

These studies reveal, although unintentionally, that the concept of natural area is hard to use in cities because social and cultural groups seldom live exclusively in local areas but are, rather, intermingled with some other groups. Even when they are segregated in these areas, they move to—or, in ecological terms, invade—other areas of residence as soon as they assimilate or improve in fortunes. Thereafter their communities often dissolve, and they no longer occupy a common area. In these circumstances, the ecological importance of a local area is difficult to determine.

But a few groups are segregated in areas of residence which enhance the communities they create in them. In most large cities, Negroes occupy certain residential sections to which they are restricted by practices of involuntary segregation and racial discrimination. By continually migrating to these cities, they have filled some residential areas in them nearly to saturation and created their large biracial neighborhoods in others. Through voluntary segregation, Jews also tend to live in their own neighborhoods. Now, however, these are often in suburban cities, representing their third or fourth area of settlement. Jews comprise only a proportion of the total population in Jewish neighborhoods, however.[13]

By now ecologists have given up the concept of natural area, using instead such other terms as areas of specialized land use, areas of segregation, ecological districts, or

community areas. They consider these local areas as socio-
economic areas, identifying them by appropriate social and
economic criteria. Among the criteria they use to locate
these areas in cities are their predominant land use, types
of buildings, use and occupancy of buildings; rental values
of land and buildings; nativity, race, religion, and occupations of inhabitants; their rates of delinquency and
dependency; their economic and social classes; and the
physiographic features and lines of transportation which
bound the areas. In this way ecologists divide the residential sections of cities into a number of ecological areas,
none of which, it should be noted, fits into either circle
or sector theory. The number of areas varies with the size
and type of cities and with the scale by which investigators
determine them. To show their variations, there are 22
ecological areas in New Haven,[14] and 75 community areas
in Chicago.[15]

Another method of determining local areas, advanced
by some sociologists,[16] utilizes the census tracts into which
the census bureau divides cities. They classify the populations of tracts by three sets of significant characteristics—
social rank, level of urbanization, and ethnic segregation—
grouping the tracts with similar populations into larger
"social areas." To determine the social rank of tract populations, they use a scale based on measures of occupation
and education. They determine the level of urbanization
by an index of family status, based on fertility, number of
women in labor force, and residence in single-family
dwellings. They measure ethnic segregation by an index
based on the number of "new immigrants" from Europe,
immigrants from other American countries except English-
speaking Canadians, and Negroes.

For each characteristic, they classify the tracts into three
or four categories ranked from high to low and either
retain these measures of them separately or combine them
to classify the tracts into 9 or 16 social areas.[17] Apparently

this procedure identifies local areas as reliably as ecological methods do [18] and provides, moreover, rich descriptive data on cities, but it suffers the limitations of a geophysical or areal approach in its aspirations to determine the social organization of American cities.[19]

However local areas are determined, they denote sections of cities whose populations are comparable in their social and cultural activities and in their standards of living. We cannot assume that these areas are neighborhoods in a social sense: that is, that their inhabitants neighbor with each other or pursue a neighborhood life. Nor should we assume that status and ethnic subcommunities inhabit them. In all likelihood, individuals and families have friends and acquaintances in these areas and associate with them informally and in group activities. Locality still functions as a basis for local social life in cities,[20] even if selectively so.

Furthermore, inferences about families based on the socio-economic areas in which they live should be made cautiously. Such areas are determined by characteristics of populations which reside in them, hence on averages of group traits from which individuals vary. While populations confer their qualities on areas of residence, all persons do not share them equally. Ecological correlations between areas of residence and the individuals who inhabit them are uncertain.[21]

Within these limits, socio-economic areas are important in the ecological organization of cities. They show the dispersion of populations into localities which have a relationship to their social and cultural life, as well as to their occupational groups and economic classes.[22] Therefore they provide an ecological approach to the study of subcommunities in cities and to a consideration of their residences and neighborhoods. A determination of these areas is easily extended to suburban cities and to metropolitan areas as well.

## Cities and Regions

Another aspect of the ecological organization of cities is their functional relation with their metropolitan areas and geographic regions. Ecologists have always been concerned with metropolitan areas as well as with individual cities, because they saw in them the emergence of a new kind of regional city or an urban regionalism. They recognized also that the growth of cities depended on the settlement, natural resources, and economic development of the regions in which they stood. Moreover, cities have assumed some semblance of order in their number, size, and distribution over regions, and some regions have influenced the growth of other regions.

Ecologists think of metropolitan areas as metropolitan communities, and investigate the ecological organization of central and suburban cities in them. Therefore they devote their studies to discovering the patterns of settlement of metropolitan communities, the movements of population and economic activities in them, their paths of circulation, the various areas they enclose, their boundaries, and, finally, their interpenetration with other communities.

The shape of metropolitan communities, consisting of central city surrounded by suburban cities and villages, ideally appears circular in form, somewhat like a planet and its satellites.[23] They might also be compared to a wheel, or a series of wheels within a large wheel, with the cities and villages of the area constituting the hubs of these wheels, the network of roads and highways which connect the cities forming their spokes, and the boundaries of areas forming their rims.[24] However, their circular character is only approximate because the internal growth of communities is axial, following lines of transportation which conform to the topography of the land. Their form is also affected by the central city, in which the functional interdependencies of metropolitan communities are established and administered and, to a lesser extent, by the suburban cities.

The primary area of metropolitan communities includes the central city and the adjoining suburban and urban fringe territory, defined as the maximum radius of daily routine movements of travel. Their secondary area includes a larger trade zone, extending outward so much as 50 to 75 miles; and their tertiary territory extends still farther into the areas reached by some metropolitan services. The boundaries of communities are never fixed, but vary with lines of transportation and means of travel, as well as with the economic goods and services which are distributed in outlying areas. These boundaries assume a hexagonal, or orthogonal, rather than circular shape because metropolitan areas encroach on each other, and economic competition between or among them distorts their respective peripheries.[25]

In their studies of cities and geographical regions, ecologists have concentrated on the dominant economic role of metropolitan cities in regions, and have attempted to determine the scale of their dominance. By several methods of investigation they have amply demonstrated the economic dominance of metropolitan cities, whether by the circulation of metropolitan city newspapers,[26] the expansion of metropolitan trade areas,[27] the greater concentration of retail and wholesale trade, manufacturing, and service industries in metropolitan cities rather than in outer zones of their regions,[28] or selected sales, financial, manufacturing, and other indices of economic dominance.[29] Their studies all show that the dominance of metropolitan cities is greater in nearby areas and declines in distant areas in their regions. At the boundaries of areas, where these cities compete economically with other cities, they have the least influence.

More recently, however, ecologists have shifted their

emphasis from the economic dominance of metropolitan cities to the metropolitan functions they perform in their regions: marketing, industry, transportation, and finance.[30] Not metropolitan cities directly, however, but business, industrial, and financial corporations located in them carry on economic activities, and affect the economic growth of regions. By studying these corporations and their enterprises, ecologists analyze the economic expansion of cities into their regions, and determine the specialization of economic activities which cities and regions develop. This method of investigation compels ecologists to study the economic organization of the United States as well as the demography of its people. (See the classification of metropolitan cities in Chapter VII.)

Metropolitan cities are highly variable in their economic relations with regions. While their industries depend in some way on local and regional resources, some industries obtain raw materials, semi-finished products, industrial fuels, or other products from regions other than their own, and, it may be, from far away. These may be iron ore, coal, wheat, or other commodities, brought in by water or rail transportation. Seacoast cities import some commodities from abroad. Some cities share in the same resource-area—for example, the cities in the middle western agricultural and livestock regions—and develop industries suitable to each, with local specialization among them. Some cities are industrial centers, whose manufactures, locations, or other characteristics, limit their development of metropolitan functions.

A number of cities utilize their regions in specialized ways. Some have important food-processing activities based on specialized agriculture; others have basic industries which depend on mining, lumbering, or fishing; several have important military installations. And a few are major resort cities which attract visitors from all over the country.

Certain economic criteria are useful in analyzing urban and metropolitan economies and in evaluating the metropolitan functions of large cities: value added by manufacture, wholesale sales, business service receipts, non-local commercial loans, demand deposits, other information.[31] In this way, ecologists have discovered the extent to which business firms in these cities are active in regional and national economies. In future studies, however, they are likely to employ the more complex procedures of economists who compute the economic inputs and outputs of urban and metropolitan economies to reveal the vast importance of city-region economies in the United States.[32]

Metropolitan cities have been ranked in urban hierarchies by geographers in order to show the economic interdependence of the cities of a region. Classifying these cities by size of population and distinctive economic activities, geographers place these cities in a hierarchical order on the principle that cities of each rank perform not only their own specialized economic activities but also those of cities of all lesser ranks. Large central cities, having their own functions and the general functions of the smaller cities, are at the head of the hierarchy. They unify the cities in a regional network of activities. While geographers have applied this concept to cities in limited areas,[33] they have not ventured to classify all the cities of the United States in these terms.

## Ecology and City Planning

City planners attempt to guide the physical growth of cities by an orderly arrangement of their streets and highways, business sections, industrial zones, residential areas, and lines of transportation. In their work, they deal with sub-communities, local areas, transitional zones, shifts of population, and other matters which also concern ecologists. They tend, too, like ecologists, to regard urban populations

as aggregates rather than as individuals, and to believe
that an ordering of their spatial and areal relations contributes to their social order.

The Chicago World's Fair of 1893 first interested
Americans in modern planning. Its buildings and grounds
won their admiration and aroused the hope that cities, too,
might be made as attractive. Their approbation led some
of the fair's architects, landscape designers, and engineers
to launch a city planning movement, with the objective of
bringing order and beauty to American cities. They were so
successful that after the turn of the century they were
able to persuade Chicago to adopt a master city plan and
to put it into effect. Thereafter they prevailed on a few
other cities to plan for their future growth by hiring private
firms to draw city plans for them. On the whole, these
early city plans were sound and creditable but limited in
perspective. They dealt mainly with zoning, streets and
highways, transportation, public buildings, civic appearance, and public recreation, in keeping with the architectural and engineering training of planners.

During the 1930's, however, planners had to concern
themselves with the welfare of the people who lived in
cities and not only with cities in their physical sense. For
virtually the first time, they became interested in the
housing and social conditions of urban dwellers. Thereafter
they gradually incorporated social and economic considerations of cities in their thinking and advanced to what
we now call comprehensive city planning. Now city planners deal with zoning, subdivision regulations, population densities, neighborhood rehabilitation, building codes,
suburban sprawl of population, and other matters which
bear on the people and their lives.

To the public acceptance and organization of planning,
the federal government contributed immensely through its
various programs to alleviate the distresses of the depression. Government officials required cities to adopt city

planning as a municipal function in order to qualify for federal grants of money for public projects. Their concern was to ensure the proper location of housing developments, public buildings, new highways, and other projects in cities, and to safeguard the expenditure of public funds. But, in addition, they wanted cities to assume responsibility for their own planning and rehabilitation, and to coordinate their private and public construction through master plans. Under their pressure many cities established planning commissions and hired staffs of planners and other technically trained personnel. Since then, most cities have done likewise, and planners have become a professional group.

Today planners work with cities already built up, which grew largely without planning or with the minimal planning of engineering and highway departments and of real estate firms. Therefore they deal with cities whose physical structure is determined by streets and avenues laid out in gridiron pattern, with buildings and houses aligned along them, fixed lines of transportation, and most land and buildings privately owned. They confront also the present ecological organization of cities and the location of business, industrial, and residential districts in them. Many problems with which they contend—traffic congestion, slums, areas of mixed land use, undesirable industrial zones, defilement of water fronts, and narrow streets—existed in cities long before planners arrived on the urban scene.

Under such circumstances, planners are limited. For the most part, they devote most of their efforts to repairing or eliminating the worst faults of cities in order to increase livability in them and to make them better places for business and industry. This involves, among other things, the complete clearance of seriously deteriorated areas and replacement of their structures with new business, industrial, or residential buildings; the rehabilitation of other deteriorated areas by less drastic measures; and the conservation of still other areas by means which forestall blight. Recently planners have attempted to restore vitality to central business sections by urban renewal projects and street improvements and to initiate other renewal projects to provide industrial zones.

Planners utilize certain principles like zoning, which is a first step in planning. Zoning refers to the division of cities into zones or districts, and the public regulation in each of them of the height, bulk, and use of buildings, the use of land, and the density of population, in order to protect the lives, health, safety, morals, and general welfare of the people. The zones are designated as central and sub-business districts, light and heavy industrial areas, and single-family and multiple-dwelling neighborhoods, with further subdivisions in large cities. In imposing these controls over buildings and land, zoning restricts the property rights of their owners.

American cities accepted zoning, like planning, relatively late. New York, in 1916, was the first city to adopt city-wide zoning, and other cities followed its lead, especially after 1926 when the Supreme Court upheld the constitutionality of zoning.[34] While planners advocated zoning, not planners but property owners and real estate firms succeeded in persuading cities to enact zoning ordinances and to undertake zoning. They supported it largely for economic reasons: to stabilize commercial areas and residential neighborhoods in order to protect their investments. Early zoning commissions sometimes laid out zones with more concern for such considerations than for the planned growth of cities. They zoned too much land for business and industry and inflated its value, permitted nonconforming business uses in residential areas, and protected upper-class neighborhoods by restrictive regulations. Planners therefore oppose some details of city zoning plans but not, of course, the principles of zoning when they are employed to promote the purposes of planning.

As zones are laid out, they largely coincide with the

existing land-use areas and areas of segregation in cities. In built-up cities, zoning must accept the actual physical and ecological organization of cities. Its purpose, in fact, is to perpetuate the existing structure of cities, but, over the course of time, to achieve a uniformity in land use and in buildings in zones. It accomplishes these objectives by designating the principal land use as the sanctioned land use in zones, forbidding nonconforming uses thereafter in it. Thus, zoning intends to prevent the invasion of alien land uses in zones, whether brought about by business and industrial firms or by subcommunities of people, and to stop ecological succession in them. It restricts these changes further by enforcing standards in the construction of buildings and in the occupancy of land to maintain the existing character of the zones.

But zoning does not succeed as well in interior sections as it does in outer sections of cities. Business buildings, industrial plants, single- and multiple-family dwellings, and other buildings occupy the inner areas in often considerable confusion: i.e., mixed land uses prevail. Zoning must accept this condition and is committed to continue it because while zoning designates the major land use, it nevertheless permits other land uses in inner zones. Thus, in areas which are business districts, residence also exists; in industrial zones, both business and residence continue; in residential areas, both business and industry are present. In the latter case, this means that working class families live in neighborhoods with mixtures of businesses and industries which reduce residential amenities in them. Zoning accomplishes its mission of enforcing a single land use only in the better single-family neighborhoods, from which business and industry are barred. In its different application to inner and outer belts of cities, zoning appears to subscribe to the concentric circle theory of urban growth.[35]

Another principle of planning, much advocated by

planners now, is the transformation of the residential sections of cities into a series of neighborhood units. By neighborhood units planners mean residential areas having either 5,000 or 10,000 inhabitants and possessing enough physical unity to provide the basis for neighborhoods. This unity is derived from the uniform features of the area: houses of similar kind, comparable lots and land values, and only local traffic on its streets. Planners advise that such areas should include an elementary school. They ordinarily plan to enhance these elements of homogeneity by providing children's playgrounds, parks, perhaps a community building, and by directing through-traffic around rather than through neighborhoods. Finally, they suggest that shopping centers, service industries, and high schools be located along streets which are contiguous or convenient to several or many neighborhood units. In this way they hope to promote a series of business areas throughout the residential sections of cities.[36]

In laying out neighborhood units, planners are guided by principles which determine an efficacious arrangement of living space and physical facilities in cities. They have no other social or political objectives.[37] They hope, however, that persons and families residing in such areas will convert them into actual neighborhoods by an increased tendency to neighbor inspired by these innovations. Planners therefore try to make the areas pleasant for family living and for the growth and nurture of children. Thus they act on the ecological premise that physical association induces social association. However, they do not consider neighborhood units to be ecological communities, or status or ethnic subcommunities. They hope only that families in them will develop a sense of community, and, in some cases, even become residential subcommunities.

But small neighborhood units are impractical in large, built-up cities for they are unsuitable for heterogeneous populations. Also, they are impossible to achieve in cities with complex systems of streets and highways, internal congestion, extensive areas of decay, areas of mixed land use, and overcrowding or deterioration of buildings in older sections. Planners therefore advance area planning as a way of dealing with sections of cities requiring other and more drastic remedies than neighborhood planning. They select for area planning whatever localities are in need of major renewal or rehabilitation. These may be the older parts of central business districts, water fronts, market places, industrial zones, slum areas, or obsolescent neighborhoods. When such areas include slum or other residential sections, as many as 50,000 inhabitants and many acres or even square miles of land may be involved. To restore these areas requires large public expenditures and large-scale planning and enterprise, which, in the latter case, entails razing of old buildings, preparation of cleared land for re-use, construction of new buildings, use of superblocks in laying out residential areas, realignment of streets and avenues, introduction of parks and boulevards, and other changes. The financial resources and leadership to undertake area planning often come from urban renewal agencies, public housing authorities, public construction, highway, and other projects in which local and federal governments cooperate.

As planners see them, these areas are localities having specialized business, industrial, residential, or other functions, whose utility is impaired by narrow, congested streets, substandard buildings, and other defects. Thus they are not ecological districts or socio-economic areas as sociologists use these terms, or even zones of segregation. But planners nevertheless follow ecological principles in restoring these areas. They have to consider the importance of location and economic function in the innovations they introduce, which include changing land use, regrouping buildings, designing shopping centers, constructing single- and multiple-family dwelling units, improving traffic lanes, and developing parks and other recreational facilities.

Another principle of planning which is indispensable to the success of the other three is control by planners of city circulation systems, i.e., of streets and highways. This requires that planners improve the existing streets and avenues, locate new streets and highways to facilitate the flow of traffic, differentiate major and minor streets for rapid transit and local traffic, establish cross-town, circumferential, arterial, collector, and other specialized streets, fit interstate and interregional highways into urban street systems, and make still other innovations when necessary or feasible. It also necessitates the integration of local systems of transit and transportation by land, rail, water, and air so that people and goods can travel rapidly. In handling these matters, planners also provide for off-street parking of cars, loading and unloading facilities for freight removed from streets, a system of railroad, airport, and bus terminals, and other facilities which improve circulation in and about cities.

Planners and ecologists alike thus recognize the vital importance of transit and transportation to cities, and to the distribution of business, industry, and residence in them. Urban dwellers must be relatively accessible to each other and move about cities freely in their economic pursuits and in social and cultural activities. Therefore the use they make of land and the value they impute to its location depend considerably on the local transportation system and their particular use of it. When streets and roads are inadequate and impede movement, cities are afflicted with traffic congestion, high densities of settlement, mixed land-uses, overcrowding of land by buildings, and other problems in friction-of-space, as ecologists call it. To the extent that planners succeed in improving cities' circulatory systems, they reduce not only present difficulties but guide the future growth of cities in such directions as they deem desirable.

## NOTES

1. Amos H. Hawley, *Human Ecology* (New York: Ronald Press, 1950), pp. 66–74.
2. Don Martindale, *The City*, by Max Weber, pp. 29–30.
3. Amos H. Hawley, *Human Ecology*, p. 236.
4. Robert M. Haig, *Regional Survey of New York and Its Environs* (New York: Regional Plan of New York, 1927), I, p. 21.
5. Ernest W. Burgess, "The Growth of the City," *Proceedings of the American Sociological Society*, XVIII (1923), pp. 85–89; reprinted in *The City*, edited by Robert E. Park, Ernest W. Burgess, and Roderick D. McKenzie (Chicago: University of Chicago Press, 1925), pp. 47–62.
6. Robert E. Park, Ernest W. Burgess, and Roderick D. McKenzie, *The City*, pp. 54–56.
7. Homer Hoyt, *The Structure and Growth of Residential Neighborhoods in American Cities* (Washington: Federal Housing Administration, 1939), pp. 76–78, 112–122.
8. Leo Kuper, *Durban: A Study of Racial Ecology* (London: Cape, 1958).
9. Walter Firey, *Land Use in Central Boston* (Cambridge: Harvard University Press, 1947).
10. Maurice R. Davie, "The Pattern of Urban Growth," in *Studies in the Science of Society*, edited by George Peter Murdock (New Haven: Yale University Press, 1937), pp. 133–161; and Chauncy D. Harris and Edward L. Ullman, "The Nature of Cities," *Annals of the American Academy*, 242 (November 1945), pp. 7–17.
11. Robert E. L. Faris and H. Warren Dunham, *Mental Disorders in Urban Areas* (Chicago: University of Chicago Press, 1939); and Clifford Shaw and H. D. McKay, *Juvenile Delinquency and Urban Areas* (Chicago: University of Chicago Press, 1942).
12. Louis Wirth, *The Ghetto* (Chicago: University of Chicago Press, 1929).
13. Cf. Erich Rosenthal, "Acculturation without Assimilation? The Jewish Community of Chicago, Illinois," *American Journal of Sociology*, 66 (November 1960), pp. 275–288.
14. Maurice R. Davie, "The Pattern of Urban Growth," p. 145.
15. Social Science Research Committee of the University of Chicago.
16. Eshref Shevky and Marylin Williams, *The Social Areas of*

*Los Angeles* (Los Angeles: University of California Press, 1949); and Eshref Shevky and Wendell Bell, *Social Area Analysis* (Stanford: Stanford University Press, 1955).

17. Eshref Shevky and Wendell Bell, *Social Area Analysis,* pp. 26–27.

18. Maurice D. Van Arsdol, Santo F. Camillieri, and Calvin F. Schmid, "The Generality of Urban Social Area Indexes," *American Sociological Review,* 23 (June, 1958), pp. 277–284; and Theodore R. Anderson and Lee L. Bean, "The Shevky-Bell Social Areas: Confirmation of Results and a Reinterpretation," *Social Forces,* 40 (December, 1961), pp. 119–124.

19. Eshref Shevky and Wendell Bell, *Social Area Analysis,* pp. 3–19.

20. Scott Greer, *The Emerging City* (New York: The Free Press of Glencoe, 1962), pp. 109–120.

21. W. S. Robinson, "Ecological Correlations and Behavior of Individuals," *American Sociological Review,* 15 (June 1950), pp. 351–357.

22. Otis Dudley Duncan and Beverly Duncan, "Residential Distribution and Occupational Stratification," *American Journal of Sociology,* 60 (March, 1955), pp. 493–503.

23. R. D. McKenzie, *The Metropolitan Community,* p. 71.

24. Amos H. Hawley, *Human Ecology,* pp. 234–235.

25. Amos H. Hawley, *Human Ecology,* pp. 234–235, 238, 245–258.

26. R. E. Park and Charles Newcomb, "Newspaper Circulation and Metropolitan Regions," in *The Metropolitan Community,* by R. D. McKenzie, pp. 98–110.

27. R. D. McKenzie, *The Metropolitan Community,* pp. 76–78; and Amos H. Hawley, *Human Ecology,* pp. 405–431.

28. Donald J. Bogue, *The Structure of the Metropolitan Community* (Ann Arbor: University of Michigan Press, 1949).

29. Rupert B. Vance and Sara Smith, "Metropolitan Dominance and Integration," in *The Urban South,* eds., Rupert B. Vance and Nicholas J. Demerath (Chapel Hill: University of North Carolina Press, 1954), p. 127.

30. Otis Dudley Duncan, *et al., Metropolis and Region.*

31. Otis Dudley Duncan, *et al. Metropolis and Region,* pp. 259–275. See also Rupert B. Vance and Sara Smith, "Metropolitan Dominance and Integration," in *The Urban South,* pp. 124–132.

32. Walter Isard and Robert Kavesh, "Economic Structural Interrelations of Metropolitan Regions," *American Journal of Sociology,* 60 (September 1954), pp. 152–162.

33. John E. Brush, "The Hierarchy of Central Places in Southwestern Wisconsin," *Geographic Review,* 43 (July 1953), pp. 380–402.

34. Village of Euclid, *Ohio* v. *Ambler Realty Company*, 272 U.S. 363, 1926.

35. *Cf.* Arthur B. Gallion, with Simon Eisner, *The Urban Pattern* (New York: Van Nostrand, 1950), pp. 170 and 174.

36. Clarence A. Perry, "The Neighborhood Unit, a Scheme of Arrangement for the Family-life Community," in *Regional Survey of New York and Its Environs* (New York: Regional Plan of New York and Its Environs, 1929), Vol. 7, pp. 22–129.

37. Arthur B. Gallion, with Simon Eisner, *The Urban Pattern*, p. 278.

# · X ·

# *People and*
# *Groupings in Cities*

## The National Population

Although economic explanations are useful in interpreting American cities, cities are made up of people, who do not act solely for economic reasons. They also employ social and cultural organizations to organize their activities and to maintain the social order of cities. An analysis of their social life and order is made in this and the next two chapters, with consideration first of their social groupings in this chapter.

With four out of five Americans resident in cities or in suburbs, the American people are, in general, urban dwellers. They consist of a white population, an amalgam of European peoples who came as colonists and immigrants and their present descendants, and a non-white population composed of Negroes, Indians, Japanese, Chinese, and others. At present, nine out of ten Americans are white and one in ten Negro. Their precise proportions in 1950 were: whites, 89.5 percent; Negroes, 10 percent; and other non-white races, .5 percent. These proportions have been approximately the same since 1920. All these racial groups, with the exception of Indians who live on reservations or on farms in the western states, are highly urbanized.

The white population is derived mainly from countries of Western Europe and predominantly from the British Isles. In 1790, according to a special report made by the Bureau of the Census in 1909, 83.5 percent of the people were of English descent, 6.7 percent Scotch, 1.6 percent Irish, 2 percent Dutch, 5.6 percent German, 0.5 percent French, and 0.1 percent Jewish and other.[1] While these exact proportions have been disputed, they indicate nevertheless that the early American population was composed of slightly more than 90 percent British stock, taking English, Scotch, and Irish together, 2 percent Dutch, and 6 percent German. This composition of the people changed with the mass movement of immigrants from Europe in the nineteenth and twentieth centuries, although the British and Germans continued to preponderate in the population.

In 1920, the census bureau computed the national origins of the American people for purposes of the National Immigration Act of 1927, which set quotas for immigrants based on their countries' contribution to the American population, and reported them as follows: Great Britain and Northern Ireland, 41 percent; Germany, 16 percent; Irish Free State, 11 percent; Canada, 4 percent; Poland, 4 percent; then, Italy, Sweden, Netherlands, France, Czechoslovakia, Russia, Norway, Mexico and Switzerland.[2] These proportions, hard to determine reliably, were approximate for 1920 and are more so for 1960; but they are the best available indication of the present ethnic composition of the American people.

These figures also indicate the character of immigration to the United States and the role of immigrants in the growth of the national population. In 1790, after a colonial period of 180 years, the population was not quite 4 million, one fifth of whom were Negroes; in 1960, 170 years later, the population was 179 millions. During America's national existence, the total immigration was over 41 millions: from 1776 to 1820, estimated at 250,000; [3] from 1820 (when immigrants were counted for the first time) to 1940, 38 millions; since 1940, 3 millions, most of them displaced persons and refugees. Except for Negroes who were imported from Africa as slaves, immigrants came freely as individuals and families rather than organized groups, most of them intending to stay.

In the nineteenth century, as earlier, most immigrants came from countries of Western Europe, the British Isles, Germany, the Scandinavian countries, the Netherlands, Switzerland, and France. They composed the "old immigration" which predominated in the immigration to the United States through the 1880's, although the English, Germans, and Scandinavians continued to arrive in large numbers thereafter. After 1890 an increasing proportion of immigrants came from the countries of south and east Europe, notably Italy, former Austria-Hungary, and Russia. They were the "new immigration" of Latin and Slavic peoples, who were largely Catholic in religion and peasant in origin, with some of them, indeed, not long freed from serfdom. They predominated in the immigration to the United States until the Congress shut off free immigration in 1921. Since then, the largest numbers of immigrants have come from Canada, Mexico, and the West Indies. Their movement to this country is not restricted by immigration quotas.

By 1890, the United States was well advanced in urbanization and industrialization. The "new immigrants" therefore settled principally in large cities of the northeastern and middle western states, where they found work in industries. In these cities they and their children sometimes constituted half or more of the population. At times more members of some ethnic groups—the Irish, Italians, Jews, and Negroes, for example—lived in New York than in the big cities of their own countries. As a result, these cities took on a foreign aspect.

In contrast, the "old immigrants," especially those who arrived in the early nineteenth century, located on the land, where economic opportunity existed for them. Only the Irish and the Jews stayed in cities. The former, whose mass immigration began in the 1840's, settled in Boston, New York, and other eastern cities; the Jews, while concentrated in New York, dispersed more widely. The "old immigrants" and their descendants predominated in the rural populations of the United States, which made them seem like "native Americans," a reputation they have maintained to the present time. This is true especially in the southern states, which later European immigrants generally avoided because of the Southerners' reported hostility to them, and to avoid economic competition with Negroes.

There have been some exceptions. For example, many German and Scandinavian immigrants, coming after 1900, settled on the land, principally in Wisconsin, Minnesota, and the Dakotas, and in various western states, adding to the foreign stock of their rural populations. Since 1890, however, native rural populations have migrated to cities in increasing numbers, and their proportions in urban populations have risen accordingly. This is revealed in the comparative percentages of native- and foreign-born persons in cities: only 28.2 percent of native populations resided in cities in 1890, but 47.8 percent in 1930, and 62.7 percent in 1950. The percentages of foreign-born whites for these same years were 61.8, 80.3, and 83.5 respectively.[4]

With immigration controlled and reduced since 1921, certain demographic changes have occurred among ethnic groups. One is the steady decline of foreign-born persons. Within the total white population, the percentage of foreign-born whites was 14.6 in 1890 and 14.5 in 1910, but 11.4 in 1930 and 6.7 in 1950. Their number in 1950 was 10 million;[5] their median age was 55.4 years as compared to 30.1 years for the total American population. In percentages their countries of origin in 1950 were: Italy, 14; Canada, 9.7; Germany, 9.7; U.S.S.R., 8.8; Poland, 8.5; England and Wales, 5.8; Ireland, 5.2; Mexico, 4.4; Austria, 4; Sweden, 3.2; Czechoslovakia, 2.7; Hungary, 2.5; Switzerland, 2.4; and Norway, 2.[6]

Another result of restricted immigration to the United States is the continuing aging of the foreign-born white population. In the period of free immigration, there was a high percentage of immigrants in the productive years of life, from 15 to 64, fluctuating between 84 and 88 percent between 1890 and 1930. In 1950 it was 72 percent. The percentage of immigrants 65 years of age and older was about 15 percent in the decades from 1890 and 1930; in 1950, it was 28 percent.[7]

A third change is that the native-born children of immigrants predominate in the foreign stock of the United States, as the census bureau calls the foreign-born whites and children of foreign or mixed white parentage. But with the passage of time they too steadily reduce in the population. In 1890, they were 11.5 million persons, about a half of them less than 15 years of age; in 1930, they were 25.9 million; in 1950, 23.6 million, a decrease of 9 percent from 1930 to 1950. This decrease was selective of age in 1950: the age groups less than 25 years declined, but those over 25 years increased, with greater increase with advancing age.[8]

As the foreign stock diminishes, the native white stock— the native-born persons of native white parentage, as the census bureau uses this term—increases in the population. In 1950, the native stock was 67.1 percent of the white population; but 82.3 percent of children under 5 years of age, 79.3 percent of those 5 to 14 years, and 73.9 percent of those 15 to 19. In contrast, the percentage of native stock in the white population was 57.3 percent in 1930, and 54.9 percent in 1890.[9] This native stock represents the amalgamation of the millions of immigrants who have come to the United States and the growth of a national population.

Two thirds of American Negroes reside in the southern and southeastern states and one third in northeastern and middle-western states, with some dispersed in far western states. Like the whites they have urbanized at accelerating rates since 1900 and comparable proportions have settled in cities: 48.6 percent in 1940, and 62.4 percent in 1950. In the south they are quitting the land to settle in southern cities: only 26 percent of them lived on farms in 1950; between 1940 and 1950, rural farm Negroes decreased 30 percent in the country. When Negroes leave the south, they migrate to metropolitan cities in the north and west. Thus they are concentrated in cities with one million inhabitants or more, with less than 2 percent of their numbers in small cities or villages in northern states. More than 80 percent of Negroes in all sections of the country except the south live in urbanized areas.[10]

## Cultural Majority and Minorities

As the native population increases, the subcommunities of Americans change. The great bulk of them belong to the cultural majority of the people: they are Americans by nativity, nationality, and citizenship, active in American society. While many are aware of their national origins and have pride of ancestry, they have long since lost their ethnic ties, and associate in indigenous social and cultural groups. However some cultural minorities also exist, notably among Italians, Poles, and other immigrant groups which still have large foreign stocks, and among recent immigrants from Mexico, Cuba, and Puerto Rico. These groups comprise ethnic minorities, in contrast to racial minorities composed of Negroes, American Indians, Chinese, Japanese, and other Asiatics.

Calling the latter groups cultural minorities suggests that they exist in the society separated from the majority population by their different culture, religion, race, or other characteristics, and as a result are discriminated against and accorded inferior status.[11] The ethnic minorities still hold in some measure to their cultures and languages. Many are Catholics or Jews; some are peasant peoples transplanted to cities; more recently, they include displaced persons who have suffered the ravages of war or other alienation. Other minorities comprise Spanish-speaking peoples, mostly Mexicans and West Indians who cling to their native cultures, are Catholics, and commonly are poor, semi-literate migrants from rural communities. Negroes are treated as a racial minority by practices of segregation and discrimination which have continued from their period of slavery to the present.

These groups are by no means unique in their status and treatment as minorities. All immigrants who ever came to the United States were, in their time, similarly discriminated against and disdained by the native population. At the start, English colonists opposed Scotch, Irish, German, Dutch, and Swedish settlers. Moreover, they persecuted religious minorities of their own nationality, Quakers and Catholics, for example. In the nineteenth century, Americans similarly contended with the German, Irish, Scandinavian, and other immigrants who settled among them, and were sometimes active in nativist movements against Catholics and foreigners. After 1890, they were hostile to the "new immigrants" who entered the country in great numbers, and, since then, to recent immigrants. In this persistence of conflict with ethnic groups, Americans developed attitudes to which they still adhere. They evaluate more highly, in the main, those groups which came as colonists rather than as immigrants, belong to the "old" rather than the "new" immigration, are of British rather than other stock, emigrated for religious or political rather than for economic reasons, and are whites rather than non-whites.

But the national policy of the United States has been to

welcome, and eventually to amalgamate, each immigrant group, the non-white races excepted, and thus to resolve its minority status. The American means for assimilating ethnic groups are: citizenship through naturalization of the foreign-born, universal suffrage, public education, civil rights, freedom of work, and other privileges. Immigrant groups have commonly availed themselves of these opportunities in the first generation to effect their assimilation to this country. By their second generation they are often politically active or they may utilize legal means to remove discriminations against them and to improve their status in the society.[12]

How rapidly the various immigrant groups have assimilated has depended on their own cultural traits as well as their reception in the United States. They have fitted into the society relatively soon when their culture and living standards have approximated those of Americans. Also, when they have not been too numerous, or have arrived over a long time and dispersed over the country, they have tended to assimilate quickly. On the other hand, when large numbers of them have concentrated in big cities, they have formed immigrant colonies which have retained their foreign cultures and retarded their assimilation. At the same time, native hostility against them has built up.

Thus some groups assimilated in a single generation— English-speaking immigrants from the British Isles or Canada for instance; others from Europe in two or three generations; still others over a longer time. Recent refugees and displaced persons from Europe have tended, on the whole, to assimilate more rapidly than did previous immigrants of their countries.[13] Other immigrants still coming, notably French-Canadians, Mexicans, and West Indians, however, assimilate slowly.

At present, the second- and, in some cases, the third-generation comprise the adult population of ethnic minorities, which are therefore predominantly native-born. They are assimilated Americans who attended the public schools, speak the English language, live and work in American cities or villages, and know no other country than the United States. To a large extent, they reside in older residential neighborhoods of cities and retain some ethnic activities. But as they advance economically, many of them move to better neighborhoods or to the suburbs, where they complete their assimilation. Their presence in cities thus differs greatly from that of immigrants at the turn of the century.

But racial, in contrast to ethnic, minorities are excluded from these expectations of amalgamation into the native white population. They are prohibited from inter-marriage with whites by custom and in many states by law, and discrimination and segregation hold them in a minority status. This is certainly true of Negroes. Toward Indians, there is some ambivalence in attitudes. They are citizens but they are also wards of the state. The majority reside on reservations but are free to leave them. Sometimes their assimilation into white society has seemed a solution of their minority status. There is also a similar relaxation of attitudes toward Chinese and Japanese minorities. Neither group is populous, most of them are native-born, and earlier animosities toward them have abated.

While restricted from amalgamation, racial minorities do not resign themselves to permanent inferior status. Negroes, Americans by birth and culture, have advanced materially in their standards of living and made notable progress in many areas of activity in the last decades. When they leave the southern states, they are removing themselves from the restrictions they have lived under in southern rural communities. When they settle in cities, whether southern or northern, they have improved opportunities for education, vocational training, industrial employment, and housing. Moreover, in cities they organize Negro associations to promote their interests in American society. Thus they have been active in politics and initiated litigation in the courts to eliminate the legal sanctions which have supported acts of discrimination against them. In the cities, middle and upper status classes have emerged as important groups among Negroes, leading them in their efforts to win social and political rights. These advances by Negroes redound to the benefit of other racial minorities and serve as models to emulate.

Americans liken the amalgamation of immigrants to the reduction of diverse peoples in a "melting pot" into a single population. While this analogy is correct in the main, it oversimplifies and somewhat disguises certain aspects of the process of amalgamation.

For one thing, successive immigrant generations differ in their reactions to absorption into American society. The foreign-born immigrants, their native-born children, and their children's children co-exist as three generations stratified into age groups and they experience their lives in the United States differently. Each generation has its own problems of existence, and possesses different cultural resources with which to solve them. Moreover, one generation raises the next generation to live an existence which is fundamentally different from its own. This produces tensions which affect assimilation into the society.[14]

In these terms, the immigrants leave their countries for the United States, settling in cities or on the land. They find employment, establish their families, and progress in enculturation to American life; but they also stay in ethnic groups, and never give up their native cultures entirely. Therefore they rear their children, who are the second generation, in homes in which both foreign and American cultures exist, with the result that children grow up marginal in some respects to both of them. But the native-born children are reared in American communities. They experience the hold of alien cultures as liabilities. Therefore they largely abandon them, hastening their own enculturation. They raise their children, who are the third generation, as

Americans, scarcely distinguishable from other Americans of their age and social level. For this reason, the third generation has few ties with ethnic groups and few worries about immigrant origins. Its concern, like that of other Americans, is to make its way in the society and to achieve some modicum of wealth, status, and power.

In most ethnic groups native-born members predominate, and the groups exist at some stage of assimilation, whether second- or third-generation. If mainly second-generation, then adult populations have largely Americanized but engage in some ethnic activities, although not in the insurance lodges, protective associations, and foreign-language newspapers their fathers found necessary. If third-generation, they have hardly any ethnic activities at all. But whether second- or third-generation, they still belong to the churches of their fathers, and through them they retain some social and ethnic consciousness of kind.

This attachment to their churches creates a second factor which affects the amalgamation of ethnic groups into the American population. On coming to the United States, most immigrant groups resist assimilation to American Protestant religion, establishing instead their own churches where they continue to worship in their accustomed ways. In this they have the approval and, indeed, the applause of most Americans, who favor religion and regard it as a stabilizing moral influence in human life and affairs. Later on, immigrant groups lessen the foreign character of their churches by Americanizing some of their practices, for example, by using English in services, employing native-born clergy, changing public worship services, and instituting social action programs.

Conversely, the churches attempt to promote the assimilation of members of congregations by founding or supporting secular organizations which aid them in participation in the American society, including classes in the English language and programs of social activities. Still later, when second- and third-generation members have dropped most of their ethnic activities, they continue to be active in churches as their remaining important ethnic association; or they use the churches as meeting places for such few associations as they still have. Thus churches keep their congregations as members of socio-religious groups which are aware of their ethnic origins even after they are thoroughly assimilated into American society.

Under these circumstances, members of immigrant groups value both ethnic and religious ties when they marry. This determines, of course, the process of their amalgamation. They marry largely within their ethnic groups when this is possible, even into the second generation. Three out of four persons, taking the two generations together, have married within their foreign stock in recent decades.[15] When they marry outside their ethnic groups, they prefer someone at least of their own religion, if not of their own descent. Thus immigrant groups which belong to Protestant churches tend to intermarry among themselves rather than with non-Protestants. Similarly Catholic groups—Irish, French, Italians, Poles, and some Germans—intermarry among themselves more than with non-Catholics. Jews likewise intermarry among themselves, eliminating their national distinctions which derive from their different countries of origin. At present, 93 percent of Jewish, 91.5 percent of Protestant, and 78.5 percent of Catholic marriages are endogamous in respect to religion.[16] Not a single but a triple "melting-pot" fuses the ethnic groups into three religious subcommunities in the United States—Protestant, Catholic, and Jewish.[17]

## Religious Subcommunities in the United States

Protestants, Catholics, and Jews form important subcommunities in American society. In the early days of the republic, when most Americans came from the British Isles, the nation was predominantly Protestant in religion. But as Catholic and Jewish populations grew rapidly after 1890, their churches became important: the Catholic church, with 36 million Catholics in 1958, is the largest church in the United States. At present, about 55 percent of Americans claim church membership. In 1957 the religious preference of persons 14 years of age and older was: Protestant, 66.2 percent, Roman Catholic, 25.7 percent, Jewish, 3.2 percent; other, 1.3 percent; no religion, 2.7 percent.[18] American Christianity is no longer solidly Protestant; moreover, the Protestant, Catholic, and Jewish churches are accepted as American churches today.[19]

American churches, with the notable exceptions of the Christian Science and Mormon churches, originated in Europe. Colonists and immigrants brought them here, establishing them as independent churches controlled by their clergy and congregations. Since immigrants came from many countries, they transplanted many churches on American soil; and their diversity has persisted to the present. In the colonial period, English settlers made Protestantism the American religion. It acquired a distinctive character through their churches of dissenting or separatist tradition. These nonconformist churches prevented the establishment of a state religion later on; and the Anglican, Presbyterian, Lutheran, and Catholic churches, which were state churches in certain European countries, became denominational churches.

The Protestant churches multiplied by fission. Dissident minorities in their congregations quarreled over theological issues or divided on social and economic matters and withdrew to found churches of their own. The Presbyterian and Baptist churches especially gave rise to many new sectarian churches. At present, some 250 Protestant denominations and sects exist in the United States, although the bulk of Protestants belong to seven major denominational churches: Baptist, Methodist, Lutheran, Presbyterian, Episcopal, Disciples, and Congregational.

Other English colonists established the Catholic church in Maryland and German settlers did so in Pennsylvania. Later French Catholics in Louisiana and Spanish-speaking Catholics were added to their number through territorial acquisitions. But the Catholic church remained small in the United States until the mass movement of Irish and German immigrants in the 1840's. The Irish especially replenished and revitalized the church and came to predominate in its clergy. They enabled the church to absorb the vast numbers of immigrants who came from south and east Europe after 1880 and to expand into the cities in which they settled. Some Jews, mostly Portuguese and Spanish Jews, were settled in the colonies and established synagogues in several cities. But their large increase also occurred with the immigration of German Jews after 1848 and of Russian Jews after 1880.

With this diversification of churches and religions, Americans adopted a policy of religious toleration, which had already taken strong root in the colonies. Specifically they made the doctrine of state-church separation the legal means to grant religious freedom to churches. As stated in the first amendment to the constitution: "Congress shall make no law respecting an establishment of religion, or prohibiting the free exercise thereof." Churches are independent religious associations in the United States, controlled by their clergy and congregations, free to carry on their own worship and other activities, recruit followers, and possess properties. But they are not supported by taxes and cannot give religious instruction in the public schools.

Protestants, Catholics, and Jews adhere to different religious institutions. Thus, all Protestant churches accept Jesus Christ as the sole head of the church and substitute the Bible for the church as a source of authority. They define the church as a community of believers united by a common faith. They assume the universal priesthood of Christian believers, not only of the ordained clergy, and believe that God reveals himself directly to individual believers and that their trust in Him transforms their lives. This is called justification by faith: to show their faith in Him, they engage in good works or vocation.[20]

In addition, Protestant churches follow other institutionalized practices. They strongly support religious individualism, enjoining upon believers the duty of reading the Bible. They have popular church governments and accept strong lay leadership and participation in church activities. Whether the form of church government is episcopal, presbyterian, or congregational, they support the autonomy of local congregations and favor religious activism over religious doctrine. In brief, they make Protestantism a layman's and not a theologian's religion.[21] The various Protestant churches differ in how they put these principles into practice, some preferring a conservative, others a liberal construction of them, and they differ, too, in their conceptions of the secular functions of religion.

In general, Protestantism is highly accommodated to American society. Conversely, it has also enormously influenced the society, especially through its advocacy of religious individualism and church democracy. Therefore it is often regarded as constituting the national American religion. Protestant churches have supported the doctrine of state-church separation, consenting to the state's control not only of government but of marriage and family, education, and welfare institutions as well. But their congregations have always been active in secular activities which infringe this doctrine, founding charitable enterprises, organizing reform movements, establishing schools and colleges, participating in civil life and organizations and leveling moral criticism at the society and the state. Thus they seldom observe the separation of state and church so completely as it appears at first, nor would most Americans want them to.[22]

Their institutions are a clue to the way in which Protestant churches function in the social life of the people. Despite their denominational and sectarian differences, the churches are sufficiently alike to unite their members in a Protestant subcommunity which differs from the Catholic and Jewish subcommunities. At least they have similar organizations of religion, and their congregations share in their governance and activities. This gives them a feeling of kinship. In point of fact, denominational barriers between churches have lessened in recent times. This is attested to by the ecumenical movement among Protestants to merge churches which originally were united or are similar in doctrines, and to struggle toward a reunited Church. Moreover, on moving to other cities or suburbs, individuals and families often change churches when their own church is absent and some other church which is conveniently at hand is congenial in its worship and congregation. A similar apostasy by Protestant clergy at some time in their careers is not infrequent.

Nonetheless the Protestant churches also exist independently, unifying their members in separate socio-religious groups. They are national religious bodies with congregations and adherents in cities and regions of the United States and comprise denominational or sectarian groups of persons affiliated with them through common creed and faith, rituals of baptism, historic tradition, family membership, often ethnic descent. Because Protestants maintain the autonomy of individual churches, congregations often develop into well-knit local groups. Their members know each other through participating in worship services, associating in church activities, residing in local neighborhoods, through marriage and burial rites in the church, and through secular activities as well.

Moreover, congregations, or denominational churches more largely, commonly have social rank or confer prestige in the system of classes in cities, which has some effect on the cohesion of members. In social terms, the churches of English or colonial origin, the Episcopalian, Presbyterian, and Congregational churches for example, have socially prominent congregations. Such churches as the Methodist, Baptist, Lutheran, and Disciples follow them. Sectarian churches ordinarily have inferior status.

Most Negroes are Protestants, mainly Baptists and Methodists, who maintain their own segregated churches and pursue a separate religious life and worship. Their religious preferences, stated for persons 14 years of age and older in 1957, were: Protestant, 87.5 percent; Roman Catholic, 6.5 percent; other, 1.5 percent; and no religion, 3.5 percent.[23] Historically their churches arose in the south and provided a ministry for rural Negroes who were illiterate, and wanted a personal, highly emotional religion. Since then, Negroes have established their churches in cities where they are busy centers of social, economic, and political activities, as well as places of religious worship. Thus they resemble white Protestant churches in taking on programs of social action and in the increasing sophistication of their worship services. More than white Protestant churches, however, they hold their congregations and Negroes in general in firm subcommunities.[24]

The Catholic church is an international church with its world center in the Vatican and an American church under the control of the Vatican. It is the original Christian church which developed its organization and institutions of worship in the early centuries of the Christian era. Its basic institutions include: the Pope as absolute head of the church; a liturgical worship based on participation in the sacraments of baptism, confirmation, holy communion or the Eucharist, confession, matrimony, holy orders, and extreme unction; the sole authority of the church to administer these sacraments; absolute clerical control of all activities of the church, religious and secular; interpretation of the scriptures exclusively by holy orders (for laymen the Bible is a devotional book to read but not to interpret); and weak lay leadership in church affairs.

While the Vatican does not concur in the doctrine of state-church separation, the American Catholic church does so in the United States. However, the American Catholic church, like other Catholic churches, has responsibility for the marriage and family life, education, social welfare, and morals of Catholics, and does not surrender these functions willingly to the state.[25]

As a sacramental religion, Catholicism requires a church and a vast body of priests to conduct its liturgies of worship. On this basis the Catholic church has become the most highly organized and powerful church in the world, with a great number of clergy and religious orders to discharge its multifold duties and activities. Its control and administration rest in the Vatican, where the Pope, cardinals, curia, congregations, tribunals, and offices compose a government which rules the church as a religion and as a state. The Vatican sends an Apostolic Delegacy to Washington to represent it in the United States. But a hierarchy of cardinals, archbishops, and bishops, governing archdioceses and dioceses into which the country is divided, administer the work and worship of the American Catholic church. This clerical control of the church stands in stark contrast to Protestant churches, whose polity is shared by clergy and congregations, and which decentralize power and authority to maintain the autonomy of congregations and the religious individualism of Protestant believers.

To minister to Catholics in their family and social activities, the church maintains a great and varied number of organizations. The Catholic schools are foremost among these in the United States. In 1961 there were 10,594 Catholic elementary schools with 4,402,410 students; 2,433 high schools, with 886,295 students; and 267 colleges and universities, with 321,999 students.[26] They make it possible to educate young people in parochial schools from the first to the last class, under the tutelage of priests and sisters. Other important church enterprises are its Catholic Chari-

ties, family agencies, hospitals, orphanages, old people's
homes, and other welfare organizations. The National Catholic Welfare Conference provides guidance for these activities of the church.

In addition, the church encourages the organization of
Catholic laymen's associations, some in connection with welfare enterprises, others dealing with their activities in
American society, but all of them led or influenced by
priests or religious orders. These organizations exist at
parish, diocesan, and national levels of the society, and
attract Catholic men and women at various stages of their
lives or careers. They include Catholic associations of teachers, students, doctors, lawyers, and other professional persons; Catholic leagues of policemen, firemen, and sanitary
workers; Catholic medical and hospital associations. Young
people join the Catholic Youth Organization, Newman
clubs, and other associations.

The Knights of Columbus, the Holy Name Society, and
other organizations enroll adult men and women in their
specialized activities. There are also Catholic organizations
in journalism, communications, the arts, literary activities,
and the sciences. National bodies attempt to determine the
books and movies which Catholics are permitted. The
church does not neglect any area of human activity in its
effort to minister to Catholics and keep them true to their
faith.

Despite its imposing organization and diverse religious
and temporal enterprises, the core figure in Catholic worship is the priest, and his area of activity is the parish. Usually an appointed priest and several assistant priests serve
urban parishes. In his parish church the priest conducts
the liturgies of worship, administers the sacraments, serves
as spiritual leader, supervises parish activities, and helps
parishioners with personal and family problems. In addition,
the priest represents his church in the larger Catholic subcommunity and encourages parish members to participate

in Catholic-sponsored organizations and activities. A total of 16,552 parishes with more than 50,000 priests existed in the United States in 1958.[27]

Priests control the religious life of parishioners more than Protestant ministers. Catholics are required to attend mass, the main liturgical form of worship, each Sunday, therefore to be constant in their devotions. But priests exert authority mainly through administering the sacraments. Each infant must be baptized, and becomes a Catholic thereupon. As he grows up, he is confirmed in the Catholic faith. He goes to confession at certain times, and at least once a year. He also participates in the holy communion. Later on, he marries, preferably, from the church's point of view, a fellow Catholic; but, if not, the spouses agree to rear their children as Catholics. At the last, he dies and is buried with the rites of the church. The great occasions of life are infused with religious meaning and content; and the church, having charge of the sacraments associated with them, sustains their significance.

But parish priests strive to keep entire families and not only individual members faithful in their religious duties and actively participating in Catholic life and social affairs. According to canonical rule, children must attend parochial school if they are locally available, and priests compel parents not only to consent to this but to pay for it as well. They require parents also to reinforce their authority to secure the children's compliance to their church duties as well as attend to their own. For the latter, this includes participating in Catholic activities, whether in trade unions or sodalities or reading Catholic journals and displaying Catholic sacred emblems in their homes. As necessity arises, adult Catholics resort to Catholic hospitals, welfare agencies, or other organizations. Even more often, they consult the priest about personal or family problems.[28]

As a religious subcommunity, Catholics maintain a solidarity among themselves based on their church and the multiplicity of their religious and secular organizations. Through them, they are able to live in a Catholic world, as it were, and to practice a Catholic way of life. Moreover, they do so without eliminating entirely those ethnic and cultural distinctions which still exist. Many Catholics belong to ethnic minorities—Italian, Polish, French-Canadians, Slavs, and others—and often the minorities have their separate churches and priests of their own nationality. In the parishes of some metropolitan cities, two or three different Catholic churches and possibly a Negro Catholic church sometimes coexist.[29]

This enclosure of Catholics in their own subcommunity is far from a complete definition of their position. Catholics are Americans also, and participate as well in the activities of American society. In the main, they associate as Catholics in their religious and parochial activities, but as Americans in their employment, political activities, military service, and other secular enterprises. As one church among many in the United States, they could not attain or even desire absolute separateness.

Their existence in American society, moreover, makes inroads even on their religious life. In the large cities, where the Catholic population is considerable, parish priests supervise their congregations with difficulty: some individuals and families move to other localities, affiliate with other groups, or drop away from the church. The church calls the loss of Catholics who become inactive "leakage." [30] Moreover, as the social status of Catholics rises in the society, their religious fervor declines. At least wealthy upper classes are less amenable to the authority of priests in their nonreligious activities and tend to lapse into secularism. This is true also of ethnic congregations when they begin to assimilate and lose their immigrant character. Finally, the out-marriage rate of Catholics is about one fifth of all their marriages; and marriages of mixed faiths dilute the religious convictions of both spouses.

Judaism differs from Protestantism and Catholicism because it is the religion of a specific people, the Jews, and probably could not survive were they to cease to exist. Judaism is intimately associated with Jewish history and civilization in antiquity, which is recounted in the Old Testament. It comprises a body of laws, doctrines, and customs which commemorate their past life and its great events, and serves them both as a religion and a way of life.[31] Judaism was the first monotheistic religion in the world. It rests on the Jews' belief in a transcendent God, the Creator and His law, the Torah, given by Him to Moses, leader of the Israelites, whom God had chosen as His people. This law, given in the five books of Moses, prescribes rules of behavior, with religious sanctions, concerning the dress, food, family living, occupations, and, indeed, all activities of Jews.

During their exile in Babylon and return to Palestine and their subsequent dispersion after its downfall, the Jews intensified their observance of the law in order to preserve themselves as a people. Scattered in small minorities in many countries, they clung to Judaism as a means of continuing as Jews. They assimilated to the societies in which they lived but did not amalgamate and disappear into their populations. Thus they persisted as a religious subcommunity, evolving the various present forms of Judaism.

Historically, the institutions of Judaism include: an intense sense of monotheism and a belief in a universal ethical God who reveals Himself to man; His covenant with Moses and the Jews making Him their God and they His chosen people; the practice of circumcision as a sign of this covenant; the revelation of God's will through His laws, the prophets, and the scriptures; the faithful observance of these rules and prescriptions of behavior as the principal means of worship; the commemoration of festivals, holidays, and other occasions in Jewish history to intensify their faith in God and in themselves; a study of Talmudic Law to determine what the right and proper rituals are; hence a veneration of the rabbi, a scholar and teacher of

Judaism, after the decay of the old priesthoods; the replacement of the old temples by synagogues, which became
places of worship, study, and assembly; and a concern for
ethics and social justice in human behavior. In brief, Judaism was a ritualistic religion with secondary interest in
doctrines of theology.[32]

In the United States today, the Jews are highly assimilated
and have accommodated Judaism so much to American society that they no longer agree on all these institutions or
observe all the rituals of their religion. As American Jews,
they are not a persecuted people, segregated in ghettoes,
who cherish Judaism as a means to retain their ethnic
identity. They are instead a relatively prosperous group,
employed in commercial pursuits and in the professions,
and residing in stable neighborhoods of cities and suburbs.
Their way of life is American and not that of ancient Jews
or of German or Russian Jews, and is remote in its patterns
and ethos from those of the Israelites whose history is related in the Old Testament. In consequence, they have
Americanized Judaism in many ways and made their synagogues to resemble Protestant churches.[33]

At present, American Jews belong to three separate Judaic denominations, the Orthodox, Reformed, and Conservative synagogues. The first of these is the historic Jewish
church, preserved by the Jews in their European ghettoes.
It was first established in the United States by Sephardic
Jews in the colonial period and was predominantly the
church of the Russian Jews whose mass immigration occurred after 1880. The Reformed congregation was founded
by Jews in Germany in the early nineteenth century. Emancipated from ghettoes and incorporated into German society, they were motivated to modernize their synagogues
to adapt them to their changed modes of life. German Jewish immigrants transplanted Reformed Judaism to this
country after 1848. Their descendants, and many successful, educated Jews who are concerned with Americanizing
their synagogue, compose its congregations today.

Conservative Judaism is intermediate between the Reformed and Orthodox Judaism. American Jews founded it, in the late nineteenth century, in an effort to preserve a traditional Judaism modified sufficiently to fit American society.[34] Jews prefer the Conservative and Reformed synagogues, but they have not entirely left the Orthodox synagogue, which gradually has transformed itself into an American Orthodox synagogue.

Without differentiating the synagogues, we may note some innovations which they have adopted. These include the organization and control of the synagogue by its congregation and not by the Jewish community at large, which sustains the local autonomy of each synagogue and prevents strong, national, denominational organizations; the transformation of the rabbi from a scholar immersed in Talmudic law into a preacher, pastor, priest, educator, youth worker, counselor, and civic representative of his synagogue, roles similar to those of Protestant and Catholic clergy; the organization of the worship service in the manner of Protestant services, its focus on the sermon, with choir music, congregational singing, responsive services, benediction, etc.; many church-connected organizations and activities, including sodalities, men's clubs, education projects, "young marrieds" activities, and numerous youth enterprises; and church and Hebrew schools, part-time and full-time, with instruction in Judaism, the Hebrew language, and secular subjects. These activities, taken together, indicate a considerable secularization of Judaism, again in the manner of Protestant churches.[35]

Today the synagogues are busy centers of Jewish life and activities. About 60 percent of Jews are affiliated with them,[36] and perhaps more attend services during the High Holidays or take part in their activities at some time or other. But their motivations are apparently secular as often, or more often, than religious. They are attracted to the social, cultural, educational, and recreational activities of the synagogues and not only to worship services.

More generally, they belong to synagogues in order to have an opportunity to participate in Jewish activities as Jews, and sometimes to gain status as members of a congregation with high prestige. Parents too welcome the opportunity to send their children to synagogue schools to acquire some training in Judaic rituals and in Jewish history.

Jews pursue social and cultural activities in other organizations also. Next to the synagogues in importance, the Jewish Community Centers carry on many enterprises, as well as provide offices for local organizations. Jewish charities —family welfare agencies, hospitals, orphanages, old people's homes, and others—are numerous; and the fund-raising programs to support them also have become important activities. The National Jewish Welfare Board, American Jewish Congress, Anti-Defamation League, and B'nai Brith are national organizations which have local chapters in many cities. The workingmen's movements, which led to the formation of important radical trade unions after the turn of the century, have diminished in importance as a means of mobilizing Jewish life and activities.

Clearly the Jews constitute a subcommunity in American society, unified in their religious and cultural existence, and aware of themselves as Jews. At present, they live in the better neighborhoods of cities and suburbs, thus removed several times from the ghettoes in which first-generation Jews settled, but segregated in their own residential areas, although voluntarily so for the most part.[37] They have lost most of the ethnic and cultural traits which divided first-generation Jews into national groups, and native-born Jews have little knowledge of the Old World origins of their ancestors. How much Jews are enclosed in the Jewish subcommunity is hard to say. All of them participate in American society, and many successful Jews are prominent, well-known Americans, but some middle-income Jews are also contained largely in their own social world.[38] Since they are highly endogamous in marriage, they assimilate without amalgamation and persevere as a subcommunity.

In this last respect, some Jews regard their situation in the United States as anomalous and are uncomfortable about it. The Jews choose to continue to be Jews and maintain an active Jewish life; but some have also so secularized their religion that their historical reasons for persisting as a Jewish subcommunity are called into doubt. In brief, they are, in some and increasing degree, Jews without Judaism. Jewish leaders and thinkers are worried about whether their highly organized social and cultural life will be enough to perpetuate them as Jews, and, even if it is, whether this is a desirable outcome of their covenant with God as His chosen people.[39]

Between Protestants, Catholics, and Jews, there are deep fissions which segregate them in their subcommunities. But the earlier antagonisms which existed among them, revealed in anti-Catholic and anti-Semitic movements of the nineteenth centuries, have declined, although they are not gone completely. Protestants still distrust Catholics because of the clerical control of their church; but their fear also diminishes as Catholics become assimilated, and advance to important places in the society. Nor do Protestants and Catholics display serious hostility to Jews, especially since World War II. While Jews still retain organizations to fight anti-Semitism, they are concerned, as often as not, with social acceptance rather than ethnic discrimination in American society. The three subcommunities include Americans who engage in many activities without concern for religion at all, and the secularism of modern times helps to promote a growing tolerance among them.[40]

## The Negro Subcommunity

Negroes are enclosed in their racial subcommunity much more than whites, and pursue their separate social life and

cultural activities. As a people, they have been American
longer than any ethnic group except colonists from the
British Isles; but they came in slavery, and since their
freedom up to the present time they have continued sub-
servient to whites.

In most American cities, except in some southern cities
where local conditions or historical circumstances dictate,
Negroes live in areas of residential segregation. Their poverty commonly compels them to dwell in substandard
buildings in the older sections of cities. But white practices
of discrimination, including the refusal of real estate firms
and banks to sell or rent housing to them outside Negro
districts, the use of restrictive racial covenants by property
owners, and the hostility of white families whose neighborhoods are invaded by Negroes, also keep them confined to
certain areas of residence. Negro Harlems, or Bronzevilles,
or whatever local name prevails for their sections, exist in
all metropolitan cities.

This residential segregation of Negroes leads to segregation of their social and cultural enterprises also. They
locate their homes, stores, industries, churches, and organizations in Negro areas and spend much of their time
and energies in their subcommunity. Their children also
attend the public schools nearest to their places of residence,
which tend, because of their racial concentration, to be
Negro schools in Negro districts. Similarly their access to
municipal services, recreational facilities, hospitals and
urban amenities are determined by their segregation in the
interior sections of cities. Negroes are thus isolated physically and culturally from much association with whites,
which keeps them socially inferior also.

Moreover, Negroes are discriminated against by other
practices which reinforces these patterns of segregation.
At present, the legal sanctions which support discrimination against them are under attack, but Negroes still are
seriously handicapped by customs which restrict their ac-

tivities. In the southern states, with their legacy of customs which survive from the period of slavery, whites tend to deprive Negroes of civil rights and to treat them in social relations as servile people. To these ends, they have provided Negroes with "separate but equal accommodations" in housing, schools, transportation, and public services, which in actuality are much inferior to the accommodations of whites, and which keep Negroes in subordinate positions. Whites discriminate against Negroes in northern states more often by economic and residential practices, but grant them civil rights and do not insist on racial etiquette in their social contacts.[41] Nevertheless, like southern whites, they exclude Negroes from their status groups and social activities, and show little desire for social equality with Negroes.

With their participation in American society restricted by segregation and discrimination, Negroes maintain their subcommunity. But they fight, of course, the many restraints under which they exist, and their segregated churches, press, and schools are important organizations through which they do so. This builds their sense of race solidarity. In addition, they carry on social and cultural activities through a multitude of voluntary associations: social clubs, insurance lodges, occupational associations, recreational groups, fraternities and sororities, and civic bodies. In comparison to whites, they have a larger relative number of these associations, and in this respect are "exaggerated" Americans.[42] They also support many Negro businesses and service industries, but lack sufficient capital and business experience to develop them into major size.

About two thirds of Negroes work as unskilled and semi-skilled workers in industries, earning an income substantially below whites. In 1960 the median family income of urban Negroes was $3,894, compared to $6,163 for urban whites.[43] Their comparative poverty reflects their recent urbanization and shows itself also in their rates of crime and public dependency.

Negroes hold to their subcommunity by endogamous marriage practices. At present, 29 states have laws which make intermarriages between whites and Negroes illegal and void; in other states such marriages are legal but tolerated with hard grace. Little intermarriage occurs between the races in the states which allow it. Several studies of intermarriage in New York State and some New England cities indicate that they constitute 3 percent or less of Negro marriages.[44] Through inbreeding, the Negro, white, and Indian "blood" of American Negroes becomes distributed throughout all of them, and they are apparently evolving into a stable hybrid of brown Americans. While they lose extreme African features in this process, Negroes nevertheless remain a "visible" people, which makes them convenient objects of racial prejudice.

Within their subcommunity, Negroes are stratified into status classes, with an estimated 10 percent constituting an upper class, 20 percent a middle class, and 70 percent a lower class; a class of "shadies"—persons who earn their livelihood in "protected businesses" of the underworld—also exists. In general, Negroes place more emphasis on social distinctions than whites do, which reflects both their segregation behind a color line and their necessity to climb socially in their own social world.[45] They depend largely on criteria of achieved status to determine such distinctions —mainly success in business, professions, education, and public entertainment—although some upper status groups nourish social pretensions which derive from ancestry or other family ascription. Some upper class Negroes sometimes appear to support the segregation of Negroes since this protects their own positions behind the color line.

In general, upper class Negroes comprise the leading business and professional people, some public entertainers, university professors, some ministers, writers, and civil service employees. For the most part, they are well-educated, earn large incomes, own their own homes, and have stable families and comfortable domestic lives. Many emulate their white peers in practicing deportment and speech befitting the gentry. Fashionable Negro society is centered in Washington, but New York, Philadelphia, Atlanta, and other cities with large Negro populations are important society locales too. Negro society usually belongs to the Republican party, attends Protestant churches of English derivation, sends its children to northern white universities or leading Negro colleges.

Middle class Negroes include lesser business and professional persons, white-collar workers, civil servants, and skilled workers who have relatively steady employment and good incomes. They have risen from the Negro masses through economic means, but have some amount of education, stable families, own their homes, and engage in church activity. Often they make conscious efforts to advance socially, and many of them are marked by tensions of striving and, to some extent, of frustrated ambitions.

Lower class Negroes constitute the unskilled and semi-skilled Negroes who are relatively impoverished and often illiterate, at least in the older generations. They have unstable families, with common-law marriages and high rates of illegitimacy, with some tendency for mother-children families to predominate among them. Their crime rates are high, as are their rates of public dependency. However, many of them are active in churches, especially in those which provide an emotional religion. The number of "Black Puritans" among them is considerable.

## NOTES

1. *A Century of Population Growth* (Washington: Bureau of the Census, 1909).

2. Maurice R. Davie, *World Immigration* (New York: Macmillan, 1936), p. 44.

3. Maurice R. Davie, *World Immigration*, p. 12.

4. Donald Bogue, *The Population of the United States* (New York: The Free Press of Glencoe, 1959), p. 126.

5. Conrad Taeuber and Irene B. Taeuber, *The Changing Population of the United States* (New York: Wiley, 1958), p. 77. Data cited by permission.

6. Donald Bogue, *The Population of the United States*, p. 361.

7. Conrad Taeuber and Irene B. Taeuber, *The Changing Population of the United States*, pp. 77–78.

8. Conrad Taeuber and Irene B. Taeuber, *The Changing Population of the United States*, p. 81.

9. Conrad Taeuber and Irene M. Taeuber, *The Changing Population of the United States*, pp. 82–83.

10. Donald Bogue, *The Population of the United States*, pp. 126–127, 130–131, 139–140.

11. Louis Wirth, "The Problem of Minority Groups," in Ralph Linton, ed., *The Science of Man in the World Crisis* (New York: Columbia, 1945), p. 47.

12. Howard M. Brotz, "Social Stratification and the Social Order," *American Journal of Sociology*, 64 (May 1959), 571–578; and Samuel Lubell, *The Future of American Politics* (Garden City, New York: Doubleday Anchor Books, 1956), pp. 79–85.

13. Maurice R. Davie, *Refugees in America* (New York: Harpers, 1947).

14. Karl Mannheim, "The Problem of Generations," in *Essays on the Sociology of Knowledge*, edited by Paul Kecskemeti (London: Routledge and Kegan Paul, 1952), pp. 276–322; Judith R. Kramer and Seymour Leventman, *Children of the Guilded Ghetto* (New Haven: Yale University Press, 1961), pp. 21–34; and Will Herberg, *Protestant-Catholic-Jew* (New York: Doubleday Anchor Books, 1956), pp. 6–23.

15. James H. S. Bossard, "Nationality and Nativity as Factors in Marriage," *American Sociological Review*, 4 (December 1939), 792–798.

16. Donald Bogue, *The Population of the United States*, p. 695.

17. Ruby Jo Reeves Kennedy, "Single or Triple Melting-Pot?" *American Journal of Sociology*, 49 (January 1944), 331–339.

18. Donald Bogue, *The Population of the United States*, p. 689.

19. Will Herberg, *Protestant-Catholic-Jew*, pp. 38–39.

20. William Adams Brown, "Protestantism in Creed and Life," in *The Religions of Democracy* by Louis Finkelstein, J. Elliot Ross, and William Adams Brown (New York: Devin-Adair, 1941), pp. 173–237.

21. William Adams Brown, *The Religions of Democracy*, p. 204.

22. H. W. Schneider, *Religion in the Twentieth Century* (Cambridge: Harvard University Press, 1952), pp. 58–59.

23. Donald Bogue, *The Population of the United States*, p. 689.

24. E. Franklin Frazier, *The Negro in the United States* (New York: Macmillan, 1957, rev. ed.), pp. 334–366.

25. J. Elliot Ross, "The Roman Catholic Religion in Creed and Life," in *The Religions of Democracy*, pp. 88–169.

26. *National Catholic Almanac* (Paterson, N. J.: St. Anthony Guild, 1962), pp. 508–511.

27. *Catholic Directory*, 1958.

28. Joseph H. Fichter, *Social Relations in the Urban Parish* (Chicago: University of Chicago Press, 1954); and *Dynamics of a City Church* (Chicago: University of Chicago Press, 1951).

29. Joseph H. Fichter, *Dynamics of a City Church*, p. 12.

30. Joseph H. Fichter, *Social Relations in the Urban Parish*, pp. 68–69.

31. Nathan Glazer, *American Judaism* (Chicago: University of Chicago Press, 1957), pp. 6–7, 133.

32. Louis Finkelstein, "The Jewish Religion, its Beliefs and Practices," in Louis Finkelstein, ed., *The Jews, Their History, Culture and Religion* (New York: Harpers, 1949), II, pp. 1327–1389.

33. Will Herberg, *Protestant-Catholic-Jew*, p. 191.

34. Marshall Sklare, *Conservative Judaism* (New York: The Free Press of Glencoe, 1955).

35. Will Herberg, *Protestant-Catholic-Jew*, pp. 191–192; and Albert I. Gordon, *Jews in Suburbia* (Boston: Beacon Press, 1959).

36. *American Jewish Year Book*, 1958, p. 115.

37. Erich Rosenthal, "Acculturation Without Assimilation? The Jewish Community of Chicago, Illinois," *American Journal of Sociology*, 66 (November 1960), 275–288.

38. Judith Kramer and Seymour Leventman, *Children of the Gilded Ghetto*, pp. 75–120.

39. Nathan Glazer, *American Judaism*, pp. 127–149; and Will Herberg, *Protestant-Catholic-Jew*, pp. 196–198.

40. *Cf.* Gerhard Lenski, *The Religious Factor* (New York: Doubleday, 1961), pp. 55–67.

41. St. Clair Drake and Horace R. Cayton, *Black Metropolis* (New York: Harcourt, Brace, 1945), p. 117.

42. Arnold Rose, *The Negro in America* (New York: Harpers, 1944), p. 299.

43. *Income of Families and Persons in the United States, 1960.* p. 35.

44. Maurice R. Davie, *Negroes in American Society* (New York: McGraw-Hill, Whittlessey House, 1949), p. 410.

45. Maurice R. Davie, *Negroes in American Society*, p. 416.

# · XI ·

# *Social Stratification*
# *in Cities*

### The Nature of Classes

Not only subcommunities but classes divide the American
people into social and cultural groups, a stratification
which is an important factor in their social life and organization. While subcommunities and classes are based on
different principles of human behavior, they are nevertheless related to each other. Subcommunities exist within the
classes which are prevalent in the United States, and subcommunities are stratified into classes of their own. But
social stratification exists apart from subcommunities and
may be analyzed in its own terms.

"Classes" refers to groups of individuals and families who
occupy a common position in a system of classes in the
society. They are unified by similar occupations, education,
religion, often descent, and regard themselves as a class.
This definition denotes several features of stratification.
One is that classes comprise groups of people and not
categories of individuals. Another is that classes are ranked
from superior to inferior on a scale based on socially
accepted criteria of evaluation. A third is that this hier-

archical order of classes signifies inequalities among them. Indeed, stratification institutionalizes these inequalities and perpetuates them. Finally, these inequalities mean that classes have different access to occupations and wealth, prestige, and social power, and that their members have therefore unequal possessions and endowments.

The appearance of classes in the cities of Mesopotamia (see Chapter II) suggests that they are universal in urban communities: city dwellers are socially and culturally heterogeneous and divide into many groups. But urban classes are, of course, never uniform the world over. They differ in type and number, the criteria which distinguish them, their ascription by family, the mobility and hence the achieved status they allow, finally, in the composition of their members. Nor are classes ever permanent. New groups arise which seize power and elevate themselves to high status and wealth, altering the previously existing system of classes.

In the United States, open, competitive classes displaced the colonial system of classes in the nineteenth century. After the Revolutionary War, the pro-English upper class lost its rank and much of its property. Thereafter Americans acted to prevent the formation of another such aristocratic class by weakening some of the legal means which made a landed aristocracy possible. Specifically they prohibited the practices of primogeniture and entail of estates, and provided further for the equality of inheritance of descendants when persons died intestate. They also destroyed the legal means to subordinate individuals by enacting legislation which established equality of persons before the law, stipulated fair and equal punishments, broadened the suffrage, established public schools, naturalized immigrants, and emancipated Negro slaves. Their common citizenship and nationality have continued since then to level the social distinctions among them, as well as to equalize their opportunities in the society.

For these reasons, it is difficult to make a reliable determination of classes in the United States. Classes are not
organized, although their members affiliate in organizations
and carry on organized activities. Nor are they recognized
in the law. They are not national in membership, although
there is some tendency for a national upper class to form:
rich, powerful persons and families encounter each other
in social and economic activities, and nurture sentiments
of superiority.[1] But existence of such a class is tenuous,
and classes generally are discontinuous over the land and
local in cities and regions. Even social classes, in the sense
of composite groups of persons and families which have
common economic, social, and political rank, do not occur
in the society.

Instead there appears to exist concurrently two forms of
stratification in the United States, creating two different
kinds of classes and evaluations of social rank and worth.[2]
One of these is economic stratification, which forms economic classes; the other is status stratification, which creates status classes. Both kinds of stratification afford access to wealth, prestige, and power. Consequently a
correlation exists between the two sets of classes, but never
an invariably high or predictable one. For example, all rich
persons are not socially important, because wealth is only
one measure of status and they may have acquired their
money in some ignoble way. Also, some prominent families
may be reduced in economic but not social circumstances.
For considerations of this kind, economic and status classifications should not be merged into a single system of
social classes, or their identities otherwise confused.

As their name implies, economic classes comprise individuals and families who perform similar economic functions, and are unified by comparable occupations, size and
source of income, the share of economic goods and services
which their income buys, and such prestige and power as
job and wealth give them. Thus, they are persons bound
by common economic interests into classes. Economic

classes are aggregates rather than social groups. Their members are too numerous, culturally diverse, and geographically dispersed to know each other or to associate in social and cultural activities. They join organizations, however, which protect or advance their common economic interests. Thus they acquire a sense of class and a class consciousness among themselves.

This definition of economic classes suggests that their number and kind in various countries of the world depends on the prevailing character of economic production and technology. In the cities of antiquity, with their economic base in agriculture and trade, classes comprised landowners, merchants, workers, peasants, and slaves. Only merchant and artisan classes, in contrast, lived in the commercial cities of medieval Europe. On the basis of their relation to property and technology, Marx differentiated classes in the western world of the nineteenth century as landlords, capitalists, and workers.[3]

At the present time, the economic classes in the United States perhaps approximate the following aggregations.[4] An upper class of individuals and families controls the giant corporations and determines policy for them; thus it also influences large sectors of the economy, and in some matters possibly the entire economy. Its members are wealthy industrialists, important bankers, large business owners, and a few professionals. Some of them belong to powerful family dynasties which control major industries in the country.

A second upper class comprises persons who actually manage the corporations and administer the economy. While they are employees and take orders from the controlling class, they are superior in ability, knowledge, education, and achievement to all others in the society. This class includes top corporation officials, major government officials, large manufacturers, prominent business, financial, and industrial leaders, and successful professionals.

Third, an upper middle class of persons resembles those

of the second class, but are of lesser attainment. Nevertheless they consist of relatively successful, well-educated
persons: middle-level corporation, government, and military officials; middle-sized industrialists, business owners,
and manufacturers; professional persons; and large farm
owners.

Fourth is a lower middle class which consists of lesser
corporation and government officials and supervisors; small
business owners; beginning professionals; clerical, office,
and sales personnel; some skilled workers and foremen; and
small farm owners.

The last, the working classes, with the class immediately
above them, contains the bulk of the American population.
Their upper level consists of skilled workers, foremen, and
line supervisors, small businessmen, and small farmers. At
their lower level are semi-skilled workers, factory operatives,
and marginal farmers. Below them, partially declassed, are
persons who work infrequently or are unemployable.

Status classes, as their name implies, comprise persons
and families who enjoy the same social status or prestige
because they have a certain style or level of living, belong
to similar organizations, engage in common social and
cultural activities, are unified by family and religious ties,
and are accorded comparable esteem. While status classes
are based on social, not economic, distinctions, the occupations and incomes of members nevertheless contribute to
their prestige, and, in any event, determine their patterns
of consumption. They acquire sentiments of status class
through their continuous association with each other and
through the recognition they win as a class in the society.
Their children, too, usually attend similar schools and pursue social activities which socialize them to their own class
and serve therefore to perpetuate it.

In concrete terms, status classes consist of socio-economic
and socio-cultural groups, including subcommunities, which
exist among the people. These groups occur among native

Americans and new (or recent) Americans, whites, Negroes and Indians, Christians and Jews, ethnic groups, and other segments of the population. They are numerous and diverse because Americans are heterogeneous and segregate into many groups based on social and cultural affinities. The people hold these groups in various estimation of their characteristics, and accord high status to groups of white Americans of the cultural majority, and lesser status and descending rank to groups of the cultural minority.

While groups and subcommunities are ranked socially, their hierarchical order is seldom clear or exact except in the uppermost and lowermost groups. A number of reasons account for this imprecision. One is that so many groups now exist, especially in metropolitan cities and areas, that an accurate evaluation of them is unrealistic. Another reason is that groups are identified with different institutions not readily comparable in prestige: for example, their churches, families, education, occupations, and subcultures. Third, Americans have no consensus on what constitutes prestige and hence rank among them. Status groups tend to overestimate their own virtues and to deprecate those of others, and upper status groups to assume that lower status groups want to emulate them, which is often not the case. A fourth reason is that status is mostly achieved and not inherited; Americans place high value on social mobility, which ultimately, of course, reduces distinctions between status groups. Finally, religious and racial subcommunities are stratified internally, which further complicates the existence of status groups in the society.

Consequently, the fusion of status groups into status classes is never uniform, nor is the number of classes the same, although five or six classes usually are identified in American cities.[5] It is possible, nevertheless, to generalize about classes. Upper status classes comprise Americans whose families have been rich and prominent for several generations and who confer their social qualities on their class. These characteristics include, with exceptions here and there, Old American family lineage, English descent, important occupations and large incomes, endogamous class marriage, private school education, membership in Protestant churches of English or colonial origins, hence mainly Episcopal, Congregational, and Presbyterian churches. Their other attributes include residence in exclusive urban and suburban neighborhoods, membership in important social clubs, and manners and speech befitting their class.

In the upper middle class, status groups try to emulate the elite groups, but, having to achieve their successes rather than acquire them through partial ascription by families, they have fewer social distinctions and symbols of status. However they commonly derive from families which are important if not illustrious, and they live comfortably in stable families and good homes in the better neighborhoods. They attend both private and public schools and universities, belong to Protestant, Catholic, and Jewish churches, hold important jobs, and have moderate incomes. Often they are active in the social and cultural activities of cities and metropolitan areas, and belong to social, professional, service, and other organizations.

Lower middle status groups also imitate the status groups above them, but with less success and fewer distinctions. They too enjoy stable employment with fair incomes and establish good homes in residential neighborhoods at more modest levels. They attend public schools, with some finishing colleges or universities, and perhaps a larger proportion attend but do not graduate. They belong to Protestant, Catholic, and Jewish churches in which they are reasonably active, and some affiliate with secular organizations also.

Below them are the status groups of the lower class whose modes of life and levels of achievement are those of the working classes, with gradations among them. For the

most part, they have steady employment and earn creditable if modest incomes, and live in modest homes and
apartment houses. They attend Protestant denominational
and sectarian churches, Catholic churches, and Jewish
synagogues. Usually they attend high school, and the
brighter and more ambitious children go on to public
colleges or universities. Men belong to trade unions and
veterans' associations; women also join these organizations,
but, more often, the sodalities attached to their churches.

At the bottom are the status groups of the poor, dis-
possessed, and afflicted: white, Negro, and Indian families
who are socially submerged in the cities in which they
dwell. They are manual workers, occasionally employed.
They seldom join churches or other organizations, their
children often attend school reluctantly. The police and
welfare departments of cities often know many of their
members.

## Economic Classes in Cities

While stratification is national in character, classes are, for
the most part, local social groups in the United States.
The people live and work in the cities and regions of the
country, have a domestic and social life in them, engage
in their cultural activities, and acquire worldly goods and
station in them. Invariably they divide into classes on the
basis of social and economic distinctions, pursue different
modes of existence, and take on different attributes. Thus
they experience classes as real and tangible entities which
affect their achievement of wealth, prestige, and social
power. The study of classes should be made, therefore, in
the cities and metropolitan regions of the United States.

We have already discussed some aspects of economic
classes in cities, noting the importance of the economic
organization of cities to their social organization: the basic
industries or mixtures of industries determine the corporate

organization, labor forces, occupations, income levels, technical skills, and other economic traits of urban populations. Urban economic organization also affects the social and cultural characteristics of urban workers: their levels of education, standards of living, status subcommunities, often ethnic descent. Consequently it influences the number and size of economic classes in cities.

Moreover, the organization of metropolitan economies serves to account for the distribution of economic classes in metropolitan and suburban cities. While all classes are represented in metropolitan economies, their employment and residence vary among cities. Members of middle and upper classes commonly work in metropolitan cities, but many of them live in suburban cities; members of the lower classes work and live in metropolitan cities, and are usually not able to reside outside them. Classes are influenced by their particular urban locations and by the specialized economic activities in metropolitan regions.

For most persons who work, their stratification initially involves membership not in economic classes but in economic groups. They segregate into occupational groups based on their work and the technical skills, income, styles of life, access to status, and other characteristics which their employment entails. These groups may be functional or organizational. In the first case, people divide into groups related to their economic functions. These involve specialized tasks in administration, office work, technology, factory labor, and others. In the second or organizational case, they divide into groups related to their place in the business firms which employ them: management, white-collar workers, factory workers, and others.

At a second level, workers tend to segregate into industrial groups. Not only are there many industries, but each one has its own organization of production, markets, finance, work enterprise, and other activities. They are variously food processing, heavy manufacturing, chemical, drug, electronics, metal fabricating, automobile, airplane, newspaper, radio and television, lumbering, wheat milling, and still other industries. Each industry employs specialized labor forces and determines their conditions of employment, income levels, modes of life, and access to prestige and power. Hence it attaches workers to their industry and to industrial firms which employ them, and develops unique skills and attitudes in them.

Occupational groups which perform similar functions in several industries coalesce into still larger economic groups. They have economic interests in common which transcend their employment with particular business firms or industries and are unified by similar training, comparable incomes and modes of life, and occupational ethos. These groups occur among specialized workers at all levels in the economy. Thus they include associations of corporation executives, manufacturers, bankers, newspapermen, TV and radio personnel, professions, schoolteachers, building trades, and government workers. Sometimes occupations impose a highly unique way of life on their employees which forms them into well-knit economic groups: for example, structural steelworkers and circus performers.

Finally, economic groups stratify into economic classes which extend throughout the society and take on distinctive class attributes. Economic classes are related, again, to the possession of wealth, prestige, and power which derive from economic activities and economic organizations. Large business and industrial owners and important financiers thus compose upper classes; their various employees, at descending economic levels, form middle and lower classes.

At all economic levels except the lowest, economic groups maintain organizations to protect their economic interests as classes and to develop a sense of class consciousness among members. These class-linked associations occur in both urban and national economies. Thus, the owning and managerial classes are organized into Chambers of Commerce, National Association of Manufacturers, and trade associations. Professional groups have legal, medical, architectural, scientific, and other associations. Skilled and semi-skilled workers are organized into trade unions; some trades also form semi-professional bodies, or other kinds of associations.

Even when their economic group and class are unclear, as is often the case in metropolitan cities and regions, individuals and families are identified by economic criteria. What they do for a living, their employer, size of income, the quality of home and possessions—these become clues to and labels of economic status. At least these are indications of achieved economic status, important to know when social status is unknown or claims to status cannot be validated. Thus persons are known by the work they do, their places of residence, the cars they drive, and other evidences of wealth. They are doctors, lawyers, merchants, or thieves, as the doggerel goes, and have the prestige of these occupations. In hard times or when social unrest is great, economic status becomes especially significant. Possession of job and income then provides better means to maintain or win social position than when the society is stable and status subcommunities are entrenched in power.

## Status Groups and Classes

When Americans speak of social classes or assign themselves to social classes, they mean, in most cases, status groups or status classes, as these terms have been defined here. Social classes, if they signify individuals and families who occupy a social position which combines similar economic, social, and political status, do not exist in the contemporary United States. But status stratification is real enough, and status groups and classes exist as social and cultural groups in the society.

In some sense, status groups and classes are nominal strata, consisting of particular persons and families and specific to the cities and metropolitan areas in which they occur. For this reason, they are related to the economic classes of cities. A few observations will illustrate the connections. If local families own and manage the basic industries of cities, they most likely compose upper status classes in them. Their superiority is threatened, however, when national corporations control these industries. Some officials of corporations remain aloof from local society or participate indifferently in it, preferring to be active in status groups of their own. Their administrative, technical, professional, and scientific personnel—the so-called new middle classes—also segregate into their own status groups. They are concerned with pursuing business careers in the corporations and not social careers in the cities in which they reside. Corporations often also employ large numbers of semi-skilled factory operatives or manual laborers and affect the number and distribution of status groups in cities.

Factors other than economic also affect status stratification in cities. The older cities of the United States have classes which are more clearly defined than those in newer cities in recently settled sections of the country. In older cities, upper class families generally have formed into relatively rigid elite groups and influence, to some extent, the lesser classes also. Thus proper Bostonians, Philadelphia gentlemen, and similar groups exist in cities of the eastern and southern United States. Their traits include family ascription, inherited wealth, endogamous marriages, genteel occupations, and private education. To some extent, well-defined classes exist in other older cities, in St. Louis, New Orleans, and San Francisco, for example.

Some upper status families in middle western and far western cities migrated from eastern cities where they were of some importance.

A related consideration is that some status groups also have unique social and cultural characteristics. In New England cities, for example, many families trace their origins to English colonists and to ancestors who were prominent in early American society. Similarly, elite groups in southern cities take pride in ancestors who were pre-Civil War gentry. In general, people in the south tend to emphasize family and kinship as sources of status more than do Americans elsewhere in the country. In addition, derivation of families from other important groups not always distinct now—Yankees, Quakers, old Dutch families —confers prestige. Some older immigrant groups have risen to high status in cities where they settled early and in large numbers: for example, Irish in Boston, Jews in New York, Germans in Milwaukee and St. Louis, Scandinavians in the Twin Cities, and Spanish in West Coast cities.

Keeping in mind variations in local evaluations of prestige, we can still generalize about status classes in cities. One or more sets of families exist as upper status groups and merge into upper classes in them. A number of status groups, whose members are unified by various combinations of family, educational, religious, occupational, and residential ties, constitute middle classes in them. Many status groups, similarly bound by institutional ties but with religious and ethnic affiliations especially important, form their lower classes. Some status groups also belong to Protestant, Catholic, and Jewish subcommunities and to Negro and ethnic subcommunities. Other status groups are sufficiently self-enclosed to approach becoming subcommunities. The elite class is an example. Others occur among business, academic, military, entertainment,

and religious groups. The underworld of crime is a subcommunity.

To generalize further, some status groups expand into
metropolitan areas and are not confined to metropolitan
cities. Elite groups especially are likely to develop into
metropolitan elite because many members dwell in suburban cities but are socially active in central cities also.
Similarly business, professional, and university groups
often are metropolitan in composition. Moreover, important persons in government, eminent judges, celebrities
of stage, screen, radio and TV, and some professional
athletes are usually socially acceptable in even the exclusive society of the very rich.

Several points about status stratification emerge from
this enumeration of status groups and classes. First, so
many status groups exist, especially in large cities, that
their social rank is difficult to determine; their further
assortment into five or six status classes is even more
tentative and uncertain. Second, the higher status groups
are active in metropolitan and national communities and
not only in urban communities. Cities do not function as
social arenas to contain more than a part of their enterprise.
And third, classes are fluid because mobile persons enter
them. Therefore they are variable in social traits also. This
obscurity in social distinctions tends to diminish the importance of status classes.

The volume of social mobility is an important characteristic of American society. At present, the prime
vehicle for mobility is education, both amount and source.
For important positions in government, business, and
industry, college, university, or professional training is
necessary; skilled trade and service industries demand
high school and technical training; students who fail to
complete high school are destined for the lower classes. In
terms of mobility, private education is superior socially to

public and parochial education; it may be academically superior also. Negroes are mobile in the society as they eliminate the barriers to their education and their employment in industry. These evidences of mobility rest on important changes in the society: upgrading of jobs and occupations, transition of families from tenancy to home ownership, the migration of families to cities where opportunities exist and identification with older generations is gone, and, above all, the affluence of the economy which makes secure employment and rising incomes possible.

While mobility is desirable and legitimate, it has its untoward side, the intense struggle to acquire the symbols of status, whether these are material possessions, elegant homes and furnishings, personal adornment, or other preferment. This status seeking occurs in all classes and conditions of the people. Sometimes it is explained as a reaction to the control that corporations and large organizations exercise over economic mobility because social mobility is still in the hands of individuals and families and amenable to their efforts to climb. The prosperity of the society, the existence of mass markets, the urging of advertisers, mass literacy, and the positive encouragement of mobility by Americans are general factors which promote status seeking. It is aggravated by the lack of consensus on what is accounted as prestigeful.

In their studies of stratification, sociologists have joined other Americans in deploring the excess of status striving. Discovering that the process of social mobility is fraught with emotional dangers to persons who rise to higher station, sociologists have stigmatized parvenu families and persons as "strainers." In doing so, they are, unfortunately, aligning themselves with upper status groups and classes, whose self-interest is served by a system of rigid classes which keeps them on the top.

Some members of upper status groups, living on inherited wealth and busy in its enjoyment, compose a *rentier* class which performs few useful services in the society. But status classes ultimately rest on entrepreneurial functions performed by their members and not on their consumption activities. Status groups of the idle rich, in American as in other societies, eventually face downward mobility. This changes the composition of the upper classes and enables new families to enter them.[6]

## Impact of Classes on Cities

Classes are important because they signify that people stratify into status hierarchies and power structures which affect their opportunities to get wealth, prestige, and social power. Based on social and cultural inequalities among them, classes further augment their differences. Thus stratification divides the people, creates schisms among them, aggravates conflicts between classes, separates them into exclusive groups, and penalizes the poor. Even in American society, with its open, fluid classes and access to mobility, factors of class exert an enormous influence. Sociologists have worked out correlations between class position of persons and family stability, child-rearing practices, voting behavior, church attendance, recruitment of leaders, educational expectations, size of income, and other patterns of behavior.[7]

The role of classes in urban life can be understood if they are considered as status groups: that is, as socio-economic and socio-cultural groups with status ranking. Defined in this way, status groups and subcommunities are basic types of groups in American cities. As such, they are important in reducing the magnitude of urban and metropolitan communities to human scale. They comprise relatively small groups which contain members in some order, give them individual and social identity, provide them with primary relations, and support their subcultures. In effect, status groups constitute miniature social worlds. We can accept the services which status groups provide without having to justify their existence by attributing excessive functions to them.

But status groups exercise an impact on cities in other ways, too. For example, such groups engage in social and cultural activities which constitute cultural amenities in cities. We have noted the American tendency to organize voluntary associations to achieve individual and social goals. We now see that principally middle and upper class Americans are active in them. Moreover, these activities still belong to the private sector of the society. Americans are unaccustomed to turning to government to fulfil them.[8]

These voluntary organizations are numerous and diverse in kind. They involve private welfare agencies, community chests, fund drives, voluntary doctors' hospitals, cultural enterprises such as symphony orchestras, art galleries and theaters, social clubs, service organizations, playground groups, summer camps and recreation, hobby groups, reform organizations, and others. As this enumeration of them indicates, some associations are public and cater to the common good; others are restricted to particular groups and meet limited purposes; still others are exclusive and carry on social activities. Taken together, however, they enroll many urban dwellers in enterprises which unify them in status groups or occupy them in good works which benefit all the people in cities.

Voluntary associations have other uses; they enable persons active in them to fulfill their roles as citizens and to cultivate a sense of social responsibility. Moreover, they afford opportunities for persons to develop into community leaders, or to become known as ambitious for mobility. In some activities, upper-class families designate their members to assume community leadership or responsibility; in others, persons seize the opportunity to advance themselves socially or professionally. Whether their motives are pure or class-seeking, they nevertheless undertake activities which involve humane endeavor and expenditures of time and effort. They are, at all events, the American way of encouraging individual enterprise in activities which nurture individualism in the people.

Lower class individuals and groups take little or indifferent part in voluntary associations. Such persons experience inferior class status as an impediment to participation. If they join organizations at all, the men affiliate with trade unions or veterans' associations, the women with churches or associations interested in children and with auxiliaries of men's organizations. But many of them belong to no organizations at all.

Still, voluntary associations provide an opportunity for persons of different classes or subcommunities to associate with one another. Persons and families form social sets or circles which have the same cultural interests or engage in similar social activities. Several social sets of several status groups or subcommunities join in voluntary activities, or encounter each other at concerts, theater, sports events, or other occasions. Thus they become acquaintances and even friends with each other; but they usually continue to meet each other only in these situations. This compartmentalization of social roles is characteristic of the modern social order.

Among the malign effects of classes is the tendency of status groups to segregate in residential neighborhoods, both in cities and in suburbs, and to be ecologically isolated from each other. This is especially harmful to metropolitan cities when the upper classes leave them, causing the lower classes to preponderate. This situation presents the cities with higher costs of police and fire protection, higher rates of public dependency, increased crime and delinquency rates, and other burdens, and with fewer tax resources with which to pay for them.

When cities lose prominent families, they also lose the leadership, political activity, participation in voluntary

associations, and other contributions which members of
these families have made. Conversely, these families, enclosed in exclusive suburbs, sometimes are converted into
conservative groups which oppose the cities in efforts to
undertake low-cost housing, urban renewal, and other
public projects which might ease urban problems. A
segregation of classes and decay of communication among
them may lead to community conflict, excessive crime,
management-labor strife, interracial hostilities, and other
distresses.

## Who Governs the Cities?

Since stratification rests on inequalities—of wealth and
occupation, prestige, and access to power—some sociologists who have pursued stratification studies have declared
that the upper classes, like the colonial aristocracy, control
the cities in which they dwell; or, if they do not rule them
as a class, at least they determine who the important
public officials are and command them to do their bidding.[9]
This claim of a power structure in cities has led to much
research into its existence in the last decade.[10]

Among those stirred to investigate have been some
political scientists who know more than sociologists about
urban political organization. Moreover, they lack presup-
positions about classes which would cause them to venerate
or fear the upper status groups or to stigmatize public
officials for their middle- or lower-class origins. Their
studies, which have concentrated on how key political
decisions are made, have failed to discover clear evidence
of power structures. Instead, they have found that power
is dispersed among many persons and groups rather than
monopolized by a few. Sets of leaders develop in different
activities without much overlapping among them. Public
officials, especially the mayor, are important leaders in
arriving at crucial decisions in cities; and professional and

specialized persons are increasingly important in them too.[11]

Several considerations which bear on urban power structures support, in the main, the contentions of political scientists. One is the absence of a single ruling class both in cities and in the United States. Instead there are both economic and status classes, with some but never a certain correlation between them. Therefore classes disperse rather than consolidate power in coalitions of individuals and families. Status classes, which are the kind sociologists usually investigate in cities, are based on the social distinctions of members which affect their access to power but do not invariably bestow it on them. Therefore, it is not true that upper status classes are, by definition, the ruling classes in cities.

A second consideration is the diversification of power among many organizations and persons in the society. Today political power is the critical power, but economic, intellectual, religious, and other forms of power are significant also, and they are likely to occur in many combinations. Large-scale organizations, specialized in their institutional spheres, wield these kinds of power in their activities, and endow their officials with enormous authority of office. But it has yet to be established that the leaders of organizations also belong to upper status classes in the cities in which they reside.

Third, business corporations, or the business classes, which are imputed to have political power because they have economic power, do not invariably use their powers in cities. Many corporations refrain from intervention in the government and politics of the cities in which they have plants and facilities; indeed they may be profoundly indifferent to them (see Chapter VIII). Their plant managers and officials seldom are politically active in these cities because such activity may harm their companies and, in any event, they are seldom ambitious for social or political careers. But some locally owned business firms, such as department stores, newspapers, radio and TV stations, banks, and public utilities are economically powerful, and they employ their powers for political purposes, both to advance their own interests and for the public good as they see it.[12] Analysis of the economic organization of cities should make clear the unlikelihood that businessmen dominate the cities in which they live.

Finally, power is sometimes so widely dispersed among organizations that the dispersion frustrates unity of action and prevents consensus. Thus, business, labor, political, religious, academic, and minority groups, it may be, possess power, but only power enough to veto the activities of other groups.[13] In some cases, not powerful but merely influential persons affect the activities of others through their organizational office or personal charisma, but do not command them.

## NOTES

1. C. Wright Mills, *The Power Elite* (New York: Oxford, 1956).

2. This discussion follows Max Weber, *From Max Weber: Essays in Sociology*. Translated, edited, and with an introduction by H. H. Gerth and C. Wright Mills (New York: Oxford, 1946), pp. 180–195.

3. Karl Marx, *Capital*. Translated from the first German edition by Ernest Unterman (Chicago: Kerr) III, p. 1031.

4. *Cf*. Robert S. Lynd and Helen M. Lynd, *Middletown in Transition* (New York: Harcourt, Brace, 1937), pp. 458–460.

5. For example, Hollingshead found five status classes in New Haven, Conn.; in August B. Hollingshead and Frederick C. Redlich, *Social Class and Mental Illness* (New York: Wiley, 1958), pp. 66–135.

6. C. Wright Mills, *White Collar* (New York: Oxford University Press, 1951), pp. 21–22.

7. Reinhard Bendix and Seymour M. Lipset, eds., *Class, Status, and Power* (New York: The Free Press of Glencoe, 1953).

8. Arnold Rose, *Theory and Method in the Social Sciences* (Minneapolis: University of Minnesota Press, 1954), pp. 50–71.

9. W. Lloyd Warner and Paul S. Lunt, *The Social Life of a Mod-*

*ern Community* (New Haven: Yale University Press, 1942); A. B. Hollingshead, *Elmtown's Youth* (New York: Wiley, 1949); C. Wright Mills, *The Power Elite;* Floyd Hunter, *Community Power Structure,* and *Top Leadership, U.S.A.* (Chapel Hill: University of North Carolina Press, 1953 and 1959); and Robert S. and Helen M. Lynd, *Middletown in Transition* (New York: Harcourt, Brace, 1937).

10. Wendell Bell, Richard J. Hill, and Charles R. Wright, *Public Leadership* (San Francisco: Chandler, 1961), pp. 196–216.

11. Robert A. Dahl, *Who Governs? Democracy and Power in an American City* (New Haven: Yale University Press, 1961); Linton C. Freeman and others, *Local Community Leadership* (Syracuse, New York: Syracuse University, University College, 1960); and Scott Greer, *The Emerging City* (New York: The Free Press of Glencoe, 1962), pp. 151–163.

12. Scott Greer, *The Emerging City,* pp. 155–156.

13. David Riesman, in collaboration with Reuel Denney and Nathan Glazer, *The Lonely Crowd* (New Haven: Yale University Press, 1950), pp. 234–239.

# · XII ·

## The Government of Cities

### Types of Urban Governments

If upper classes have power but do not rule cities, and the many groups which compete for power frustrate each other in exercising it, they imperil urban governments and weaken their performance of municipal functions. Government politics both involves a struggle for power and institutionalizes group conflicts. This is a normal part of political life. This struggle is never absent from cities, although its intensity varies. It is greater in large cities in which the powers of government are greater also.

From a legal point of view, cities are municipal corporations created by the states to serve as local governments. They have only such powers as the states grant them, which their legislatures may alter or revoke at will. As local governments, cities have traditionally exercised municipal powers to provide numerous public services for their inhabitants, including streets and roads, water supply, sewage disposal, fire and police protection, and schools. In recent decades, they have added tens and hundreds of new functions in government, protection of persons and property, health, sanitation, highways, public welfare, hospitals, corrections, education, parks and recreation, and municipally owned corporations.[1]

While urban governments are local and limited in powers, they nevertheless provide social services which affect the activities of urban dwellers in crucial ways. The people are compelled, therefore, to take an interest in their municipalities and to exercise their rights and duties as citizens. Through their political activities, they elect the officials of cities and share in managing the governments under which they live. But they also strive to get new or improved social services from urban governments which they deem essential to their existence or which improve their standards of living. To the extent that they succeed in these demands, they make municipal governments even more important, converting them into small welfare states after the model of the state and federal governments.

More specifically, various groups of citizens form organizations to influence urban governments to undertake specific projects: improved streets, more schools, larger welfare payments, neighborhood parks, extended water mains, zoning ordinances, more public housing, urban renewal projects, and other services. Or, more likely, they press for certain services for themselves but deny them to other groups which threaten their interests. Other groups organize to resist increases in taxes or increased tax valuations, or to maintain stable property values in neighborhoods, or to ensure good government and efficient performance of public services. These groups represent many occupational and industrial groups and all economic classes, except perhaps the lowest in urban populations. The political struggle among them is basically economic in character: they attempt through their organizations to protect or promote their economic interests and to use urban government for their own purposes.[2]

Urban governments respond to these group pressures when it is possible. Their public officials want, in the main, to make cities more livable for inhabitants and more attractive for business and industry and to administer their offices and duties efficiently. Therefore they accede to some groups and deny others, add new services and amend others. In deciding among alternatives, they consider their probable costs and effect on tax levies and municipal budgets, as well as the number and relative strength of the groups that advocate them. For these reasons, their decisions are political as well as administrative. Public officials tend to favor one economic group or another, thus affecting the balance of power which exists among them. At the same time, they try to enlarge their own powers and to win a political following. As politicians, they acquiesce to strong groups more and to weak groups less; but they strive to work compromises among them, and to pursue policies which most or at least many want.

How well urban officials perform their public duties depends on the political organization of cities. On its formal side, the organization comprises their types of government, municipal charters, hierarchies of offices and agencies, administrative bureaucracies, extent of powers, and relations with state legislatures. It includes also their tax structures and restrictions on indebtedness, which determine their finances and hence capacities to pay the costs of governments. Political organization involves urban politics and the conflict of political parties, as well as the election of mayors and other officials and the political leadership they provide.

At present, there are three types of municipal government in American cities, the mayor-council, city commissioner, and council-manager forms of government. Of these, the mayor-council type predominates in the United States, although less now than formerly. Of 3,011 cities with 5,000 inhabitants or more in 1962, 1622 cities, or 53.9 percent, had the mayor-council form of government (see Table XII). It is especially popular in large cities with 500,000 inhabitants or more and in small cities with 5,000 to 10,000 inhabitants. The commission form, introduced in Galveston, Texas, in 1900 and adopted by more than 500

## TABLE XII

Types of government of cities with 5,000 inhabitants or more in the United States, 1962

| Number of inhabitants | Number of * cities | Mayor-council | | Commission | | Council-manager | |
|---|---|---|---|---|---|---|---|
| | | Number | Percent | Number | Percent | Number | Percent |
| 500,000 and over | 20 | 16 | 80 | 0 | 0.0 | 4 | 20.0 |
| 250,000–500,000 | 30 | 13 | 43.4 | 5 | 16.7 | 12 | 40.0 |
| 100,000–250,000 | 80 | 31 | 38.8 | 10 | 12.5 | 39 | 48.7 |
| 50,000–100,000 | 190 | 69 | 36.3 | 24 | 12.6 | 97 | 51.1 |
| 25,000–50,000 | 392 | 137 | 34.8 | 50 | 12.7 | 205 | 52.5 |
| 10,000–25,000 | 1,015 | 495 | 48.8 | 104 | 10.2 | 416 | 41.0 |
| 5,000–10,000 | 1,284 | 861 | 67.0 | 66 | 5.1 | 357 | 27.8 |
| All cities over 5,000 inhabitants | 3,011 | 1,622 | 53.9 | 259 | 8.6 | 1,130 | 37.5 |

SOURCE: *Municipal Year Book, 1962* (Chicago: International City Managers' Association, 1962), p. 100.

* Of 3,054 cities with populations over 5,000, 43 cities did not respond to inquiries for information, or were excluded from the analysis for other reasons.

cities after World War I, has declined in importance since then; only 259 cities, or 8.6 percent, had commissioners in 1962. First tried at Roanoke, Virginia, in 1908, the council-manager plan continues to spread among American cities, and predominates in cities with populations between 25,000 and 250,000 inhabitants: 1,130 cities, or 37.5 percent, had this form of government in 1962.

Mayor-council governments are classified into weak and strong mayor-council types, reflecting the relative status of the mayor's office and the separation of functions and powers among mayor, council, and other officials. In the weak mayor form, the mayor is the main executive officer but has limited authority to supervise administration of city officers and of ordinances and does not prepare a budget. The council is the legislative body, but its members also have administrative duties which they usually exercise through committees. The council often appoints such officials as city attorney, city engineer, and controller, unless they are elected at the polls. This type of government, carried to an extreme in the nineteenth century, predominates in small cities, but some large cities, Minneapolis, for example, also have it.

In the strong mayor-council type, which large cities tend to adopt, the mayor has powers which make him the political leader of his administration. He appoints and removes department heads, prepares and administers the budget, and commonly has the right to veto statutes passed by the council. The council continues as a law-making group, but is largely removed from administration except for occasional inquiries into some municipal office or agency.

Commission forms of government comprise elected commissioners who serve collectively as a legislative body and individually administer the departments of cities. Usually the commissioners are five in number. One serves as mayor and performs executive and ceremonial functions of office.

Council-manager governments have councils which have the sole legislative and executive authority. They hire and supervise city managers, who administer the urban departments. Councils vary from five to nine members who are commonly elected at large on a non-partisan ballot. They elect a mayor from their own number, but he performs only ceremonial functions. City managers are professional municipal administrators who direct the activities of government as trained experts.

In practice, no two cities, even within the same class, are exactly alike in their forms of government. They have various legacies of municipal policies and practices and have improvised others to meet their contemporary needs. Also state legislatures have dealt with them differently, and sometimes quixotically, and there is a wide array of offices and powers to carry on municipal activities. Since cities are the creatures of state governments, and there are fifty state legislatures controlling American cities, there is considerable diversity among them. Cities also have independent or semi-independent boards and special districts which provide some public services apart from the mayor and council. These are variously school, library, park, recreation, welfare, and other boards. Some have elected, others appointed, officials. School boards usually have taxing powers, and other boards have relative autonomy once their budgets are set. State or federal governments rather than urban officials sometimes supervise or finance their activities. Urban governments are neither uniform nor monolithic in the United States.

But there is greater conformity among them as more and more cities adopt the strong mayor-council and especially the council-manager forms of government. Middle-sized cities have favored the council-manager plan presumably because it makes rational use of professional administrators and reduces political influence in government. Often cities have populations which are relatively homogeneous or at least lack serious class conflicts. Some cities are dominated by business classes to whom the management of cities by trained persons recommends itself. Only four cities with populations which exceed 500,000 inhabitants have city managers. Large cities have, in general, preferred a strong mayor-council plan of government because strong mayors give them a political leadership of which city managers are incapable. But such cities have sometimes also provided for deputy or assistant mayors, who are appointed officials trained in municipal administration and perform functions comparable to those of a city manager.[3]

Whatever their forms of government, most cities utilize bureaucratic practices of municipal administration and improve their operations with recent innovations in government. Among these is the use of budgets of planned revenues and expenditures, prepared by the finance department under supervision of mayor, city manager, or city council. Another is the hiring of municipal employees under a merit system based on technical and professional qualifications with a personnel office to administer a civil service system. The adoption of city planning departments and the programming of capital expenditures is a third innovation. Finally, half of the states have provided cities with some measure of home rule or the power to conduct their municipal affairs without state interference, although the courts have construed this power narrowly.

In matters of finance, cities have not progressed comparably. They are confronted by rising costs for public services but insufficient revenues to pay for them. At present, about three fourths of tax revenues of cities come from real estate taxes levied on buildings and land, hence taxes paid by home owners and by business and industrial firms. Other sources of revenue for cities are federal and state grants-in-aid, taxes collected by states and remitted to cities, and fees collected for public utilities and other services. Some cities have taxed payrolls or incomes and seek still other sources of taxable income; but invariably federal and state governments already tax these items, and taxpayers resent an additional levy.

## Governments in Metropolitan Areas

Any discussion of urban governments must take into account their metropolitan areas and the burdens which the grouping of cities and the large scale of urban agglomeration impose on them. Their organization, activities, and politics are enormously affected by whether they are central or suburban cities and by the kinds of people and the mixtures of economic enterprises which they have. Central cities face aggravated problems and increased demands for services which their own and the metropolitan populations make on them, but which their officials have limited powers and finances to handle and for which they lack authority outside their own jurisdictions. Similarly, suburban cities contend with conflicts arising from their situations in metropolitan areas and their restricted powers to deal with them.

In the growth of metropolitan areas, central cities lose a disproportionate number of the middle and upper classes but keep those of the lower class. The latter find living more difficult and have a greater need for welfare and other services but they also pay fewer taxes for them. As central cities age, their buildings and streets deteriorate, and they have great areas of slums which must be renewed or rehabilitated at nearly prohibitive expense. While their taxes continue to mount, their tax bases weaken because of the suburbanization of upper income families and the loss of business and industries to suburbs and metropolitan areas. While suburban populations reside in other cities, they commute to central cities to work or shop, using the city's streets and parking facilities, hospitals, parks, and schools, and increasing their need for police and fire protection, but not paying taxes in recompense for these services.

Although suburban cities profit from their symbiotic ties with central cities, they have problems of their own. Because many suburbs have grown rapidly in recent decades, they often lack adequate paved streets and roads, water supply, and public sewage disposal facilities, and because they have many families with young children, they need more schools, parks, libraries, and health facilities. Therefore they levy increasing taxes, which they assess principally against real property. Some suburbs are sufficiently wealthy or have a firm enough tax base to provide services in desired number and quality, but poorer suburbs, especially in the outer fringes of metropolitan areas, provide relatively few of them and perform them poorly.[4]

While central and suburban cities are integrated into metropolitan economies and communities, politically they exist as independent municipalities, with separate governments, their own officials, and limited jurisdictions. No cities have boundaries which even nearly coincide with the metropolitan areas in which they exist. In these areas cities perform same or similar public functions, thus duplicating them at high cost, uneven quality, and other waste. In services better provided on an areawide basis— planning, highways, and public utilities, for example— they cooperate with difficulty, if at all.

In the United States there are no metropolitan governments which govern a metropolitan area and provide services for its entire population. Indeed, metropolitan areas, which are a dominant feature of urbanization now, have no legal existence. The courts do not recognize them as political entities, nor are legislatures willing to consider them as ready for regional governments.

Not unification but multiplication of local governments occurs in metropolitan areas. Today such areas have a large number of cities, counties, townships, and villages, as well as school districts and nonschool special districts which are considered as local governments. City, county, and township often occupy the same land in metropolitan areas, although their boundaries do not coincide. What is more, school and special districts extend over the same areas, supplementing the municipalities in their functions. For these reasons, there are three and four layers of local government in some areas. Some local governments, moreover, extend into two and even three states.

As Table XIII shows, one in seven local governments in

TABLE XIII

Local governments in the United States
and in metropolitan areas, 1952

| Type of government | Number in United States | Number in metropolitan areas | Percent of U. S. total in metropolitan areas |
|---|---|---|---|
| All local governments | 116,694 | 16,210 | 13.9 |
| School districts | 67,346 | 7,864 | 11.7 |
| Other total | 49,348 | 8,346 | 16.9 |
| Counties | 3,049 | 256 | 8.4 |
| Townships | 17,202 | 2,328 | 13.5 |
| Municipalities | 16,778 | 3,164 | 18.9 |
| Nonschool special districts | 12,319 | 2,598 | 21.1 |

SOURCE: *Local Government in Metropolitan Areas* (Washington: Bureau of the Census, Governments Division, State and Local Government Special Studies No. 36, 1954), p. 2.

the United States was located in metropolitan areas in 1952. Their number in areas averaged 96. Populous areas had many more local governments than this: New York led with 1,071, and Chicago was next with 960. Philadelphia had 702 local governments; Detroit, 355; San

Francisco, 372; Minneapolis–St. Paul, 316; Los Angeles, 298; Cleveland, 136; and Boston, 114. Baltimore, a large city, had only 11 local governments, but Madison, a small city, had 292.[5]

Of local governments in the United States, the table shows that school districts and other special districts constituted a large proportion in metropolitan areas, 11.7 percent and 21.1 percent respectively. Such districts are accounted local governments because they have political organization, specified legal powers, and substantial administrative and financial independence with either elected or appointed officials, and are not merely parts of other governments. They exist to provide special public services which other local governments have been unable or unwilling to perform. Independent school districts which control elementary and secondary public education in the United States are well known. Other special districts less known to the public perform diverse services which include health and sanitation, protection to persons and property, road and non-road transportation facilities, public utilities, housing, natural resource and agricultural assistance, education, parks and recreation, cemeteries, and others. They are variable in their personnel, financial resources, areas, and legal powers, which suggest also their importance in cities and metropolitan areas.[6]

An important type of the special district is the metropolitan district, which provides a special service, sometimes a number of services, throughout the metropolitan area or in substantial sections of it. Over one fourth of metropolitan areas, more frequently the more populous ones, have one or more such districts, and their number is increasing in the country. They perform a large number and variety of activities which are of utmost importance to their metropolitan populations. Among their more frequent services are those concerned with water supply, sewage disposal, parks, and port facilities, but they variously own and operate airports, public housing, bridges, and transit facilities, furnish public health services, provide regional planning and a host of other services. Some districts are important governments with large budgets and labor forces, among which the Chicago Transit Authority and Port of New York Authority are well-known throughout the United States.[7]

Federal and state governments add to the multiplicity of governments and diffusion of political authority in cities and metropolitan areas. The federal government shares in the control and financing of some special districts, a number of which it has helped to establish as part of its welfare programs, and provides many other social services as well. Among special districts which benefit from its participation are public housing, urban renewal, metropolitan district planning, metropolitan airports, and other authorities. Its various programs include federal highway construction, hospital planning and construction, disaster relief, improvement of rivers, water pollution control, general welfare assistance, and civil defense. Their total number is large and impressive, and they contribute considerably to the solution of acute urban and metropolitan problems. They also involve expenditures of billions of dollars locally.[8]

State governments similarly carry on many activities in cities and metropolitan areas, some of which were enumerated earlier. Their largest contributions are to public schools, highway construction, hospitals and health, and public welfare, and are expended either through state agencies or grants-in-aid to local governments.

But despite the great importance of federal and state programs they have had certain shortcomings and have worked untoward effects on cities and metropolitan areas. In the last decades they were instituted as special district governments to deal with urban problems; now they exist as separate, autonomous organizations with their own officials and finances, and are concerned with their specialized functions. As a result, their efforts are not always coordinated and in metropolitan areas may even be at cross-purposes. Nor have their officials always been aware of or concerned with their impact on cities and areas. However, metropolitan areas have also failed to provide a unified local leadership and they have not had representatives to defend their interests before federal agencies in Washington.

Some examples of unanticipated consequences of federal programs have been: the promotion of tract housing in suburbs by the Federal Housing Authority; the impact, still largely in the future, of the federal highway program on cities and areas; and the effect of defense industries and military establishments on cities. State governments, too, have been slow to recognize the special problems of cities and areas. Their legislatures have lacked interest, funds, or authority to become much concerned with them.[9]

This profusion of local governments, with the added presence of federal and state government agencies, complicates the efforts of cities to perform their own services and to cooperate in services for their metropolitan areas. To prevent further fragmentation of local governments, and to enable them to act together to resolve their required problems, political scientists have proposed several reforms of local governments.

One remedy is for the central cities to annex some or all their suburban cities and villages and to provide them with one municipal government. In the nineteenth century many cities, as they grew in size, annexed their adjacent territories, but in the twentieth century fewer cities did so until after World War II. Since then, several hundred cities have annexed some territory and populations each year—a few of them, such as Atlanta, Dallas, Houston, and San Antonio, in considerable amount, but most other cities in small parcels of land. Most states, with the exception of Virginia, Texas, California, and Missouri, have laws which make such annexation difficult. Therefore it appears not to be a practicable solution to the multiplicity of local governments in metropolitan areas.

Another reform is the consolidation of cities and counties into a single government. Although this has been frequently proposed in recent years, only Baton Rouge and East Baton Rouge Parish have adopted it, in 1947. However there are thirty-six consolidated city-counties in the United States which were created in past decades. These include Baltimore, San Francisco, St. Louis, Denver, Philadelphia, New Orleans, New York City, Boston, Baton Rouge, and the twenty-seven first-class cities of Virginia.[10] Unless city and county contain most or all the metropolitan area, this plan has political defects. A variant form of it was adopted by Dade County, Florida, which includes Miami. There the county performs functions of local government under a city manager.

A third proposal is to combine local governments into a federal system, with a central government to provide main functions for cities and metropolitan areas and with local governments, which retain their autonomy, to perform local functions. No city has adopted this federal form of urban regional government, and none seems likely to at present.

The final proposal is to encourage the voluntary cooperation of local governments through contractual agreements to provide certain services for all of them. At present, some central and suburban cities enter into contracts with each other for common water supply, milk inspection, fire protection, health services, tax collection, and other services. These arrangements, with increased use of special districts and expansion of federal and state government activities, appear likely to increase in metropolitan areas.

## The Politics of Cities

Good organization is necessary but not sufficient to ensure the efficient administration of urban governments. The type of person who occupies the offices of government also influences the effectiveness with which they operate. While officials hold positions and fulfill roles according to the formal organization of government, they also perform their duties mindful of the politics of government and respond to political norms of conduct. They think and act politically because governments rest on political institutions, and their success as politicians determines their incumbency in office. The informal organization of government therefore affects the motivations of public officials and the quality of their performances in office.

In one sense, politics means the art of government: the control of government and administration of its affairs to fulfill public functions and to win elections in order to remain in office. In another sense, it signifies the struggle of persons and groups for wealth, prestige, and power through their participation in government and the use of political means to promote their interests. From both viewpoints, politics consists of the political activities which occur in democratic government. It includes elections, selection of candidates, political campaigns, pressure groups, voter activities, and, of course, politicians.

The politics of cities has reformed considerably since the late nineteenth century, when they reached a moral low in the country. Since then urban governments have improved their formal organization by adopting civil service, merit appointments, and budget controls. In addition, only some cities still have bosses or well-organized political machines, and perhaps none has officials who follow flagrantly a spoils system in political appointments to perpetuate their own power. For the most part, city officials handle their

public business honestly and do maintain standards in conducting their offices.

At present, there is much public sentiment to eliminate
politics from cities as unnecessary in local governments.
For this reason, many cities have adopted nonpartisan
elections to prevent candidates for office from identifying
with the major political parties: 63 percent of the cities
with 10,000 inhabitants or more had nonpartisan elections
in 1962. Moreover, 60 percent of such cities elected their
officials from the electorate at large rather than from
wards in a further effort to reduce political considerations
in their selection.[11] There has also been an outburst of
hostility against excessive use of political patronage from
the people who want to have government run with the
efficiency of business corporations and prefer public officials who are motivated by middle class moral values
rather than desire for self-aggrandizement.[12] Other evidence of public attitudes against politics comes from the
increasing number of cities that have adopted council-
manager forms of government to obtain a business rather
than a political management of their affairs.

But instead of removing politics from urban governments, these reforms merely restrain the excesses of politics, and separate the politics of cities from those of states
and the nation. In the conduct of municipal activities, city
officials make decisions which are partisan, therefore
political, in nature, even though they also consider the
efficient management and cost of these functions. Thus,
they levy taxes, fix budgets, determine public policies, or
take on new services, with main concern for the public
good but also to resolve the conflict of groups whose
economic interests are affected by their actions. Economic
groups and classes are inevitably pitted in a struggle with
each other for wealth and privilege, and often utilize the
powers of government to win prevalence for themselves.
Politics institutionalize the resolution of conflict among

groups and enable groups to influence government legitimately through their suffrage and political pressures.

The politics of cities vary with their size, economic types, and metropolitan areas. In big cities party organizations exist to nominate candidates, if possible to elect them to office, and to mobilize citizens in political activity. Thereafter elected officials, with their appointed subordinates and specialized labor forces of municipal employees, constitute the governments of cities and administer the duties of their offices. Mayor, council members, and heads of departments, having the authority of their offices, manage these activities as competently as they can. As heads of local government, mayors provide political leadership for their cities. But mayors and other officials are subject to pressures exerted by various groups of citizens which have organized to influence their political actions and are under the surveillance of newspapers and other nongovernmental groups. They tend consequently to fix on public policies and to conduct their duties by accommodating these groups and compromising their demands.

Pressure groups want special government services which promote or safeguard their economic interests: for example, street improvements, more schools, increased public housing, larger welfare expenditures, new zoning ordinances, and urban renewal projects. They organize to press their demands and to oppose those of other groups. Of pressure groups in cities, organized labor is the most numerous, but business groups are the most powerful.[13] Many urban industries are represented by pressure groups: banks and financial institutions, department and retail stores, public utilities, manufacturing groups, building contractors, transport companies, real estate groups, professional associations, theaters, hotels, and restaurants, liquor groups, and illegal occupations. Other business groups include the newspapers, radio and TV, Chambers of Commerce, and taxpayers associations. Religious and social subcommunities and specific associations within them, veterans associations, and organizations of municipal employees also constitute pressure groups. In large cities like New York, municipal employees are large, powerful groups which are organized into labor unions, public service unions, professional associations, and religious fraternities.[14] Various groups of property-owners form improvement associations to protect their interests in one or several specific projects. Finally, good government groups exert pressures to promote the general welfare of all or many of the people who reside in cities.

Only some pressure groups, such as the League of Women Voters and Citizens' Leagues, the latter variously named, are active continuously in urban politics in behalf of the programs which they advocate. Most groups organize to support or oppose specific matters which affect their interests. Scattered other groups, such as associations of property-owners, form to oppose, say, the invasion of Negroes into their neighborhoods or for some other purpose. Whether one or another group, or coalition of groups, prevails on city officials to accede to their demands depends on their importance, organization, public support, and other considerations. If business groups are well organized, not divided into factions among themselves, and alert to their common interests, they often are able to win their objectives. But frequently they cease activity after they have succeeded on an issue, or their pressures are intermittent. On particular issues, nearly any major group or combination of groups can press its demands successfully; but the composition of such groups seldom remains the same on a series of issues.[15]

In smaller cities pressure groups are much fewer in number and play less important roles in politics: business, manufacturers, and workers' associations are the principal ones among them. Urban dwellers are less divided into economic groups and classes in these cities, and de-

mand fewer services of local government. When they
want new or more services, they turn to county, state, or
federal governments as often as to their municipalities.
If they are sufficiently homogeneous in class and culture,
they often favor a council-manager form of government,
and entrust to trained persons the management of their
cities, from which they withdraw to some extent. But
politics is partisan in small cities, and elections often stir
citizens to excitement, and draw them to the polls to vote.

Political organizations, especially in the great cities, tend
to select candidates for office who belong to large subcommunities in order to give voting strength and balance to
their slates of candidates. Thus they pick Protestant,
Catholic, Jewish, and Negro candidates with the expecta-
tion that they will attract the bloc voting of their subcommunities. This practice does not preclude their selection of qualified candidates, but it tends to lessen the
likelihood of it. To the extent that it is pursued, it has
another outcome: public officials, as members of their
subcommunities, are likely to belong to middle status
groups and are inferior to the elite status groups of their
cities. Again, this status difference between officials and
prominent groups of citizens need not affect their performance of public duties, but it may do so.

Another effect is that higher status groups, although
with exceptions, find their election to office difficult, and
tend to withdraw from participation in urban government.
Still another effect, related to this one, is that many interested persons become active in state and national politics, but too seldom in urban government and politics.
Careers in city governments do not attract them, unless they
become city managers. Finally the apathy of citizens in local
government is considerable: from 30 percent to 40 percent
of eligible voters, or less, take part in municipal elections,
unless some particular local issue, or state and national

elections held at the same time and place, attracts them
to the polls in greater proportion.[16]

## NOTES

1. L. D. Upson, *The Growth of a City Government* (Detroit:
Bureau of Governmental Research, 1942).
2. William Anderson and Edward W. Weidner, *American City
Government* (New York: Holt, 1950, rev. ed.), p. 46.
3. Charles R. Adrian, "Recent Concepts in Large City Administration," *Urban Government*, edited by Edward C. Banfield (New
York: Free Press of Glencoe, 1961), pp. 441–453.
4. *Cf.* John C. Bollens, ed., *Exploring the Metropolitan Community* (Berkeley and Los Angeles: University of California Press,
1961), pp. 41–43.
5. *Local Government in Metropolitan Areas*, pp. 8–14.
6. John C. Bollens, *Special District Governments in the United
States* (Berkeley and Los Angeles: University of California Press,
1957), pp. 1–45.
7. Bollens, *Special District Governments in the United States*,
pp. 52–53, and 67–71.
8. Robert H. Connery and Richard H. Leach, *The Federal Government and Metropolitan Areas* (Cambridge: Harvard University
Press, 1960), pp. 5–6.
9. Connery and Leach, *The Federal Government and Metropolitan Areas*, pp. 199–200, and 209–220.
10. Victor Jones, in *The Future of Cities and Urban Redevelopment*, edited by Coleman Woodbury (Chicago: University of Chicago Press, 1953), p. 544.
11. *Municipal Year Book*, 1962, p. 103.
12. Frank J. Sorauf, "The Silent Revolution in Patronage," *Public
Administration Review*, XX (Winter, 1960), pp. 28–34.
13. Charles R. Adrian, *Governing Urban America* (New York:
McGraw-Hill, 1955), pp. 102–115 and p. 131; and Anderson and
Weidner, *American City Government*, pp. 45–53.
14. Wallace S. Sayre and Herbert Kaufman, *Governing New York
City* (New York: Russell Sage Foundation, 1960), pp. 75–76.
15. Sayre and Kaufman, *Governing New York City*, pp. 76–80;
and Charles Edward Merriam, *Chicago* (New York: Macmillan,
1929), pp. 90–133.
16. Coleman Woodbury, in *The Future of Cities and Urban Redevelopment*, edited by Coleman Woodbury (Chicago: University of
Chicago Press, 1953), pp. 688–689.

# · XIII ·

# *Cities Today and Tomorrow*

## The National Community

The thesis of this book is that cities constitute a particular organization of the human community. They are human aggregations which have an urban social order, culture, and institutions, and constitute complete societies. Their organization rests on the economic bases of commerce and industry and on the cultural bases of government, family, education, religion, and other institutions. This organization permits heterogeneous people to dwell in cities, and to cooperate in a division and specialization of labor which makes them highly interdependent. Cities were the form of human association which enabled men to advance from Paleolithic savagery and Neolithic barbarism to urban cultures and then to world civilizations.

Now, we believe, men have reached a higher level of community, the national community, and are groping toward an international community; and, while they hold on to urban communities, they have reduced cities to urban agglomerations of inferior status and weakened their historical character and cultural roles in societies. In

some sense, the national community, at its present stage
of development, represents a culmination of the growth of
nation-states which began in Europe five hundred years
ago. It signifies that the peoples of western countries have
become nations in fact through their attainment of common cultures, single languages, similar historical traditions, and sentiments of nationalism and nationality. As
nations, they compose national communities.

In the United States, the national community denotes
the whole American society and the existence of the people as a nation. It embraces them as Americans who
have fused into a national population despite their diverse
ethnic origins and some remaining cultural differences.
They are citizens of the United States attached to its
institutions of government, capitalism, Christianity and
Judaism, education, and family. While they dwell in fifty
states spread over a vast territory, they speak the same
language and have a common nationality. They take part
in the national affairs of their nation, and have common
concern for its welfare and security. For these reasons, they
move about in American society with relative ease and have
a remarkable social and cultural uniformity in the cities,
villages, and farms of the country.

Today American society is sometimes called a mass
society. The connotation is pejorative, but it adds to the
meaning of the national community. Its import is that the
masses have arisen in modern societies and take larger
part in their social life and cultural activities, as well as
have greater benefit of their civilizations. They are no
longer an inert, illiterate, servile, underlying stratum but
rather common people who want uncommon privileges
which the upper classes have hitherto monopolized for
themselves. Today they are free workers, educated, exercise the vote, enjoy civil rights, have improved standards
of living, and aspire to mobility. They have advanced because of the enormous progress which the United States

has made in the last century as revealed in the mass production of economic goods and services, mass education, mass media of communication, mass transportation, mass sports, and still other mass activities.

For most persons, these developments signify a widening of democracy and increased equality of opportunity in their societies. But to upper classes, faced by the mobility of the masses, they imply an assault on their entrenched positions and status pretensions. Therefore they stigmatize these developments as identified with large-scale organizations, deterioration of public and private standards of behavior, imposition of the public taste on the arts, and possible manipulation of the masses by political leaders. The derisive implication of "mass society" arises from their charges against it.

Although this book has not explicitly discussed the national community in the United States, which requires its own separate and competent treatment, it has indicated something of its nature in the analysis of American society and in the history of its people and cities. The social organization of the American national community is associational, or *Gesellschaft*, characterized by a multiplicity of specialized organizations with differentiated institutions which carry on highly diversified activities. Economic and political institutions predominate in its social order; military, educational, family, and religious institutions also are important. Other familiar features of American society are bureaucratic administration, the welfare state, professionalization of occupations, the scientific revolution, and religious and racial subcommunities. All these facets of the national community suggest its infinite variety and complexity.

We have also discussed the important role of the federal government in American society. It steadily increases the number, kind, and magnitude of its activities, influencing the society and the people in innumerable ways. Its exercise of powers of state in legislation, foreign policy, military defense, and the courts is apparent enough; but its part in regulating the economy, accelerating scientific technology, subsidizing education, welfare agencies, and hospitals, and rebuilding cities is also of enormous consequence. The national economy is of comparable significance in the life of cities.

Since most Americans live in cities and municipal governments are important and expensive, cities are politically significant in the national community. As urban communities, however, cities are incapable of mobilizing urban dwellers or guiding their energies into activities which build nations and civilizations. While they have cultures which provide inhabitants with a total human existence, the function of culture creation has passed to the national community, or, more specifically, to creative persons, subcommunities, and organizations in it. The national community determines the progress of the American people today.

## Cities in the National Community

While their roles have lessened in the national community, cities have not disappeared, nor are they doomed to. Indeed, the opposite is true; they continue to grow in number and size. Great cities exist in all sections of the country, while the urbanized proportion of the population increases steadily. Moreover, the people amass in regional agglomerations, and enlarge the scale of urbanization. In addition, as agricultural productivity expands, farm populations thin out in the rural territories. Their younger generations migrate to cities and assimilate to urban populations. A society is surely addicted to cities when 70 percent of its people live in them and another 18 percent in villages and hamlets are removed from the soil, which is the urban condition in the United States today.

There are two significant reasons for such vigorous, and even relentless, urbanization. One is that human beings require some local group in which to dwell and multiply on this earth; and cities, and not villages or other agglomerations, are the local group in modern societies. In urban groups, people can have collective strength, economic subsistence, orderly living, family life, the company of friends and associates, social and cultural opportunities, and other satisfactions of community. They also find personal identity and social security in cities, become attached to them, cherish things or activities which are familiar in them, and sink their roots deep, as it were, in the urban soil. In sum, they enjoy a total human existence in cities, which gives them some fundamental sense of meaning and continuity in their lives.

Cities are local groups prevalent in modern societies because they have a social organization which is kindred to that of the national community. Their organizations are, again, associational in character, but based on sets of institutions whose number, grouping, and rank order differ and create different kinds of communities. Nevertheless they sustain similar modes of life and types of social relations, and thus mutually support each other. People move easily between urban and national communities and experience little constraint or conflict of interest in their activities in one or the other of them.

Despite their continued vitality, the utility of cities is impaired in the national community because the national and not the urban community orders the lives and events of the people. Within the national community, a great host of autonomous organizations caters to their specialized needs in the institutional spheres of existence. In some sense, cities now exist more as urban places than as urban groups. They are human agglomerations, concentrations of business and industry, vast clutches of habitations, masses of buildings and ganglia of streets. They constitute an urban stage of life, as it were, in which the people have a civilized existence. Whether urban dwellers actually succeed in this, or lead lives of quiet desperation, depends more on the national than on the urban community, and on the troubles of the times.

If this conception is valid, cities serve three principal purposes in the national community today. One is their economic function as the workshops of the nation: they are urban and metropolitan places of business and industry; the location of markets, banks and other financial agencies, transportation and storage facilities, stores and offices, media of communication; and centers of large, highly specialized labor forces.

But cities are more than places of economic production; they contain masses of consumers whose earned income provides them a vast purchasing power to acquire economic goods and services. Since the people want the luxuries as well as necessities of life, they stimulate the growth of tertiary businesses and industries whose goods and services give a civilized quality to urban existence today. To individuals and families, cities mean, in these terms, places of employment, specialized occupations, economic acquisition, access to cultural opportunities which money affords, and job and career mobility.

Cities also have a political function. They have municipal governments which affect the lives and activities of urban dwellers more intimately and continuously than do state and federal governments. Governments make cities livable by providing essential public services, and keeping law and order in them. They enable the people to act collectively in the activities which they cannot accomplish privately. The residents of cities are never remote from urban governments for even one hour of the day.

The third service of cities is social and cultural: they provide their inhabitants with an urban society, and make a civilized life possible for them. They contain stores, offices, hotels, and restaurants, colleges and universities, churches and cathedrals, great newspapers and periodicals, movies and theaters, art galleries, and musical organizations. Thus they are centers of learning, religious centers, places of commercial entertainment, the home of innumerable organizations, places of mass communication, and the location of organized sports. In cities only, indeed, can the people enjoy the highest thought and achievement of their societies and savor the other riches of modern civilization; the legion of the poor, to stay abreast the stream of culture at all, cannot afford to live elsewhere.

## The Metropolitan Community

The majority of Americans live today in metropolitan areas, in which they enjoy the social and economic, if not the political, advantages of cities on an enlarged scale. In such areas, cities exist in a metropolitan economy in which their business and industries are specialized in their economic activities and enormously productive. The metropolitan population comprises a diversified labor force which commutes to work throughout the region, and a body of consumers of economic goods and services. To some extent, the cities cooperate through public authorities or special districts to provide public services on a metropolitan basis to some or all the people. The urban world of many city dwellers is thus a metropolitan world, in which they have livelihoods made possible by their agglomeration and collective enterprise.

Because the cities of metropolitan areas are economically interrelated, and their inhabitants are unified socially and culturally, metropolitan areas compose metropolitan communities. At present, such communities are largely nascent because metropolitan areas have grown too rapidly and so recently that their populations are not integrated in metropolitan communities. Indeed, central and suburban populations are often hostile to each other. Another reason for the slow development of metropolitan communities is that the cities of such areas are independent municipalities with their own governments and public services, which tends to keep their citizens apart from one another. A third reason is that metropolitan populations are heterogeneous, and do not readily fuse into communities.

While metropolitan communities are important, they do not represent a new form of community or a novel reorganization of human life and activities. They have no institutions which portend any major social or cultural changes in the society. Rather they represent urban communities at their present magnitude in the national community.

But to many Americans, accustomed to independent, free-standing cities, metropolitan areas appear as new phenomena because they are great clusters of cities spread over urbanized areas, in which the autonomy of individual cities is obscured or lost. Moreover they seem novel because they are massive urban agglomerations which magnify the problems of cities and complicate the lives and activities of urban dwellers on a scale never before known. Yet great cities have always expanded into their countrysides. The modern aspect of this is that outlying settlements resist annexation to central cities. But the magnitude of metropolitan areas does aggravate human difficulties, creating some fresh sense of predicament.

Metropolitan cities bear the heavy burdens of metropolitan areas. If many of them are now declining in size, as the 1960 census suggests, it is the congestion, the inconvenience, and the high cost of living or doing business in them which make people leave. These cities also suffer from inadequate and inept government and are saddled with the social problems of their populations, who are, in large part, racial and ethnic minorities.

Suburban cities have not suffered comparable hardships —for one thing because they are newer, for another because their populations belong to higher social and economic groups than inhabitants of metropolitan cities and thus create fewer social problems. The problems which suburban cities do have are increased taxes resulting from large expenditures for public utilities, new schools, streets and highways, and other facilities needed by rapidly growing populations. Many cities have sought new industries to widen their tax bases in order to pay for these public improvements, but doing so has created new problems. Since suburban dwellers must commute from home to place of work or other destination, the problems of traffic congestion, highways, parking, and railroad travel are endemic in cities of metropolitan areas.

The problems of metropolitan cities and their areas belong to the whole society. They are national problems, not just urban ones. Since most Americans are urbanized, however, they feel the distresses caused by these disorders more acutely in cities, and in ways specifically related to their urban activities.

The first major national study of cities by a federal government agency recognized that urban problems were national ones. It identified the important problems of urban communities as follows: poverty and unemployment, with drastic inequalities of income and wealth; unstable urban economies; obsolescence of physical plan and plant of cities; inadequate control over transportation; uncontrolled subdivision and speculation in urban land; substandard housing and slums; dangers to public health; ethnic, religious, and cultural heterogeneity in urban populations; inadequate facilities for vocational, higher, and adult education; increased juvenile delinquency, organized crime, and commercial rackets; urban public finance; legal control of higher political authorities; overlapping medley of independent government units never intended for sprawling metropolitan regions; and insufficient government leadership and responsibility.[1]

Commenting on the last two problems, the Urbanism Committee discussed the desirability of modernizing urban governments:[2] this touches on the next matter, which is whether metropolitan areas should have single governments. Neither the Committee nor political scientists advocate such central governments, but they recognize that the many local governments and special districts which exist in metropolitan areas create high costs, duplicate municipal services, and reduce efficiency and quality of performance in public office. Many municipalities frustrate cooperation in public projects and policy planning necessary to metropolitan areas, and they compete also for industries or other advantage among themselves.

But many urban populations do not conceive of metropolitan areas as communities, and they are not convinced of the desirability of metropolitan governments. Some central city dwellers are indifferent, apathetic, or uninformed about metropolitan areas; their public officials oppose metropolitan governments because of the threat to their own political careers; public opinion is largely opposed to consolidation of governments. No more do suburban populations want metropolitan governments, which they tend to identify with the governments of the central cities, or at least believe that regional governments will be dominated by politicians of the central cities. Many suburban cities employ professional city managers who administer their governments efficiently. Hence their citizens would regard a possible merger of central and suburban cities into regional governments as a regression.

Nonetheless, cities of metropolitan regions are functionally interrelated and likely to become even more so as their agglomerations increase. As their problems multiply, they will be, most likely, compelled to find more ways to cooperate, and they will have to consider the feasibility of metro-

politan governments. If urban communities are much
reduced in importance in the national community, then the
attachment of urban dwellers to individual cities will
diminish. In this case, they may well prefer regional governments capable of providing municipal services and managing highway, school, and other activities efficiently. If
rationality and secularity of thought characterize Americans, then they eventually must show these qualities in
their organization of metropolitan governments. Should the
prospect of such governments continue to frighten some of
them, the example of New York City, with its vast metropolitan government, demonstrates that such governments
function relatively well. State governments, in any case,
will continue to have control over them.

## Planning

The city planners' aim is to rehabilitate the urban community by making cities habitable. This is the purpose behind their projects to rehabilitate central business districts, eliminate slums, provide new housing, reduce traffic
congestion on streets and highways, rehabilitate obsolete
structures, rebuild neighborhoods, and improve amenities
in cities. They hope by these means to hold or attract business and industries, improve residential sections, lure population back from suburbs, and, in general, enhance the social and cultural life of cities. At present, vast federal funds
are being poured into urban renewal projects and housing
programs to accomplish these purposes. The business community and real estate firms, which have large investments
in buildings and land, ordinarily applaud these activities,
even though they do not approve of the intervention of the
government in other activities of cities.

Planners struggle to reinvigorate urban communities by
augmenting centralization of population in cities: they fos-
ter larger urban agglomerations, increased densities of settlement, compact and contained cities, stable property

values, and central business districts renewed as the heart of cities. They hope that greater aggregation and circulation of urban dwellers, as well as improved physical conditions of existence, will lead to better social relations and an enrichment of their cultural lives, and hence to greater sense of civic patriotism among them.

Not all planners concur in these objectives. Some advocate the opposite policy of urban decentralization: the dispersion of urban dwellers into small planned cities in metropolitan areas, where they might enjoy the combined advantages of urban and rural residence and have sufficient numbers to support cultural activities. In such more pleasant places, urban dwellers, they hope, will live and work amiably, have stable families, participate in urban activities, and, once more, be able to respond to nature. Many of these planners belong to the garden city movement, whose planning principles, if not its ideology, are firmly implanted in the practices of all planners.

Endeavors which attempt to restore the urban community are destined to fail. Now the national community is paramount, and it engrosses the energies and interests of the people. Urban communities are shells of their former being which cannot be restored by physical means. It is principally social and cultural institutions which shape the communities of men; while physical environment affects them too, its role is always secondary.

This does not mean that planners should cease their efforts to rebuild cities, but only that they should not aspire to work a social revolution through a return of the urban community. Clearly their present activities are needed in both cities and metropolitan areas and, indeed, should be augmented. But the repair of cities and sound guidance of their growth are more than enough to tax their utmost ingenuity. They should evaluate their activities by whatever criteria they desire, whether social, economic, or political, and achieve such reforms as are within their reach.

However modest their projects are, city planners expend large outlays of public funds, raising the issue of the relation of cities to state and federal governments. The federal government, in its rôle as administrator of a welfare state, contributes heavily to the costs of urban renewal, public housing, and slum clearance projects in cities; it finances the federal highway program; it pays for public buildings, school buildings, and hospitals; it contributes to public assistance programs, and to alleviating other private and public distress. In some cases it contributes outright gifts of money; in other cases it makes long-term loans at attractive rates of interest. It also contributes to projects which require state or local governments to match federal funds in some ratio. It retains responsibility to supervise how tax moneys are expended and stipulates standards of performance.

The federal government recognizes the national importance of particular city problems, and has established the appropriate public agencies to administer its welfare programs and to disperse appropriations. Sooner or later, these are likely to be assembled in a department of urban affairs in the President's cabinet. In this process the government has also made cities its creatures. City officials must turn to Washington for public funds to finance their projects; their own revenues are nearly always deficient in relation to the size of their problems. Moreover, they appeal to federal agencies for loans or grants for local distresses, increases in public assistance allotments, contracts for local industries, or other forms of aid.

In these appeals to Washington, urban officials circumvent their state governments, although never completely so. They ask for help from state governments less often, however, because state legislatures are often not willing to accede to their requests, or do so in a grudging way. Legislatures have tended to control cities negatively by restricting their powers to act for themselves, rather than by assuming the initiative and helping them with their problems. In part, this has been due to rural domination of state legislatures. Also, the states have themselves lacked funds to help the cities in their jurisdictions. However, the states have more recently assumed some responsibility in these matters: they collect taxes, for example, on a statewide basis and distribute some part of them to their cities, to the considerable benefit of the latter.

As cities depend more on federal and state governments and less on themselves, the urban community continues to be weakened in the United States.

## The Comparative Study of Cities

In this book we have compared urban organization in the cities of Mesopotamia, Rome, medieval Europe, and America, at different times and in different cultures. This method of cross-cultural study employs historical evidence to discover the processes of the growth of cities over the course of time. It permits generalizations about the cities of particular peoples or periods of time, as well as of cities in general.

But cross-cultural studies may also be made of contemporaneous cities. Either the cities of a single country or the cities of two or more countries are compared for whatever social, cultural, or political traits are desired. Existing cities may be investigated in considerable detail, with use of several research methods to test a number of hypotheses. Often the findings are highly empirical in nature and can be evaluated statistically. Both the ecological and demographic methods of investigation are useful for cross-cultural studies of this kind.

With underdeveloped countries in process of rapid urbanization and industrialization, there is particular urgency today for investigation of modern cities. In Africa, Asia, and South America, increased proportions of urbanized populations are now making the transition from village communities to national communities, bypassing the stage of urban communities which European societies underwent. As they attain national communities, they face the same economic, political, and cultural changes which western peoples experienced in the last centuries, but at a more rapid speed. Their rate of urbanization, indicating the acceleration of cultural progress in their countries, is a matter of extreme gravity to all the nations of the world as well.[3]

The study of world cities permits a wider comparative study of urban organization in countries whose peoples and civilizations differ from those of the United States and Europe. Their cities also vary from American cities, which have been treated as ideal-typical of western cities. Therefore the generalizations made about them will apply to nonwestern cities only in part. The extent to which they do apply should be known.

Recent studies indicate how greatly cities in Africa and Asia differ in aspects of their social organization from cities in western countries.[4] A wide variation occurs in African cities. Some cities built and inhabited by Europeans resemble European and American cities but native African cities, a few of which are large in size, are more like overgrown villages. Their economic base is agriculture, and clans and tribes persist as subcommunities, contesting with municipal and national governments in political matters.

Muslim cities in North Africa reflect the Arab civilization of their inhabitants. In southeastern Asian countries, one great city, which is the political capital also, often contains more than a half of the entire urban population. The bulk of the people are rural, dwell in agricultural villages, and follow tribal cultures. This urban imbalance is increased when wars, natural catastrophes, or other disasters ravage the rural peoples, some of whom thereupon migrate to the capital city in hope of employment or public assistance. Seoul, Korea, and Cairo, Egypt, with estimated populations of 1,574,868 and 2,650,000 in 1955 respectively, illustrate this over-urbanization in countries economically incapable of supporting them.[5] In Indian cities, the growth of modern industries has led to the declining importance of castes in their social organization.

Because world cities differ in many ways, it helps to classify before analyzing them. However the ideal types of cities used in this book are inadequate for that purpose; other classes of cities, probably based on their empirical traits, must be devised. But this should not be too difficult. Since these are existing cities, we can discover those essential characteristics which will provide the means to classify them. In scientific research, scholars are accustomed to construct classes of phenomena which aid their research operations in some practical manner; useful categories of cities may be similarly devised.

In this book, the use of ideal types of cities has served several purposes of analysis. First, it aids in the study of cities of the past, about whose social life and organization knowledge is deficient, or whose historical and cultural evience is fragmentary. Such hypothetical constructs as ideal types have a peculiar value when they classify human activities which are complex, insufficiently known, or obscure: they function in such cases to help an empirical analysis of the activities and to suggest hypotheses for investigation of them. Second, ideal types of cities provide a means to study social and cultural changes. Each type of city appeared in a period of history and was succeeded by another type of city when human societies achieved some major innovation in their social organization. In some sense, the use of ideal types is the sociologists' way of using historical evidence to deal with social and cultural change. Third, ideal types of cities signify important changes in their urban organization, with new or different sets of institutions predominant in their social order, and with different subcommunities likely to be in control of them.

The use of ideal types of cities has performed another service also. It has helped to explain cities as urban communities and has led to a larger appreciation of the various kinds of communities and their diverse forms of social organization. Consequently, the study of cities and societies as communities, and the comparative analysis of their social orders, appears to be a feasible and profitable method of investigating human agglomerations, and, indeed, all human life and endeavors. At present, sociologists, independently of their studies of cities, have a large and increasing knowledge of social organization, and have a body of theory, concepts, and research methods to pursue their inquiries of it. Thus they are capable of studying urban and national communities with some competence. They no longer need to use ideal types in their studies. Ideal types, their scientific mission fulfilled, may be discarded in the study of modern cities.[6]

## NOTES

1. *Our Cities. Their Role in the National Economy.* Report of the Urbanism Committee to the National Resources Committee (Washington: Government Printing Office, 1937), pp. viii–x, and 55–70.

2. *Ibid.,* pp. 48–52, 64–68, 79–81.

3. Philip M. Hauser, ed., *Urbanization in Asia and the Far East,* and *Urbanization in Latin America* (New York: Unesco Publications Center, 1957, 1962).

4. Michael Banton, *West African City* (London: Oxford University Press, 1957; A. L. Epstein, *Politics in an Urban African Community* (New York: Humanities Press, 1958); R. P. Dore, *City Life in Japan* (Berkeley: University of California Press, 1958).

5. International Urban Research, *The World's Metropolitan Areas* (Berkeley and Los Angeles: University of California Press, 1959), pp. 37 and 51; and T. C. Wilkinson, "The Pattern of Korean Urban Growth," *Rural Sociology* (19 March, 1954), 32–38.

6. Don Martindale, *The Nature and Types of Sociological Theory* (Boston: Houghton Mifflin, 1960, pp. 381–383.

# SELECTED BIBLIOGRAPHY

## I. *The Sociology of Cities*

Comhaire, Jean, and Werner J. Cahnman. *How Cities Grew: the Historical Sociology of Cities.* Madison, N. J.: Florham Park Press, 1959.

Fisher, Robert Moore, ed. *The Metropolis in Modern Life.* New York: Doubleday, 1955.

Fustel de Coulanges, Numa Denis. *The Ancient City.* Boston: Lee and Shepard, 1889.

Greer, Scott. *The Emerging City.* New York: Free Press of Glencoe, 1962.

Martindale, Don. *Social Life and Cultural Change.* Princeton, N. J.: Van Nostrand, 1962.

Mumford, Lewis. *The City in History.* New York: Harcourt, Brace, 1961.

Munro, William B. "The City," *Encyclopedia of the Social Sciences,* III, pp. 475–482.

Shevky, Eshref, and Wendell Bell. *Social Area Analysis.* Stanford: Stanford University Press, 1955.

Simmel, Georg. "The Metropolis and Mental Life," in *The Sociology of Georg Simmel.* Trans., Kurt H. Wolff. N. Y.: Free Press of Glencoe, 1950.

Sjoberg, Gideon. *The Preindustrial City.* New York: Free Press of Glencoe, 1960.

Sorokin, Pitirim A., C. C. Zimmerman, and J. C. Galpin. *Systematic Source Book in Rural Sociology.* Minneapolis: University of Minnesota Press, 1930. Vol. I.

Spengler, Oswald. *The Decline of the West.* New York: Knopf, 1928–1930. 2 vols.

Turner, Ralph. *The Great Cultural Traditions.* New York: McGraw-Hill, 1941. 2 vols.

Weber, Adna F. *The Growth of Cities in the Nineteenth Century.* Columbia University Studies in History, Economics, and Public Law, New York, 1899.

Weber, Max. *The City.* Trans. and ed. by Don Martindale and Gertrud Neuwirth. New York: Free Press of Glencoe, 1958.

Wheeler, Mortimer. *The Indus Civilization.* Cambridge: Cambridge University Press, 1953.

## II.  Cities of the Ancient World

Braidwood, Robert J., and Gordon R. Willey, eds. *Courses toward Urban Life*. Chicago: Aldine, 1962.

Braidwood, Robert J. *The Near East and the Foundations for Civilization*. Eugene, Ore.: Condon Lectures, Oregon State System of Higher Education, 1952.

Childe, V. Gordon. *Man Makes Himself*. London: Watts, 1936. *What Happened in History*. New York: Penguin Books, 1946.

Delaporte, L. *Mesopotamia. The Babylonian and Assyrian Civilization*. London: Kegan Paul, Trench, Trubner, 1925.

Frankfort, Henry. *The Birth of Civilization in the Near East*. London: Williams & Norgate, 1951.

Frankfort, H., H. A., and others. *The Intellectual Adventure of Ancient Men*. Chicago: University of Chicago Press, 1948.

Fustel de Coulanges, Numa Denis. *The Ancient City*. Boston: Lee and Shepard, 1889.

Jones, Tom Bard. *Ancient Civilization*. Chicago: Rand McNally, 1960.

Kramer, Samuel Noah. *From the Tablets of Sumer*. Indian Hills, Colo.: Falcon's Wing Press, 1956.

Morley, Sylvanus Griswold. *The Ancient Maya*. Stanford: Stanford University Press, 1946.

Sjoberg, Gideon. *The Preindustrial City*. New York: Free Press of Glencoe, 1960.

Turner, Ralph. *The Great Cultural Traditions*. New York: McGraw-Hill, 1941, vol. 1.

Wooley, Leonard. *Excavations at Ur*. London: Benn, 1954.


## III.  Cities of the Classical World

Abbott, Frank Frost, and Allan Chester Johnson. *Municipal Administration in the Roman Empire*. Princeton: Princeton University Press, 1926.

Bailey, Cyril, ed. *The Legacy of Rome*. Oxford, at the Clarendon Press, 1923.

Boak, Arthur E. R. *A History of Rome to 565 A.D.* New York: Macmillan, 1955, 4th ed.

Carcopino, Jerome. *Daily Life in Ancient Rome*. New Haven: Yale University Press, 1940.

Charlesworth, M. P. *The Roman Empire*. London: Oxford University Press, 1951.

Glotz, G. *The Greek City and Its Institutions*. New York: Knopf, 1930.

Jones, A. H. M. *The Cities of the Eastern Roman Provinces*. Oxford, at the Clarendon Press, 1937.

Jones, A. H. M. *The Greek City*. Oxford, at the Clarendon Press, 1940.

Moore, Frank Gardner. *The Roman's World*. New York: Columbia University Press, 1936.

Rostovtzeff, M. *The Social and Economic History of the Roman Empire*. Oxford, at the Clarendon Press, 1926.

Tarn, W. W., and G. T. Griffith. *Hellenistic Civilization*. London: Arnold, 1952, 3rd ed.

Turner, Ralph. *The Great Cultural Traditions*. New York: McGraw-Hill, 1941. vol. 2.

Wycherley, R. E. *How the Greeks Built Cities*. New York: Macmillan, 1949.


## IV.  *Cities of Medieval Europe*

Benson, Edwin. *Life in a Medieval City*. New York: Macmillan, 1920.

Bloch, Marc. *Feudal Society*. Trans., L. A. Manyon. University of Chicago Press, 1961.

Boissonnade, P. *Life and Work in Medieval Europe*. Trans., Eileen Power. New York: Knopf, 1927.

Hoyt, Robert S. *Europe in the Middle Ages*. New York: Harcourt, Brace, 1957.

Mumford, Lewis. *The Culture of Cities*. New York: Harcourt, Brace, 1938.

Mundy, John H. *Liberty and Political Power in Toulouse, 1050–1230*. New York: Columbia University Press, 1954.

——————, and Peter Riesenberg. *The Medieval Town*. New York: Van Nostrand, 1958.

Pirenne, Henri. *Medieval Cities*. Princeton: Princeton University Press, 1925.

Previte-Orton, C. W. *The Shorter Cambridge Medieval History*. Cambridge, at the Clarendon Press, 1952.

Taylor, H. O. *The Medieval Mind*. New York: Macmillan, 1925, 4th ed. 2 vols.

Thrupp, Sylvia L. *The Merchant Class of Medieval London* (1130–1500). Chicago: University of Chicago Press, 1948.

Tout, T. E. *Medieval Town Planning*. Manchester: Manchester University Press, 1934.

Weber, Max. *The City*. Trans. and ed. by Don Martindale and Gertrud Neuwirth. New York: Free Press of Glencoe, 1958.


## V.  *Cities of the Western World*

Ashton, T. S. *The Industrial Revolution*. London: Oxford University Press, 1948.

Barker, Ernest and others. *Golden Ages of the Great Cities*. London: Thames and Hudson, 1952.

Carr-Saunders, A. M. *World Population*. Oxford, at the Clarendon Press, 1936.

Clark, G. N. *The Seventeenth Century*. Oxford, at the Clarendon Press, 1929.

Day, Clive. *Economic Development in Europe*. New York: Macmillan, 1942.

Dickinson, Robert E. *The West European City*. London: Routledge & Kegan Paul, 1951.

Hammond, J. L., and Barbara Hammond. *The Rise of Modern Industry*. New York: Harcourt, Brace, 1926.

Heaton, Herbert. *Economic History of Europe*. New York: Harpers, 1948, rev. ed.

Heckscher, Eli F. *Mercantilism*. London: Allen and Unwin, 1935. 2 vols.

Kohn, Hans. *The Idea of Nationalism*. New York: Macmillan, 1944.

Mantoux, Paul. *The Industrial Revolution in the Eighteenth Century*. New York: Harcourt, Brace, 1927.

Tawney, R. H. *Religion and the Rise of Capitalism*. New York: Harcourt, Brace, 1926.

Weber, Adna F. *The Growth of Cities in the Nineteenth Century*. New York: Columbia University Studies in History, Economics, and Public Law, 1899.

Weber, Max. *General Economic History*. Trans., Frank H. Knight. New York: Greenberg, 1927.

## VI.    *The Growth of American Cities*

Bogue, Donald J. *Population Growth in Standard Metropolitan Areas, 1900–1950*. Washington: Housing and Home Finance Agency, 1953.

Bridenbaugh, Carl. *Cities in the Wilderness. The First Century of Urban Life in America, 1625–1742*. New York: Ronald Press, 1938.

———. *Cities in Revolt. Urban Life in America, 1743–1776*. New York: Knopf, 1955.

Bryce, James. *The American Commonwealth*. New York: Macmillan, 1896. 3rd ed., 2 vols.

Cochran, Thomas C., and William Miller, *The Age of Enterprise*. New York: Macmillan, 1942.

Fish, Carl Russell. *The Rise of the Common Man*. New York: Macmillan, 1927.

Gibbs, Jack P. *Urban Research Methods*. Princeton, N. J.: Van Nostrand, 1961.

Glaab, Charles N. *The American City*. Homewood, Ill.: Dorsey Press, 1963.

Gottman, Jean. *Megalopolis*. New York: Twentieth Century Fund, 1961.

Griffith, Ernest S. *History of American Government, The Colonial Period.* New York: Oxford University Press, 1938.

Hacker, Louis M. *The Triumph of American Capitalism.* New York: Columbia University Press, 1940.

Hawley, A. H. *The Changing Shape of Metropolitan America.* New York: Free Press of Glencoe, 1956.

McKelvey, Blake. *The Urbanization of America, 1860–1915.* New Brunswick, N. J.: Rutgers University Press, 1963.

Nettels, C. P. *The Roots of American Civilization.* New York: Crofts, 1938.

*Recent Social Trends.* Report of the President's Research Committee on Social Trends. New York: McGraw-Hill, 1933.

Reed, Henry Hope, and Christopher Tunnard. *American Skyline.* New York: New American Library, 1956.

Schlesinger, Arthur M. *The Rise of the City, 1878–1898.* New York: Macmillan, 1933.

Steffens, Lincoln. *The Shame of the Cities.* New York: Smith, 1904.

Strauss, Anselm. *Images of the American City.* New York: Free Press of Glencoe, 1960.

Thompson, Warren S. *The Growth of Metropolitan Districts in the United States, 1900–1940.* Washington: Government Printing Office, 1947.

Wade, Richard C. *The Urban Frontier.* Cambridge: Harvard University Press, 1959.

Weimer, David R., ed. *City and Country in America.* New York: Appleton-Century-Crofts, 1962.

Wright, Chester Wright. *Economic History of the United States.* New York: McGraw-Hill, 1949. 2nd ed.

## VII. *Economic Classes of Cities*

Alexandersson, Gunnar. *The Industrial Structure of American Cities.* Lincoln, Neb.: University of Nebraska Press, 1956.

Andrews, Richard B. *Urban Growth and Development.* New York: Simmons-Boardman, 1962.

Berger, Bennett M. *Working Class Suburb.* Berkeley and Los Angeles: University of California Press, 1960.

Bollens, J. C., ed. *Exploring the Metropolitan Community.* Berkeley and Los Angeles: University of California Press, 1961.

Chapin, F. Stuart, Jr., and Shirley F. Weiss, eds. *Urban Growth Dynamics in a Regional Cluster of Cities.* New York: Wiley, 1962.

Dobriner, William M., ed. *The Suburban Community.* New York: Putnam's, 1958.

Duncan, Otis Dudley, William Richard Scott, Stanley Lieberson, Beverly Davis Duncan, and Hal H. Winsborough. *Metropolis and Region.* Baltimore: Johns Hopkins Press, 1960.

Duncan, Otis Dudley, and Albert J. Reiss, Jr. *Social Characteristics of Urban and Rural Communities, 1950.* New York: Wiley, 1956.

Green, C. M. *American Cities in the Growth of the Nation.* London: De Graff, 1957.

Greer, Scott. *The Emerging City.* New York: Free Press of Glencoe, 1962.

Hoover, Edgar M., and Raymond Vernon. *Anatomy of a Metropolis.* Cambridge: Harvard University Press, 1959.

McKenzie, R. D. *The Metropolitan Community.* New York: McGraw-Hill, 1933.

Martin, Walter T. *The Rural-Urban Fringe.* Eugene, Ore.: Oregon University Press, 1953.

Mayer, Harold, and Clyde Kohn, eds. *Readings in Urban Geography.* Chicago: University of Chicago Press, 1958.

National Resources Committee, *Our Cities: Their Role in the National Economy.* Washington: Government Printing Office, 1937.

Perry, George Sessions. *Cities of America.* New York: McGraw-Hill, 1947.

Ogburn, W. F. *Social Characteristics of Cities.* Chicago: International City Managers' Association, 1937.

Solomon, Ezra, and Zark G. Bilbija. *The Economy of Metropolitan Chicago.* New York: Free Press of Glencoe, 1959.

Stein, Maurice R. *The Eclipse of Community.* Princeton: Princeton University Press, 1960.

Sussman, Marvin B., ed. *Community Structure and Analysis.* New York: Crowell, 1959.

Vernon, Raymond. *Metropolis 1985.* Cambridge: Harvard University Press, 1960.

West, Ray B., ed. *Rocky Mountain Cities.* New York: Norton, 1949.

Wood, Robert C. *Suburbia: Its People and Their Politics.* Boston: Houghton Mifflin, 1959.

### VIII. *Cities and the American Economy*

Bancroft, Gertrude. *The American Labor Force.* New York: Wiley, 1958.

Berle, A. A., Jr., and Gardiner C. Means. *The Modern Corporation and Private Property.* New York: Macmillan, 1933.

Bendix, Reinhard. *Work and Authority in Industry.* New York: Wiley, 1956.

Boulding, Kenneth E. *The Organizational Revolution.* New York: Harpers, 1953.

Calhoun, A. W. *A Social History of the American Family.* New York: Barnes & Noble, 1918, 1945.

Caplow, Theodore. *The Sociology of Work*. Minneapolis: University of Minnesota Press, 1954.

Colean, Miles L. *American Housing*. New York: Twentieth Century Fund, 1944.

Dimock, Marshall E. *Business and Government*. New York: Holt, 1957. 3rd edition.

Florence, P. Sargant. *The Logic of British and American Industry*. Chapel Hill: University of North Carolina Press, 1953.

Form, William H., and Delbert C. Miller. *Industry, Labor, and Community*. New York: Harpers, 1960.

Gross, Edward. *Work and Society*. New York: Crowell, 1958.

Mason, Edward S., ed. *The Corporation in Modern Society*. Cambridge: Harvard University Press, 1960.

Means, Gardiner C. *The Structure of the American Economy*. Washington: U.S. National Resources Committee, 1939, 1940.

Miller, D. R., and G. E. Swanson. *The Changing American Parent*. New York: Wiley, 1958.

Rossi, Peter M. *Why Families Move*. New York: Free Press of Glencoe, 1955.

Sirjamaki, John. *The American Family in the Twentieth Century*. Cambridge: Harvard University Press, 1953.

## IX. *The Ecology of American Cities*

Bogue, Don J. *The Structure of the Metropolitan Community*. Ann Arbor, Mich.: University of Michigan Press, 1949.

Burgess, E. W., ed. *The Urban Community*. Chicago: University of Chicago Press, 1925.

Davie, Maurice R. "The Patterns of Urban Growth," in *Studies in the Science of Society*, ed. George Peter Murdock. New Haven: Yale University Press, 1937, pp. 133–161.

Duncan, Otis Dudley, and others. *Metropolis and Region*. Baltimore: Johns Hopkins Press, 1960.

Duncan, Otis Dudley, and Albert J. Reiss, Jr. *Social Characteristics of Urban and Rural Communities, 1950*. New York: Wiley, 1956.

Duncan, Otis Dudley, and Beverly Duncan. *The Negro Population of Chicago*. Chicago: University of Chicago Press, 1957.

Firey, Walter. *Land Use in Central Boston*. Cambridge: Harvard University Press, 1947.

Freedman, Ronald. *Recent Migration to Chicago*. Chicago: University of Chicago Press, 1950.

Gallion, Arthur B., with Simon Eisner. *The Urban Pattern*. New York: Van Nostrand, 1950.

Hawley, Amos. *Human Ecology*. New York: Ronald Press, 1950.

Hoyt, Homer. *The Structure and Growth of Residential Neighbor-*

*hoods in American Cities.* Washington: Federal Housing Administration, 1939.

Hurd, R. M. *Principles of City Land Values.* New York: Record and Guide, 1903, 1924.

Jacobs, Jane. *The Death and Life of Great American Cities.* New York: Random, 1961.

McKenzie, R. D. *The Metropolitan Community.* New York: McGraw-Hill, 1933.

Park, Robert E., and E. W. Burgess, eds. *The City.* Chicago: University of Chicago Press, 1925.

Park, Robert E. *Human Communities.* New York: Free Press of Glencoe, 1952.

Schmid, Calvin F. "The Ecology of the American City," *American Sociological Review,* 15 (April, 1950), 264–281.

Shevky, Eshref, and Wendell Bell. *Social Area Analysis.* Palo Alto, Cal.: Stanford University Press, 1955.

Theodorson, George A., ed. *Studies in Human Ecology.* New York: Harper and Row, 1961.

Willhelm, Sidney M. *Urban Zoning and Land-Use Theory.* New York: Free Press of Glencoe, 1962.

## X.   *People and Groupings in Cities*

Anderson, Elin L. *We Americans.* Cambridge: Harvard University Press, 1937.

Bogue, Donald J. *The Population of the United States.* New York: Free Press of Glencoe, 1959.

Drake, St. Clair, and Horace R. Clayton. *Black Metropolis.* New York: Harcourt, Brace, 1945.

Davie, Maurice R. *World Immigration.* New York: Macmillan, 1936.

Ellis, John Tracy, *American Catholicism.* Chicago: University of Chicago Press, 1959.

Fichter, Joseph H. *Dynamics of a City Church.* Chicago: University of Chicago Press, 1951.

Fichter, Joseph H. *Social Relations in the Urban Parish.* Chicago: University of Chicago Press, 1954.

Frazier, E. Franklin. *The Negro in the United States.* New York: Macmillan, 1949.

Gans, Herbert J. *The Urban Villagers.* New York: Free Press of Glencoe, 1962.

Handlin, Oscar. *The Newcomers.* Cambridge: Harvard University Press, 1959.

Herberg, Will. *Protestant-Catholic-Jew.* New York: Doubleday-Anchor Books, 1956.

Kramer, Judith R., and Seymour Leventman. *Children of the Gilded Ghetto.* New Haven: Yale, 1961.

Lee, Frank F. *Negro and White in a Connecticut Town.* New York: Bookman Associates, 1961.

Lenski, Gerhard. *The Religious Factor.* New York: Doubleday, 1961.

Lynd, Robert S., and Helen Merrell Lynd. *Middletown.* New York: Harcourt, Brace, 1929.

———. *Middletown in Transition.* New York: Harcourt, Brace, 1937.

Schneider, H. W. *Religion in the Twentieth Century.* Cambridge: Harvard University Press, 1952.

Seeley, John R., R. Alexander Sim, and Elizabeth W. Loosley. *Crestwood Heights.* New York: Basic Books, 1956.

Silcox, Claris Edwin, and Galen M. Fisher. *Catholics, Jews and Protestants.* New York: Harper, 1934.

Sperry, Willard L. *Religion in America.* New York: Macmillan, 1946.

Stein, Maurice R. *The Eclipse of Community.* Princeton: Princeton University Press, 1960.

Taeuber, C., and I. B. Taeuber. *The Changing Population of the United States.* New York: Wiley, 1958.

Underwood, Kenneth Wilson. *Protestant and Catholic.* Boston: Beacon Press, 1957.

Ware, Caroline C. *Greenwich Village.* New York: Houghton, Mifflin, 1935.

Warner, W. Lloyd, and Leo Srole. *Social Systems of American Ethnic Groups.* New Haven: Yale, 1945.

Weaver, Robert C. *The Negro Ghetto.* New York: Harcourt, Brace, 1948.

Whyte, William Foote. *Street Corner Society.* Chicago: University of Chicago Press, 1943, 2nd ed. 1955.

Wirth, Louis. *The Ghetto.* Chicago: University of Chicago Press, 1929.

Wood, Arthur Evans. *Hamtramck.* New York: Bookman Associates, 1955.

Zorbaugh, Harvey W. *The Gold Coast and the Slum.* Chicago: University of Chicago Press, 1929.


## XI. Social Stratification in Cities

Baltzell, E. Digby. *Philadelphia Gentlemen.* New York: Free Press of Glencoe, 1953.

Bell, Wendell, Richard J. Hill, and Charles R. Wright. *Public Leadership.* San Francisco: Chandler, 1961.

Bendix, Reinhard, and Seymour Martin Lipset, eds. *Class, Status, and Power.* New York: Free Press of Glencoe, 1953.

Beshers, James N. *Urban Social Structure.* New York: Free Press of Glencoe, 1962.

Dahrendorf, Ralf. *Class and Class Conflict in Industrial Society.* Palo Alto, Cal.: Stanford University Press, 1959.

Frazier, E. Franklin. *Black Bourgeoisie*. New York: Free Press of Glencoe, 1957.

Hollingshead, August B., and Frederick C. Redlich. *Social Class and Mental Illness*. New York: Wiley, 1958.

Hunter, Floyd. *Community Power Structure*. Chapel Hill: University of North Carolina Press, 1953.

Kahl, Joseph A. *The American Class Structure*. New York: Holt, Rinehart, and Winston, 1957.

Lipset, Seymour Martin, and Reinhard Bendix. *Social Mobility in Industrial Society*. Berkeley and Los Angeles: University of California Press, 1959.

Lynd, Robert S., and Helen Merrell Lynd. *Middletown in Transition*. New York: Harcourt, Brace, 1937.

Mills, C. Wright. *White Collar*. New York: Oxford, 1953.

———. *The Power Elite*. New York: Oxford, 1956.

Warner, W. Lloyd, and Paul S. Lunt, *The Social Life of a Modern Community*. New Haven: Yale, 1941.

Weber, Max. *From Max Weber: Essays in Sociology*. Trans. and ed. by H. H. Gerth and C. Wright Mills. New York: Oxford, 1946.

## XII. *The Government of Cities*

Adrian, Charles R. *Governing Urban America*. New York: McGraw-Hill, 1955.

Allen, Robert S., ed. *Our Fair City*. New York: Vanguard Press, 1947.

Anderson, William, and E. W. Weidner. *American City Government*. New York: Holt, Rinehart, and Winston, 1950, rev. ed.

Banfield, Edward C., ed. *Urban Government*. New York: Free Press of Glencoe, 1961.

Banfield, Edward C., and James Q. Wilson. *City Politics*. Cambridge: M.I.T. and Harvard University Press, 1963.

Bollens, John C. *Special District Governments in the United States*. Berkeley and Los Angeles: University of California Press, 1957.

Coleman, James S. *Community Conflict*. New York: Free Press of Glencoe, 1957.

Connery, Robert H., and Richard Leach. *The Federal Government and Metropolitan Areas*. Cambridge: Harvard University Press, 1960.

Dahl, Robert A. *Who Governs? Democracy and Power in an American City*. New Haven: Yale University Press, 1961.

Greer, Scott. *Governing the Metropolis*. New York: Wiley, 1962.

Janowitz, Morris, ed. *Community Political Systems*. New York: Free Press of Glencoe, 1959.

Jones, Victor. *Metropolitan Government*. Chicago: University of Chicago Press, 1942.

Martin, Roscoe C., Frank J. Munger, and others. *Decisions in Syracuse*. Bloomington, Inc.: Indiana University Press, 1961.

Polsby, Nelson W. *Community Power and Political Theory*. New Haven: Yale, 1963.

Sayre, Wallace S., and Herbert Kaufman. *Governing New York City*. New York: Russell Sage, 1960.

Wood, Robert C., with Vladimir V. Almendinger, *1400 Governments*. Cambridge: Harvard University Press, 1961.

Woodbury, Coleman, ed. *The Future of Cities and Urban Redevelopment*. Chicago: University of Chicago Press, 1953.

## XIII. *Cities Today and Tomorrow*

Bogue, Donald J., ed. *Needed Urban and Metropolitan Research*. Oxford, Ohio: Miami University, Scripps Foundation, 1953.

Duhl, Leonard J., ed. *The Urban Condition*. New York: Basic Books, 1963.

Greer, Scott. *The Emerging City*. New York: Free Press of Glencoe, 1962.

Gutkind, E. A., *The Twilight of Cities*. New York: Free Press of Glencoe, 1962.

Hauser, Philip M., ed. *Urbanization in Asia and the Far East*. New York: Unesco Publications Center, 1957.

——— *Urbanization in Latin America*. New York: Unesco Publications Center, 1961.

Haworth, Lawrence. *The Good City*. Bloomington: Indiana University Press, 1963.

Hirsch, Werner Z., ed. *Urban Life and Form*. New York: Holt, Rinehart, and Winston, 1963.

Martindale, Don, "Preface," *The City*. Max Weber. Trans. and ed. by Don Martindale and Gertrud Neuwirth. New York: Free Press of Glencoe, 1958.

Meier, Richard L. *A Communications Theory of Urban Growth*. Cambridge: M.I.T. and Harvard University Press, 1962.

Mumford, Lewis. *The City in History*. New York: Harcourt, Brace, 1961.

*Our Cities. Their Role in the National Economy*. Washington: Government Printing Office, 1937.

Turner, Roy, ed. *India's Urban Future*. Berkeley and Los Angeles: University of California Press, 1962.

# Index